IMAGES
of America

SMITHSBURG

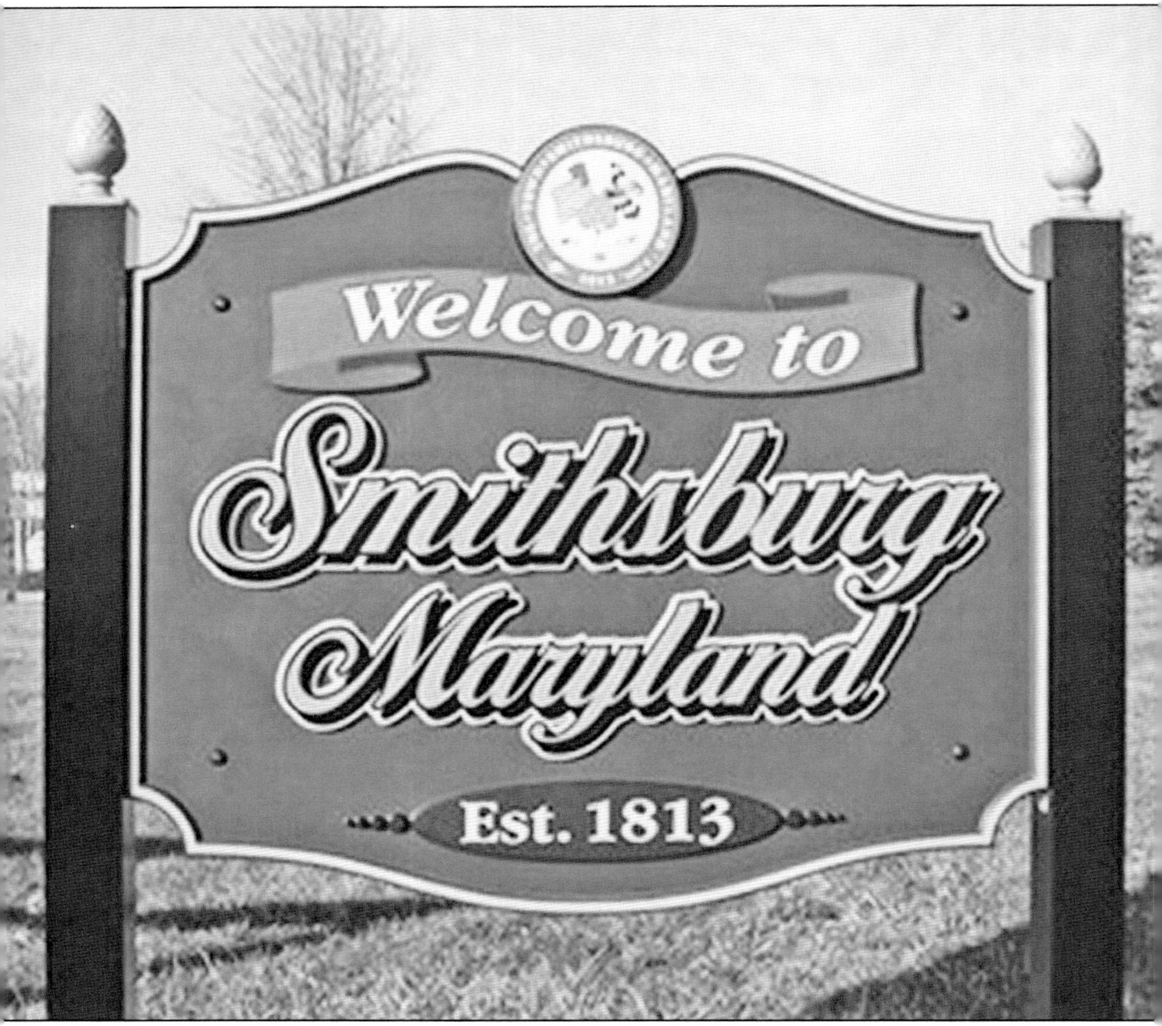

Welcome to Smithsburg! Located in northeastern Washington County, Maryland, this small agricultural community was founded in 1813 by Christopher "Stuffle" Smith. An example of a community virtually unaffected by modernization, Smithsburg still preserves its mid-19th-century charm. The only body of water within the town limits is the Smithsburg Reservoir, which is currently dormant. Summertime in Smithsburg brings the annual Steam and Craft Show as well as the annual Pride Day Festival. (Photograph courtesy of Shay Mace.)

ON THE COVER: Shipments of "Smithsburg Pride" (as the locally grown fruit is known) to various locations have grown exponentially, providing residents of other towns and even neighboring states the opportunity to experience the quality homegrown product. High demand for the locally grown fruits helped put Smithsburg on the map. This photograph was taken by James B. Minnich around 1948 and was donated by Leona and Raymond Gardenhour. (Courtesy of the Smithsburg Historical Society.)

IMAGES *of America*

SMITHSBURG

Shay A. Mace on behalf of the
Smithsburg Historical Society

ARCADIA PUBLISHING

ISBN 978-0-7385-6741-9

Published by Arcadia Publishing
Charleston SC, Chicago IL, Portsmouth NH, San Francisco CA

Printed in the United States of America

Library of Congress Catalog Card Number: 2008929307

For all general information contact Arcadia Publishing at:
Telephone 843-853-2070
Fax 843-853-0044
E-mail sales@arcadiapublishing.com
For customer service and orders:
Toll-Free 1-888-313-2665

Visit us on the Internet at www.arcadiapublishing.com

This book is dedicated to those who have considered Smithsburg their home, either short term or lifelong.

Contents

ACKNOWLEDGMENTS

I would like to thank the community of Smithsburg for the overwhelmingly positive response and support I have received in conjunction with the collection and writing of this book. Since its founding, the Smithsburg Historical Society has had a generous support team consisting of area volunteers who take pride in the history of this small town. Their operation to preserve the stories of Smithsburg is exhausting and sometimes seems never-ending. Their dedication to conservation and efforts to impart the town's history to everyone who passes through their doors has been incredibly beneficial to the creation of this book. Without the help of the devoted volunteers of the Smithsburg Historical Society, this book would not have been possible. I wish to thank Mike Rohrer, president of the Smithsburg Historical Society, and the many volunteers, including Betty Eichelberger, who have helped in the making of this book. My enormous gratitude goes to Sari Kilheffer. Sari has been an instrumental force in making available the photographs and newspaper clippings and has spent her valuable time furnishing me with plenty of comical and sustaining stories about the town's history. I also wish to thank my editors, Lauren C. Bobier and Brooksi Hudson, and the Arcadia Publishing team who have guided this work from its inception. Lauren and Brooksi's consistency and gentle guidance have been greatly appreciated and helped to keep me on task in order to produce a history of my hometown. Thank you; I am deeply grateful.

INTRODUCTION

Researching this book has truly been a remarkable experience. Though a native of Smithsburg, Maryland, I had never been aware of the history associated with my hometown. Honestly, although I lived in Smithsburg, I had not bothered to pay any attention to the local history. My interests were artistic and creative, not historical or factual. Imagine my surprise when I recently learned that many prominent and influential artists, teachers, and industrialists came from my very birthplace. Although women's suffrage would come towards the end of her life, one celebrated female artist named Emily Clayton Bishop was already blazing a trail from Smithsburg to Philadelphia to England to Greece, and by summer of 1908, she was living in Paris, France. Considered a rising star at the time in the art world, Bishop had gotten her start right here in her hometown of Smithsburg, Maryland—my hometown.

Another artist making a name in Smithsburg was Jacob Frederich Kimler. Born in the Black Forest of Germany in 1790, Kimler made his way to American in 1832. He and his family settled in Smithsburg and continued their art of making earthenware clay pottery. The last pieces were made in 1882, and only a small handful of pieces remain.

The town of Smithsburg got its start in 1813, when Christopher "Stuffle" Smith, born in the Washington County area around 1750, bought part of Shadrach's Lot from Samuel B. McClanahan of Chester County, Pennsylvania. After purchasing the land, Smith then divided it and sold the lots. A stonemason by trade, Smith had saved his money for years in the hopes of turning it into a family fortune. Making the purchase at age 63, he thought that buying the land would secure wealth for him and his family. After taking the money he had made on the land, Smith further invested in a distillery, which eventually broke him. Destitute, Smith stayed in Smithsburg as the rest of his family moved west in search of prosperity. Smith died a broken man at the age of 81. He was buried in an unmarked grave, and his only remnants are the name of the town itself and, more recently, a stone memorial next to town hall.

The first post office was built in November 1829 and served Smithsburg's 136 people. As the population of the town increased, so did the community spirit, schools, businesses, and educational prospects. Prof. George Pearson was an influential and integral factor in Smithsburg, creating more professionals than any other town in the county. Pearson taught from 1836 to 1882 and guided the education of many lawyers, teachers, doctors, bankers, writers, and artists.

Many people are not aware of Smithsburg's ties to the Civil War. Both Union and Confederate troops marched through Smithsburg on their way to Gettysburg, Pennsylvania. The town of Smithsburg even saw a bit of combat. On July 5, 1863, after the Battle of Gettysburg, J. E. B. Stuart's Confederate troops on Nicodemus Hill exchanged fire for over an hour with Hugh Judson Kilpatrick's Union forces camped out on Gardenhour's Hill. One Confederate shell hit the house of Leonard Vogel and can still be seen today in the wall of the house.

An inventor from Smithsburg, Peter Geiser, helped restructure the agriculture industry by creating a grain separator. His invention, patented in 1852, created in Smithsburg, eased the lives of farmers significantly. Smithsburg is and has been known for its farming and orchard communities due to the rich soil and excellent growing climate.

Along the South Mountain, it was discovered that our fertile soil was excellent for growing peaches. An experiment in planting in mountain land led to the thriving orchard business that we have today. By 1888, Smithsburg fruit was popular, and buyers from Baltimore and Philadelphia were placing orders for our mountain peaches.

In 1873, the Western Maryland Railroad was constructed, connecting Smithsburg to neighboring towns and cities. This enabled trade and provided transportation for the townspeople. Smithsburg at one time had one of the largest railroad yards in the county.

Smithsburg has more than doubled its population from 1990 and shows no signs of slowing. Many towns lose their charm once the growing population takes over, but not Smithsburg. Main Street looks the same as it has for hundreds of years. As the town and its community modernize, one thing is certain: the heart of this town has always been the community, and just like the appearance of the town, that will never change.

One

A History Lesson
Just the Facts

Smithsburg, Maryland, located in Washington County, was incorporated as a town in 1846. On the town's founding, the population was less than 200. The U.S. Census Bureau listed Smithsburg's population at almost 3,000 in 2006.

In 1862, during the American Civil War, Smithsburg served as a hospital town, treating wounded soldiers from the nearby battles of Antietam and South Mountain. In July 1863, Confederate general J E. B. Stuart and Union general Hugh Judson Kirkpatrick brought Smithsburg directly into battle with the exchange of artillery fire over the town. Today a Smithsburg home holds visible evidence of this battle: 25 East Water Street is also known as the "Cannonball House" because of the cannonball still lodged in the east side of the house.

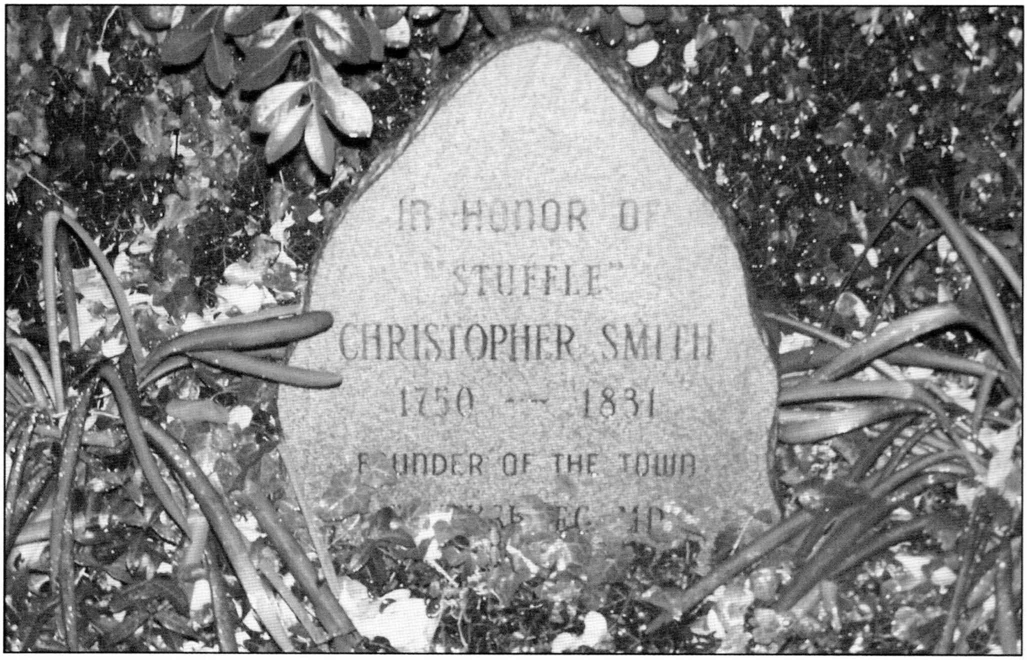

A monument to the town founder, Christopher "Stuffle" Smith, lies amidst the flowers and greens in the middle of Heritage Walk, located directly beside town hall on West Main Street. This is the only monument to the founder of Smithsburg, as Smith is buried in an unmarked grave. (Courtesy of Shay Mace.)

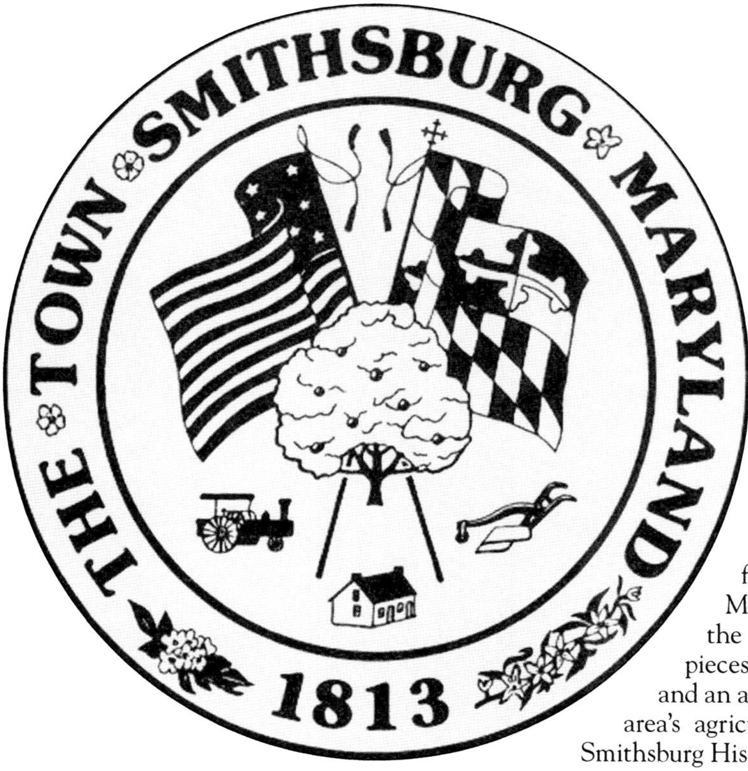

This is the official seal of Smithsburg, Maryland. The American flag is on the left, and the Maryland state flag is on the right. There are various pieces of farming equipment and an apple tree representing the area's agriculture. (Courtesy of the Smithsburg Historical Society.)

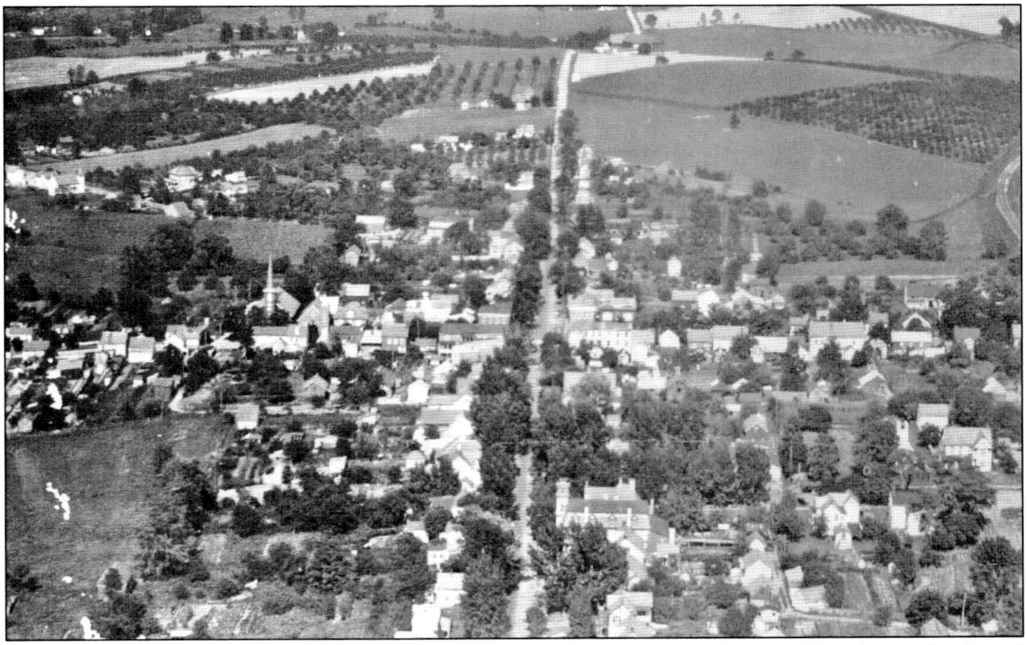

This aerial view of Smithsburg was taken in 1927. The Trinity Lutheran Church can be found to the left of center in this picture. North is to the left. The town square, located at center, is densely populated. The population thins as Main Street and Water Street lead in each direction towards Smithsburg's rolling hills. C. H. Williams took this photograph. (Courtesy of the Smithsburg Historical Society.)

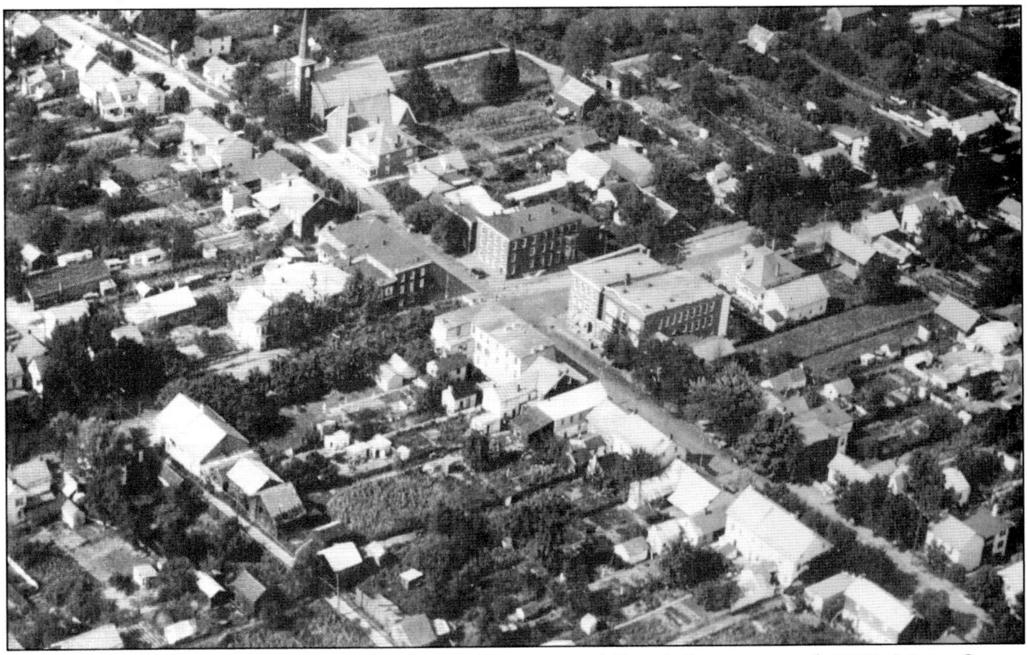

This photograph is a closer aerial view of the town of Smithsburg around 1927. Main Street and Water Street intersect at the very center of the photograph. Visible landmarks include town hall, Trinity Lutheran Church, and the old Smithsburg Bank. C. H. Williams took this photograph. (Courtesy of the Smithsburg Historical Society.)

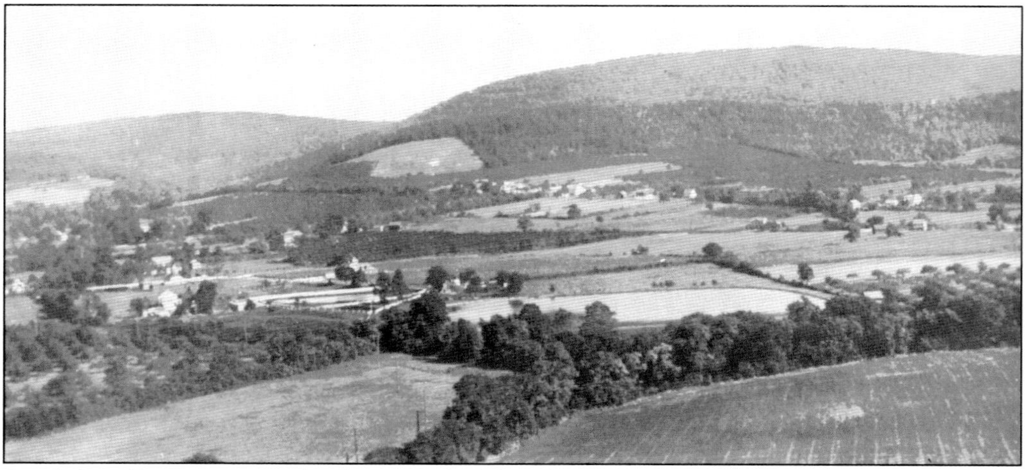

Smithsburg Reservoir is in the foreground of this photograph, which was taken from the top of the water tower. Goat Hill is seen in the background along Old Georgetown Road. The town is surrounded by lush mountains on which many fruits grow. The mountain terrain is perfect for growing mountain peaches. (Courtesy of the Smithsburg Historical Society.)

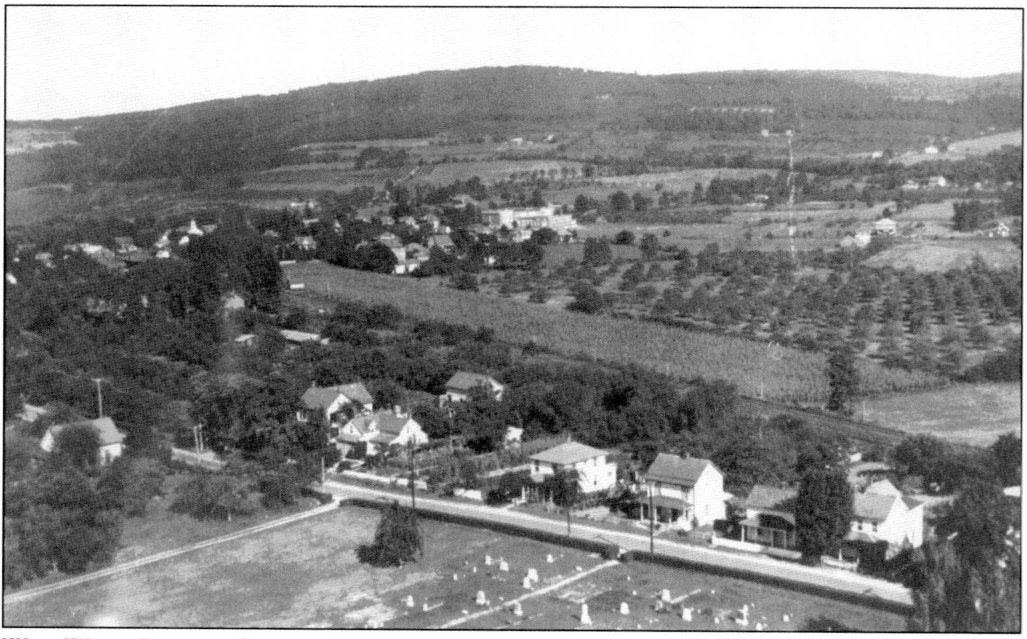

West Water Street is shown in the early 1920s. Today many of these houses still stand, as does Veteran's Park and the newly constructed Smithsburg Library. There is a car wash across the street from the cemetery, which has increased in size. C. H. Williams took this photograph. (Courtesy of the Smithsburg Historical Society.)

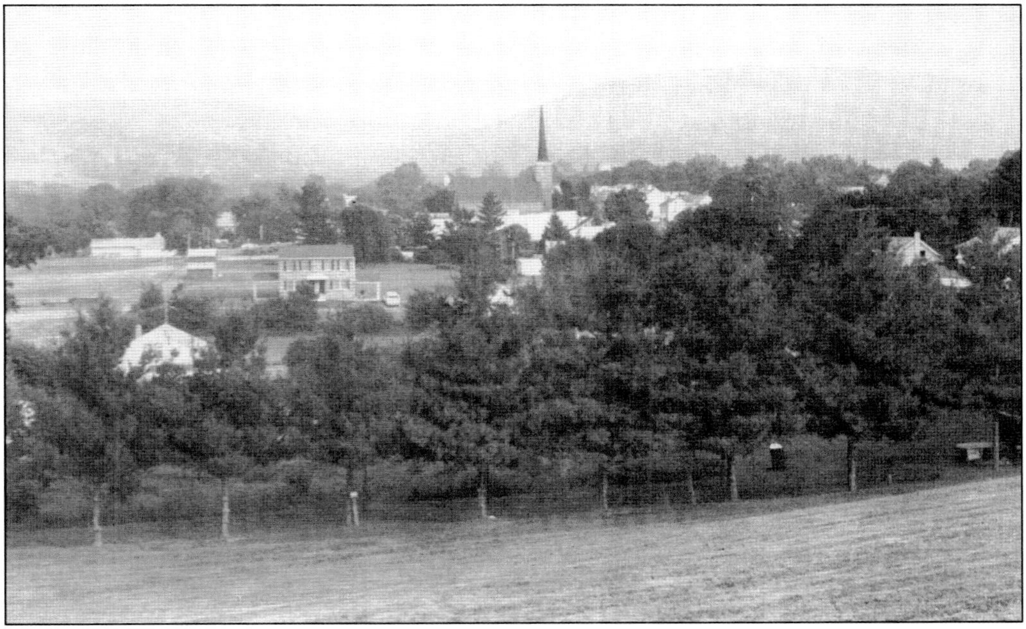

This view is from the hill directly behind Smithsburg Senior High School. Smithsburg's landscape is complete with rolling hills. The steeple of Trinity Lutheran Church can be seen in the distance in this photograph by Vernon Davis. (Courtesy of *Maryland Cracker Barrel.*)

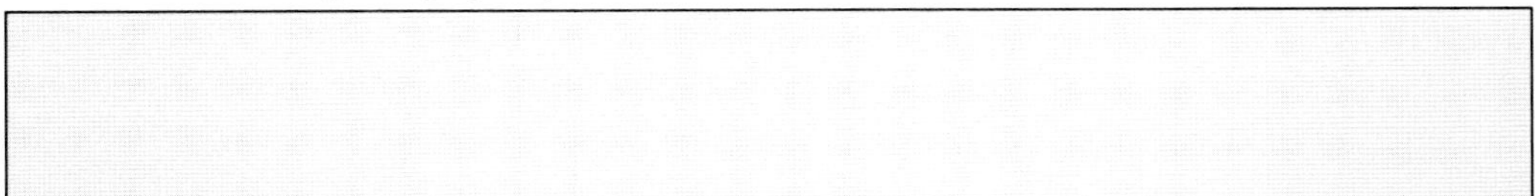

Charles Slick Jr. created this postcard from a photograph taken by Mary D. Slick. This wintry scene was the view from their house in the mid-1940s. The sun is rising in the east as the snow settles on the many tree branches surrounding the houses. Charles Slick was a prominent artist from Smithsburg. Many of his works, including this postcard, are on display at the Smithsburg Historical Society, located at 20 East Water Street. (Courtesy of the Smithsburg Historical Society.)

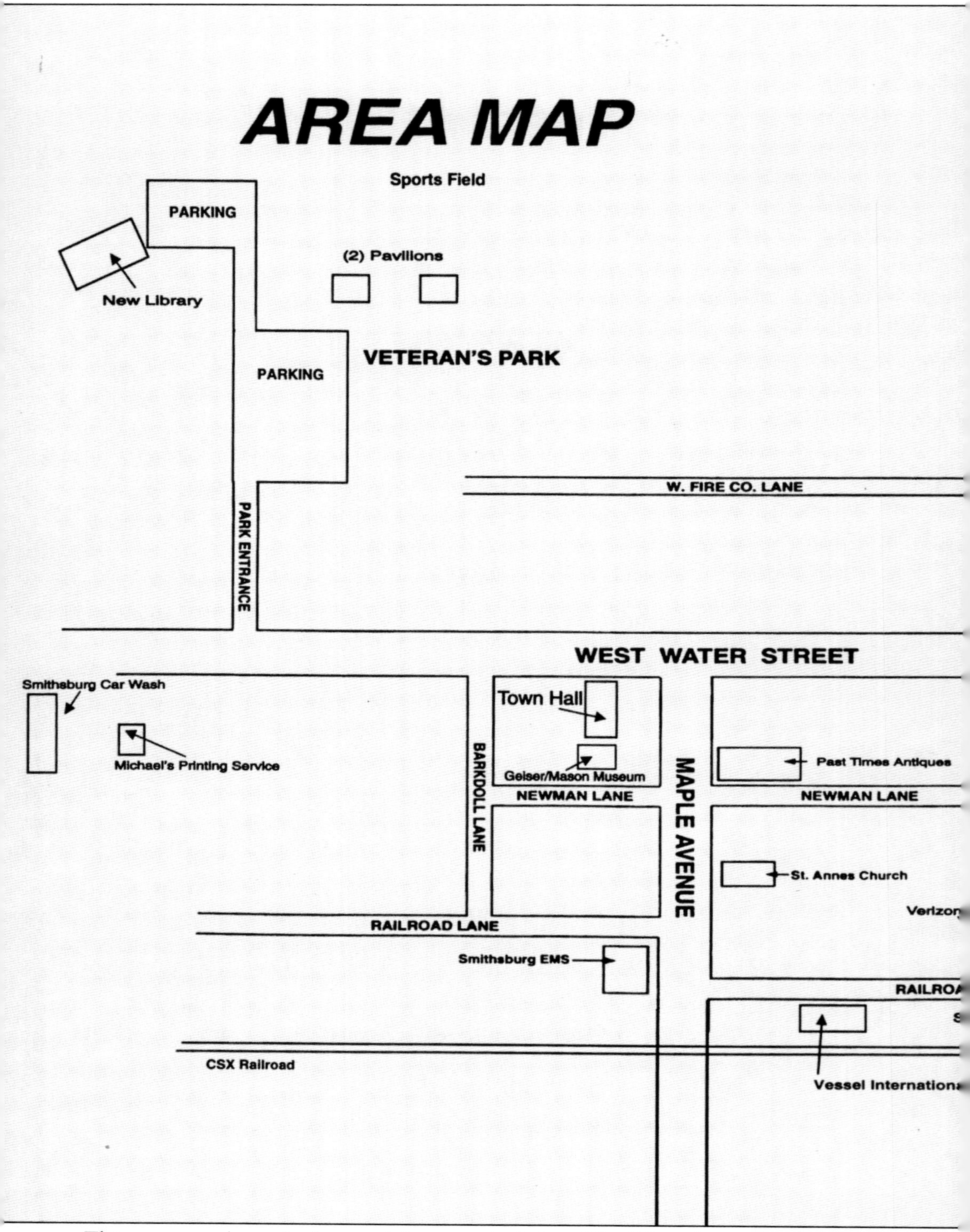

This area map shows the layout of the town, including West Water Street, Smithsburg Square, Main Street, and the outlying areas. Smithsburg Elementary School, Veteran's Park, and town hall are visible on this map found in the Smithsburg Pride Days pamphlet from 2007. The fire

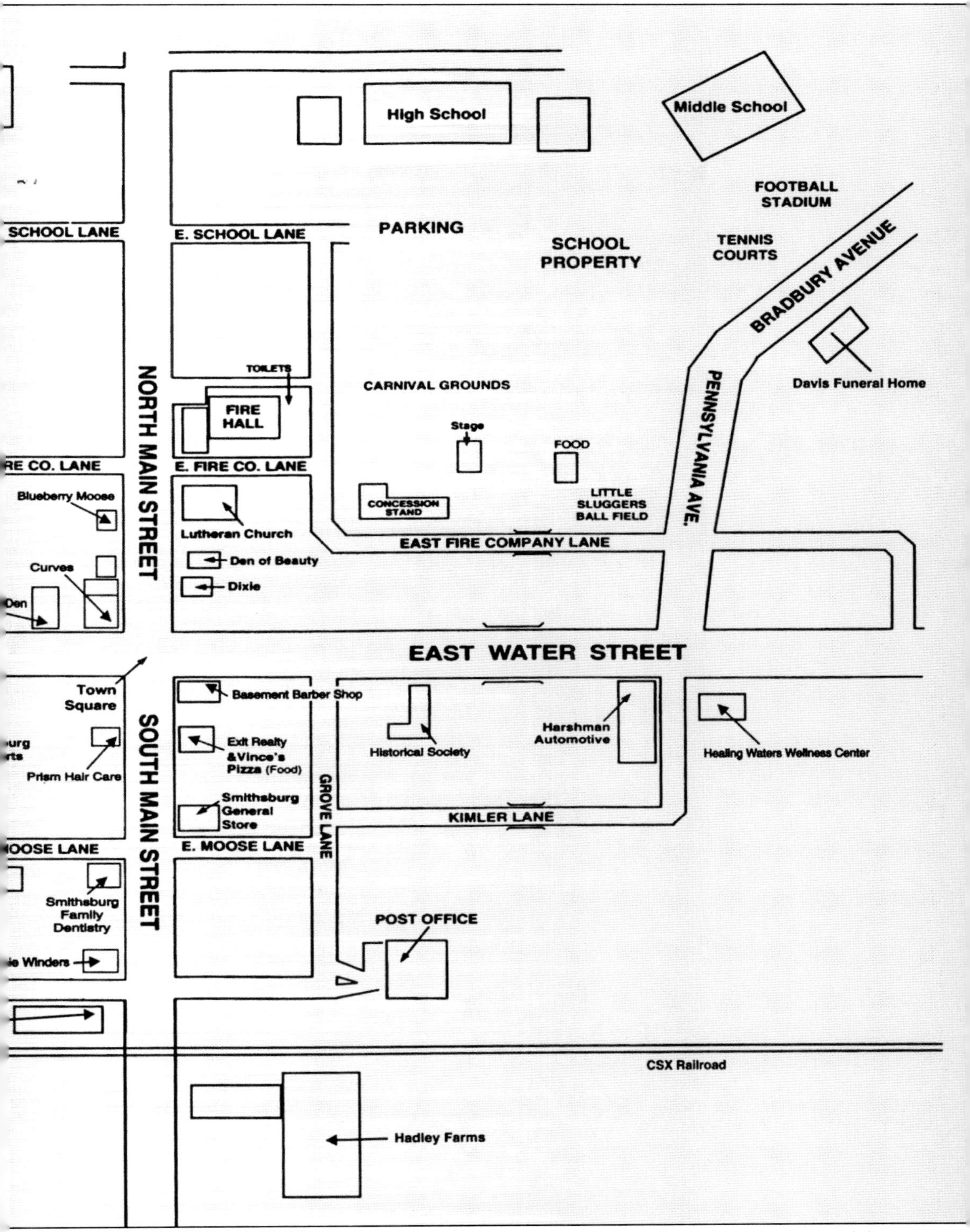

hall, Smithsburg High School, and the U.S. Post Office are visible on the right. (Courtesy of the Smithsburg Historical Society.)

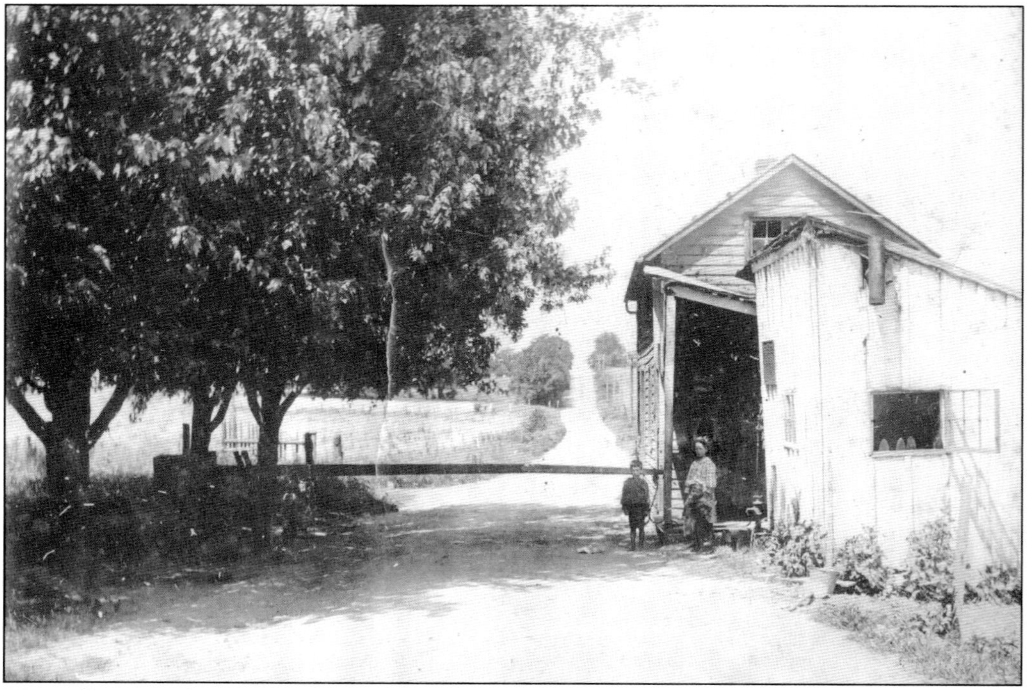

This tollgate used to stand just east of Grimm's Salvage Yard. Jefferson Boulevard, as this road is now known, was expanded to allow travel into the Smithsburg area by paying the various tolls. The people in the photograph are unidentified. (Courtesy of the Smithsburg Historical Society.)

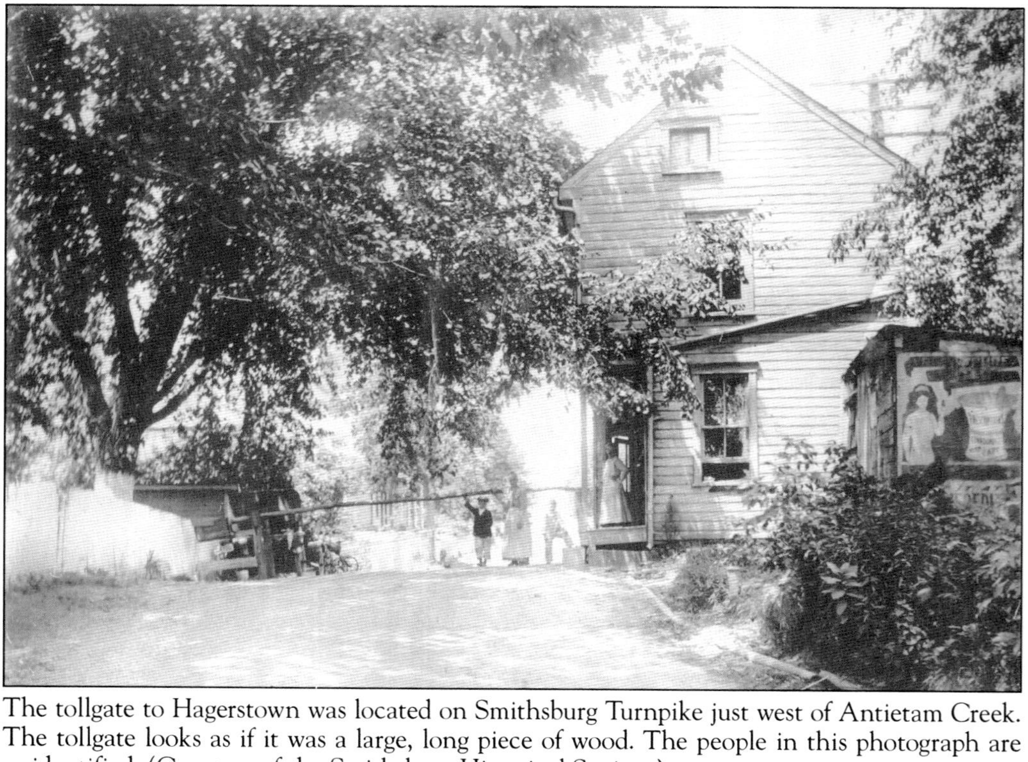

The tollgate to Hagerstown was located on Smithsburg Turnpike just west of Antietam Creek. The tollgate looks as if it was a large, long piece of wood. The people in this photograph are unidentified. (Courtesy of the Smithsburg Historical Society.)

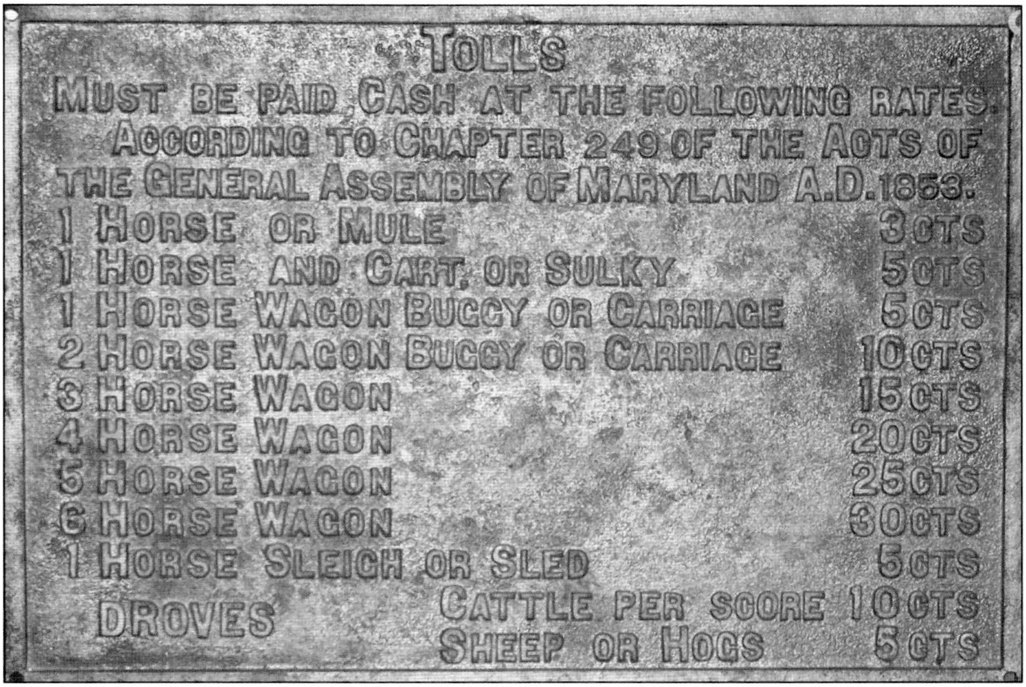

Toll rates were posted at the tollgates into town. This particular sign was created in 1835. The most expensive crossings through the tolls include five- and six-horse wagons at 25¢ and 30¢, respectively. The photograph is by Shay Mace. (Courtesy of the Smithsburg Historical Society.)

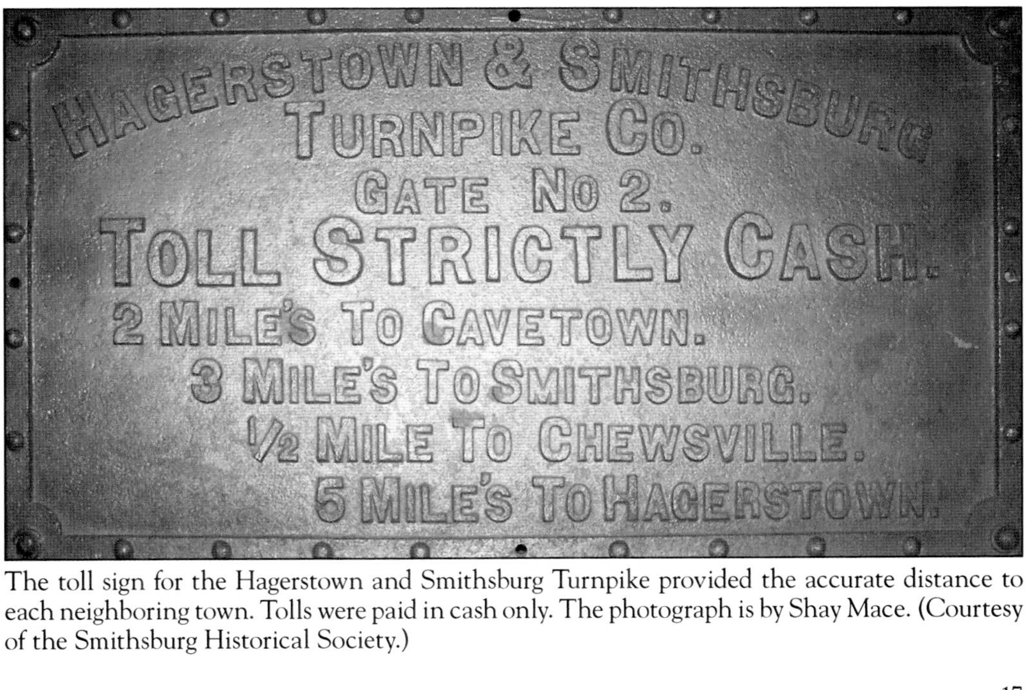

The toll sign for the Hagerstown and Smithsburg Turnpike provided the accurate distance to each neighboring town. Tolls were paid in cash only. The photograph is by Shay Mace. (Courtesy of the Smithsburg Historical Society.)

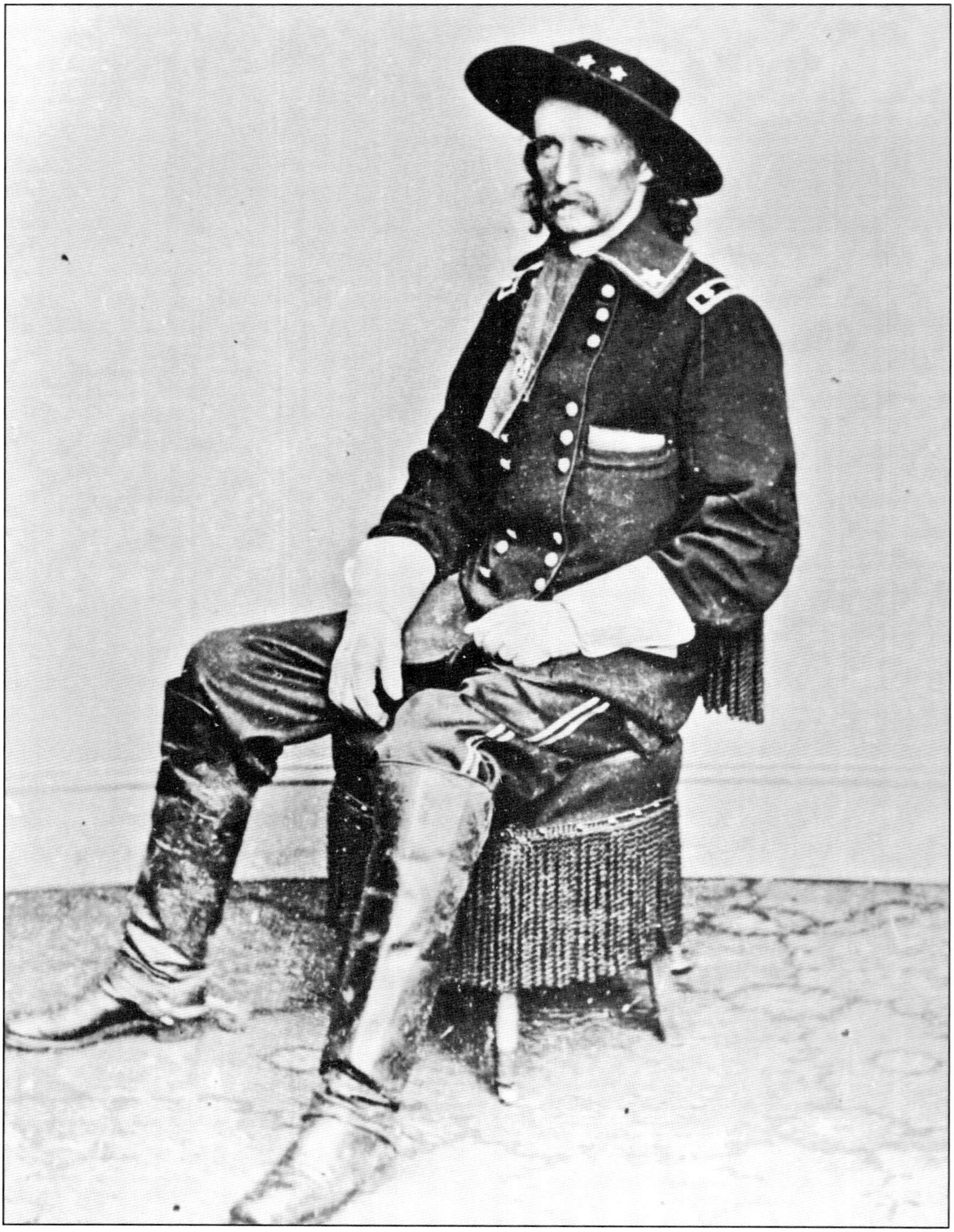

On July 5, 1863, George A. Custer celebrated his promotion to general with the residents of Smithsburg. Wooden tables were set up in the streets filled with ham, pitchers of cold milk, cakes, and pies. Soldiers and civilians celebrated together. Custer accepted an invitation to go to the home of a family on South Main Street for Sunday dinner. (Courtesy of the Smithsburg Historical Society.)

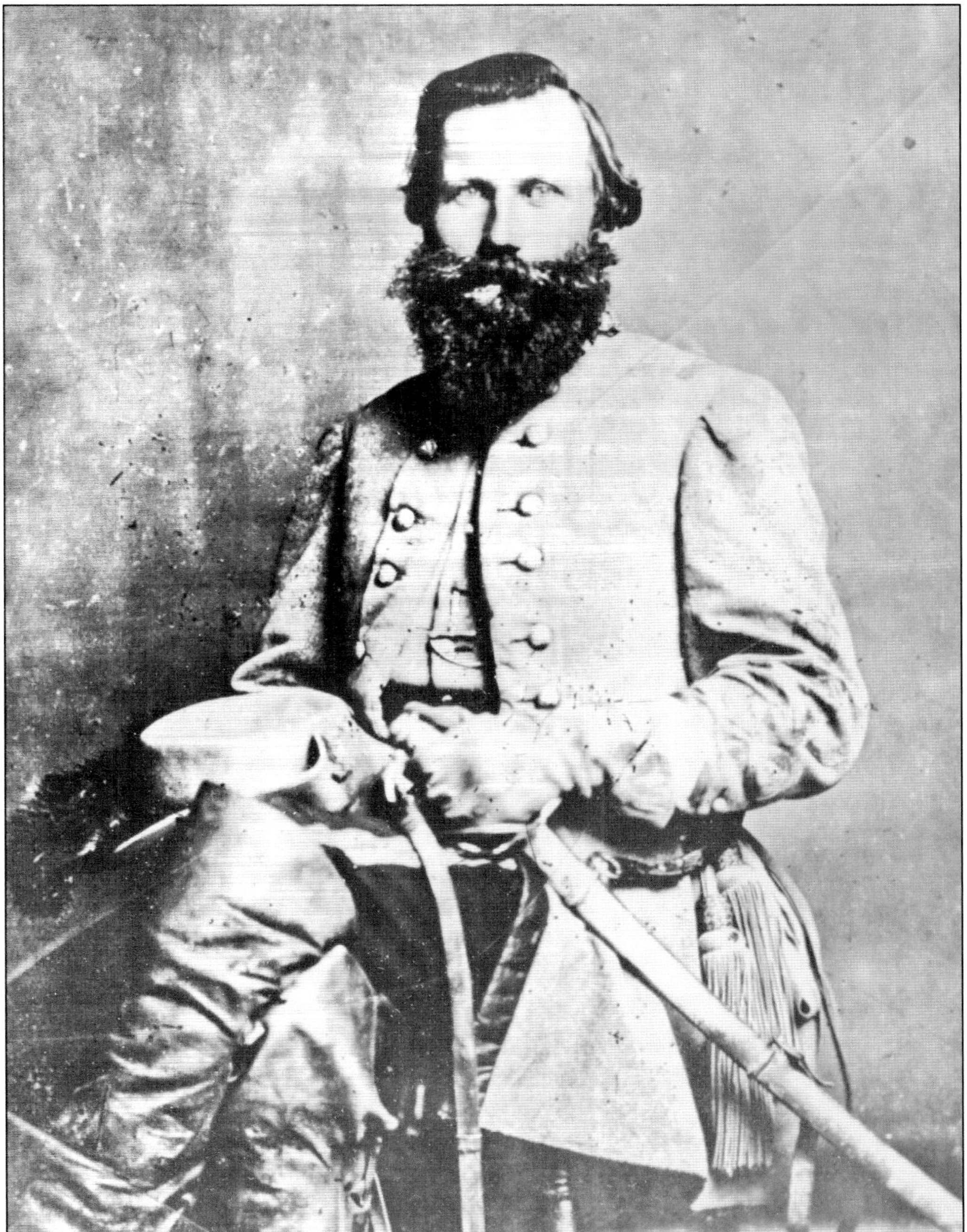

Maj. Gen. J. E. B. Stuart of the Confederate army led his cavalry into Smithsburg on July 5, 1863. After approximately one hour of artillery exchange between the Confederates and the Union under Gen. Judson Kilpatrick, each group moved on respectively—Kilpatrick to Boonsboro and Stuart to Leitersburg. (Courtesy of the Smithsburg Historical Society.)

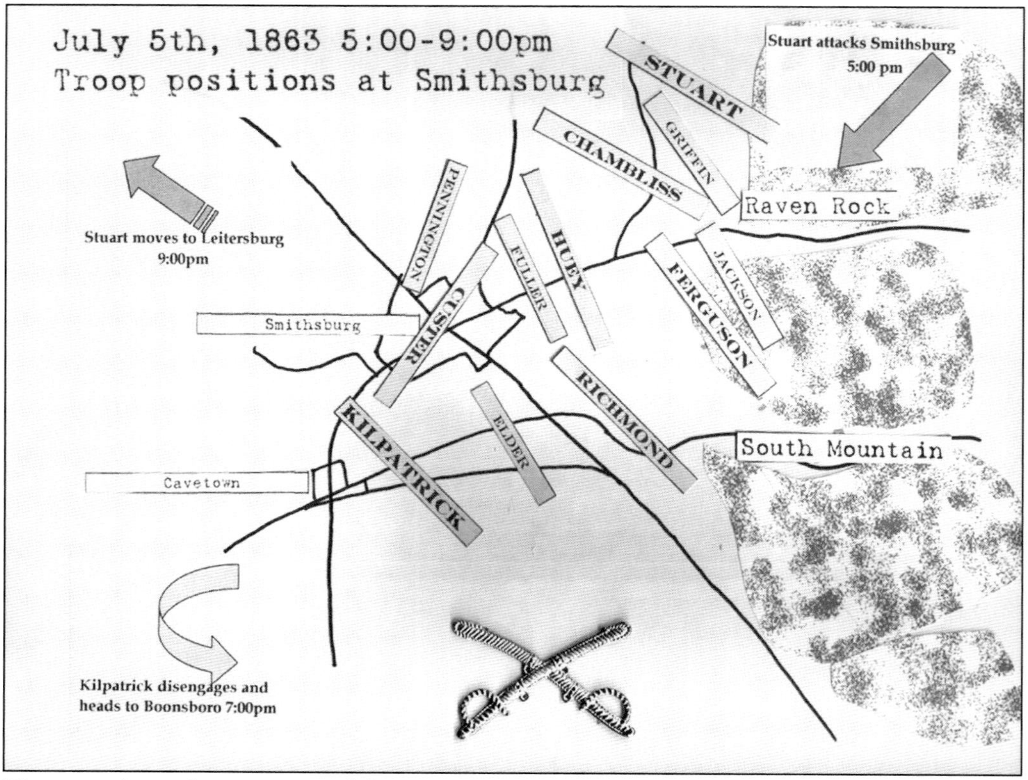

This map shows the stations and directions of Major General Stuart, Brigadier General Custer, and General Kirkpatrick. The map explains the time and places during the four-hour time span of their engagement. (Courtesy of the Smithsburg Historical Society.)

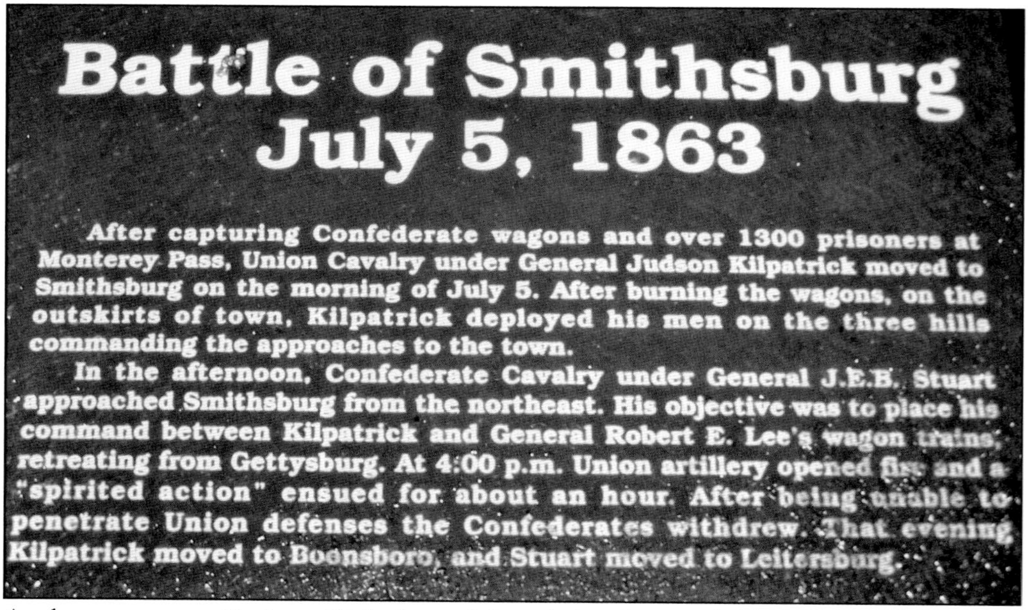

At the entrance to Heritage Walk, located directly beside town hall, this plaque stands as a historical reminder that there was artillery exchanged during the Civil War in the town of Smithsburg. The photograph is by Shay Mace.

Two

Main Street
The Main Drag

Many towns have changed their physical landscape over the years for various reasons, whether it is for new roadways or to accommodate the increasing population. While Smithsburg has evolved over the years as its population has considerably grown, the physical layout of the town has remained virtually unchanged. Most of the houses and buildings located in Smithsburg Square, comprised of Main Street and Water Street, have existed since the late 1800s. Most of the buildings in town predate World War II.

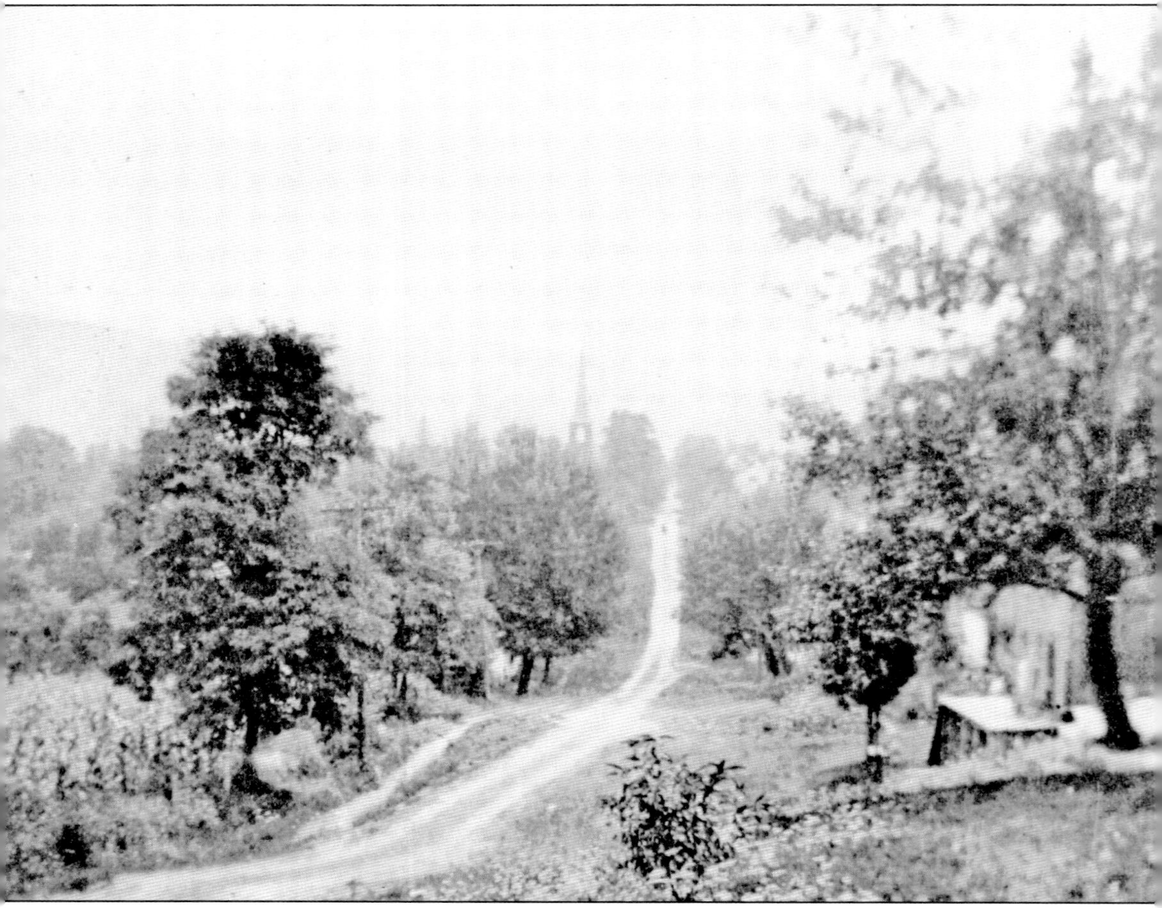

This early view of Main Street was taken from the top of Sunset Hill. In the distance, the steeple of the Trinity Lutheran Church is visible. Today many houses line both sides of Main Street. The time and date of photograph are unknown. (Courtesy of the Smithsburg Historical Society.)

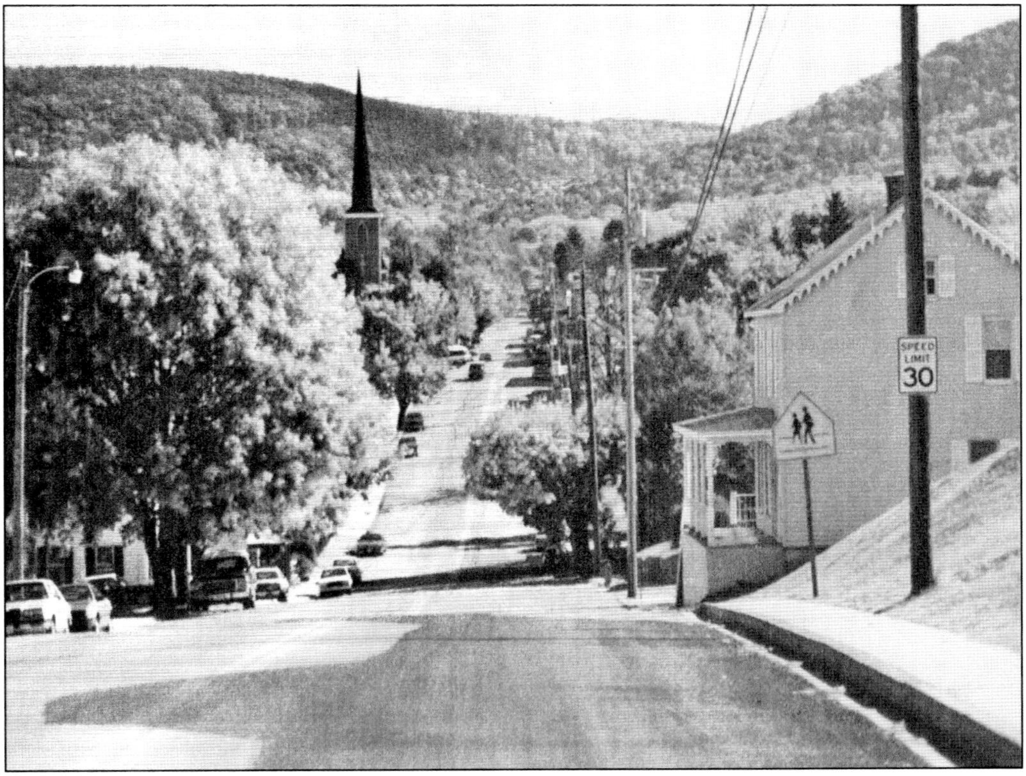

The same view was taken from the top of Sunset Hill only decades later. As one can see, the street has been widened and paved. Houses and cars are evident on the street. (Courtesy of the Smithsburg Historical Society.)

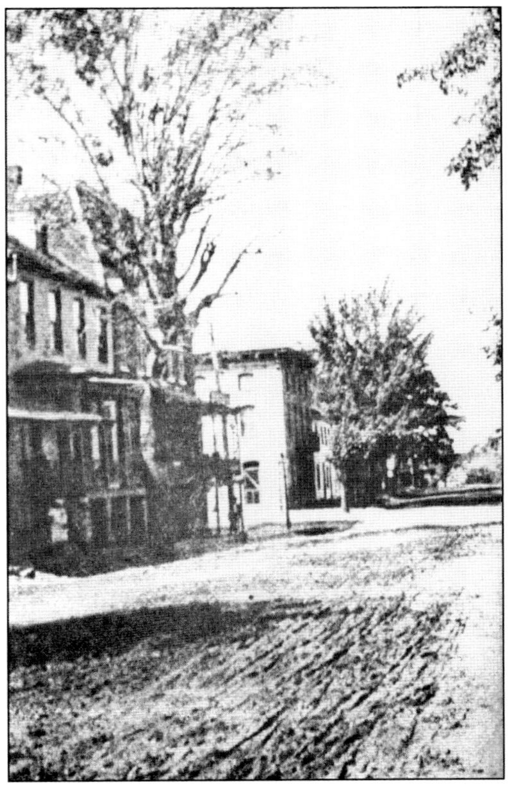

Main Street is shown in the 1890s. The corner of Main and Water Streets is in the center of the photograph. (Courtesy of the Smithsburg Historical Society.)

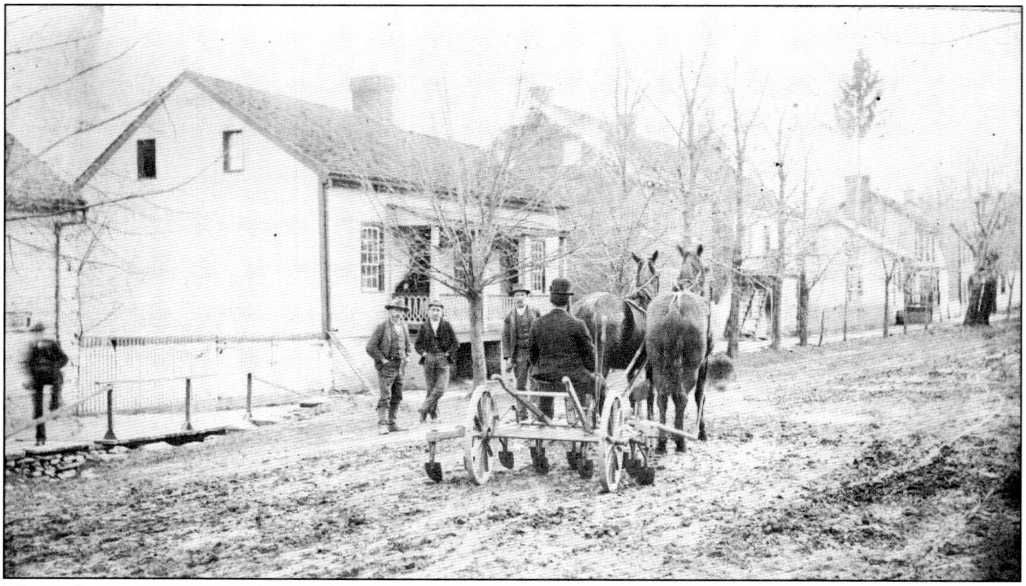

This photograph provides a glimpse into life on East Water Street in the late 1800s. Horses provide transportation up and down the dirt roads. The houses in the background are still evident today, including the Kimler Pottery House behind the three unidentified men standing beside the tree. (Courtesy of the Smithsburg Historical Society.)

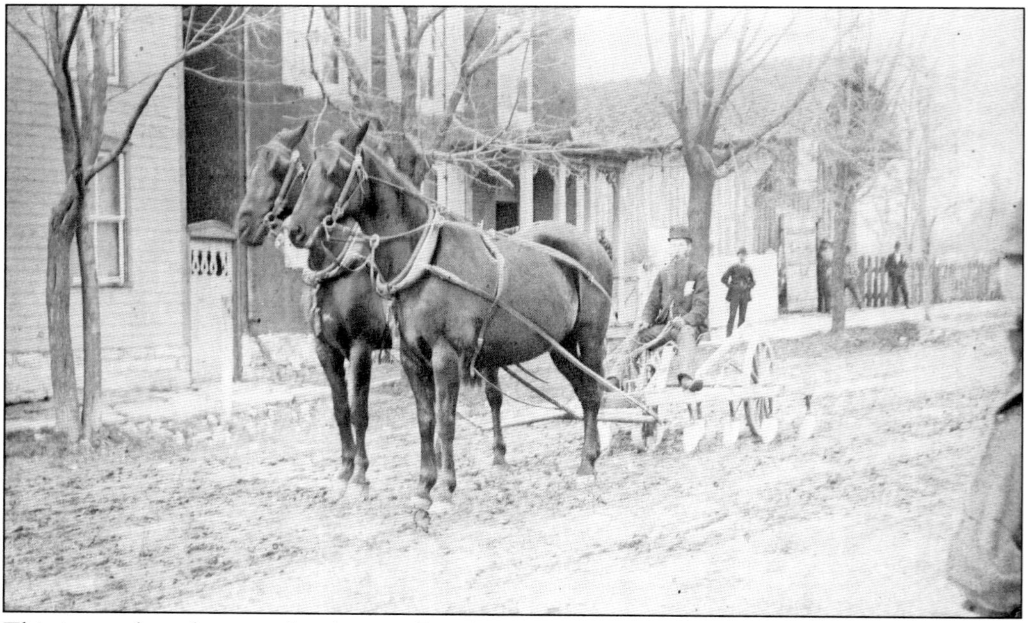

This is another photograph taken on East Water Street. The horses and driver are tilling the road. In the background is 25 East Water Street, also known as the Cannonball House. During the artillery fire of July 5, 1863, the house was struck by Confederate fire. The damage to the house is still visible today. (Courtesy of the Smithsburg Historical Society.)

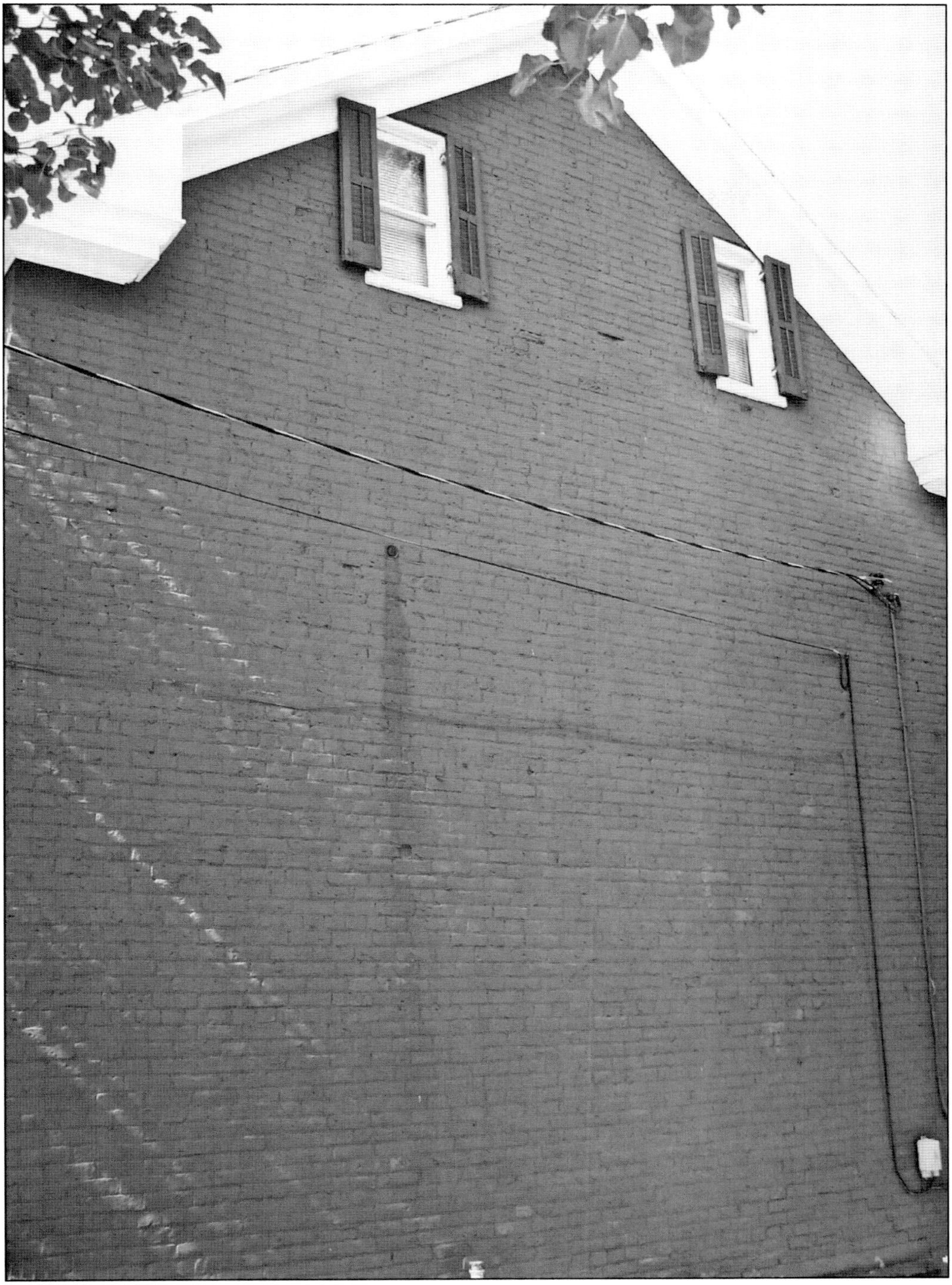

A present-day photograph of the Cannonball House shows the still-visible damage to the building. Beneath the two wires is a dark, round shape where house owners J. Leonard and Lydia Vogel patched over the artillery shell. The photograph is by Shay Mace.

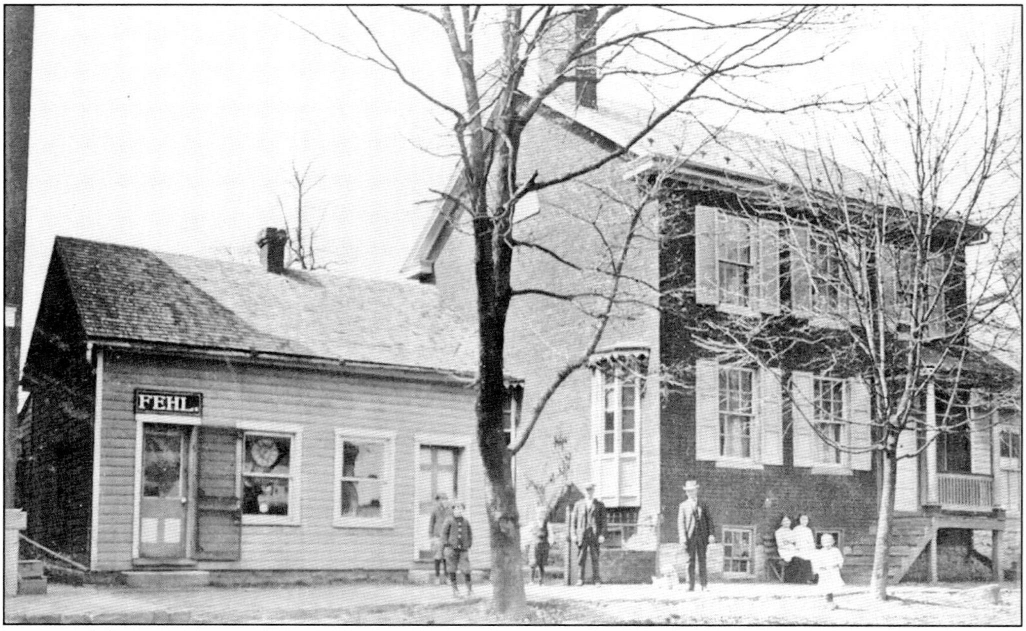

Donated by Virginia Fehl, this early photograph shows 9 and 11 North Main Street. These buildings were owned by George M. Boyer and were later sold to Dr. Elijah Bishop. The smaller building on the left has served many purposes over the years: cobbler's shop, optometrist's office, feed storage, and beauty shop. (Courtesy of the Smithsburg Historical Society.)

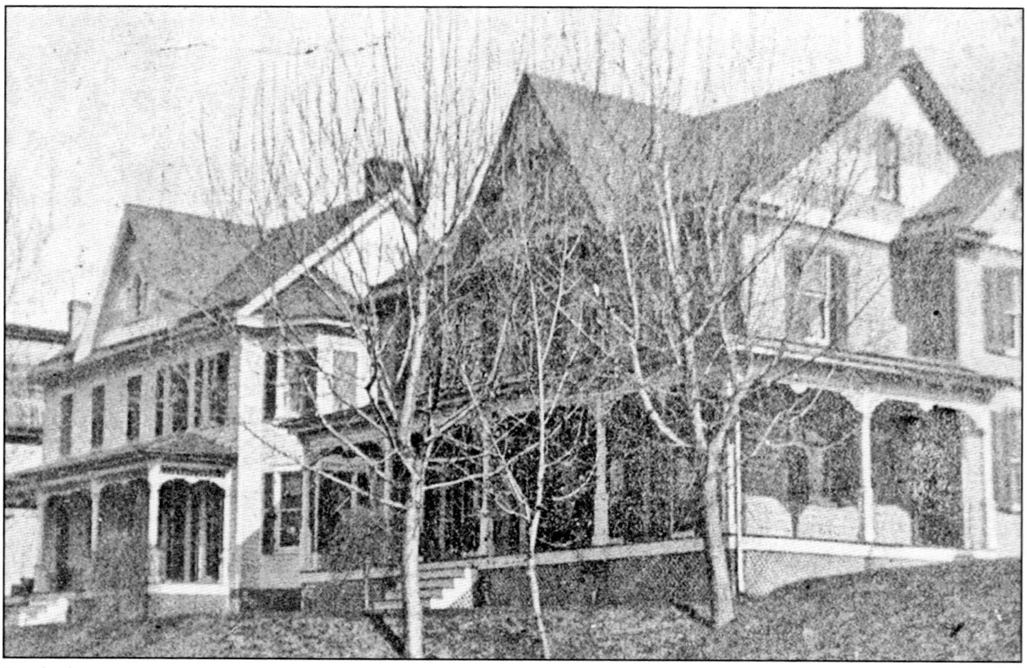

Built by B. C. Bishop in the late 1800s, 25 and 27 West Water Street are two residential structures originally owned by Samuel Hawley. In the early part of the 1900s, 25 West Water Street was inhabited by Sue and Rachel Stockslager; Elizabeth Bachtell lived at 27 West Water Street. Today these houses are still serving as private residences. (Courtesy of the Smithsburg Historical Society.)

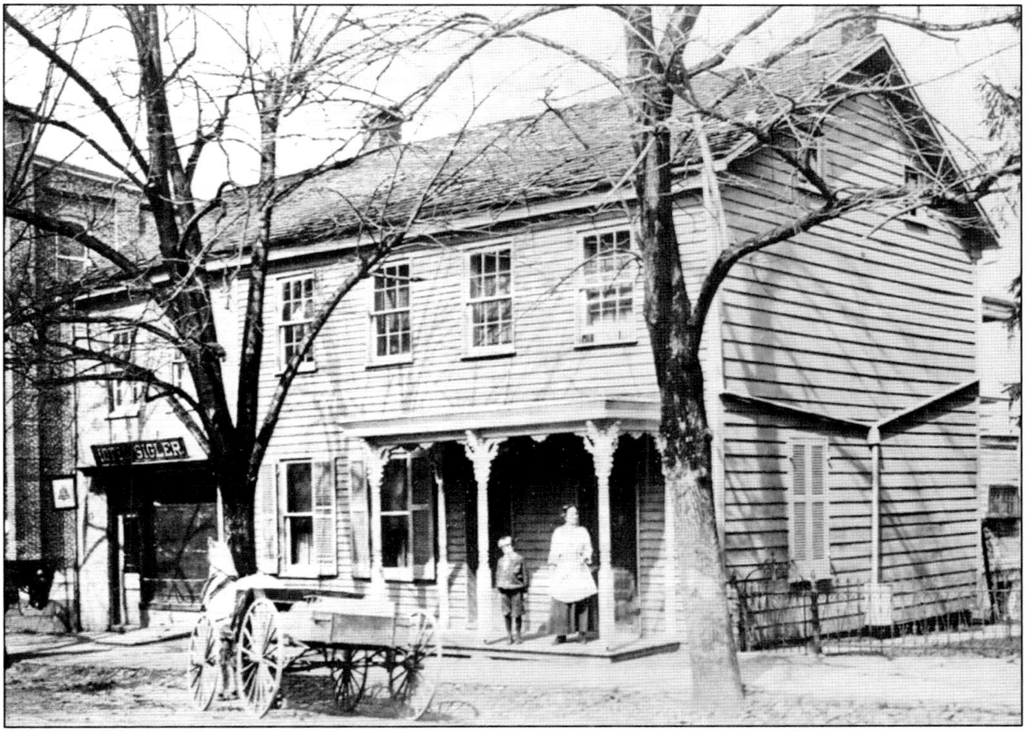

Francis Raphael and Mary Sigler stand in front of the Hotel Sigler located on Main Street. In 1910, when this photograph was taken, Main Street bustled with townspeople who could find everything from the grocery, the butcher, the doctor, and the dentist as well as a saddle and repair shop, all within walking distance. (Courtesy of the Smithsburg Historical Society.)

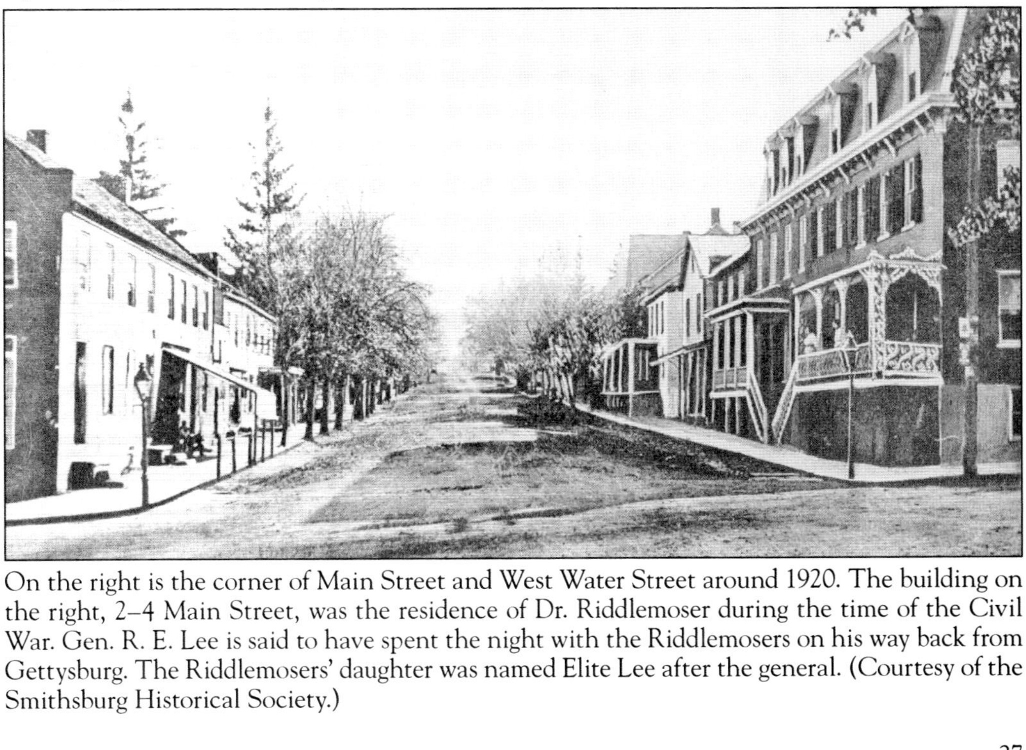

On the right is the corner of Main Street and West Water Street around 1920. The building on the right, 2–4 Main Street, was the residence of Dr. Riddlemoser during the time of the Civil War. Gen. R. E. Lee is said to have spent the night with the Riddlemosers on his way back from Gettysburg. The Riddlemosers' daughter was named Elite Lee after the general. (Courtesy of the Smithsburg Historical Society.)

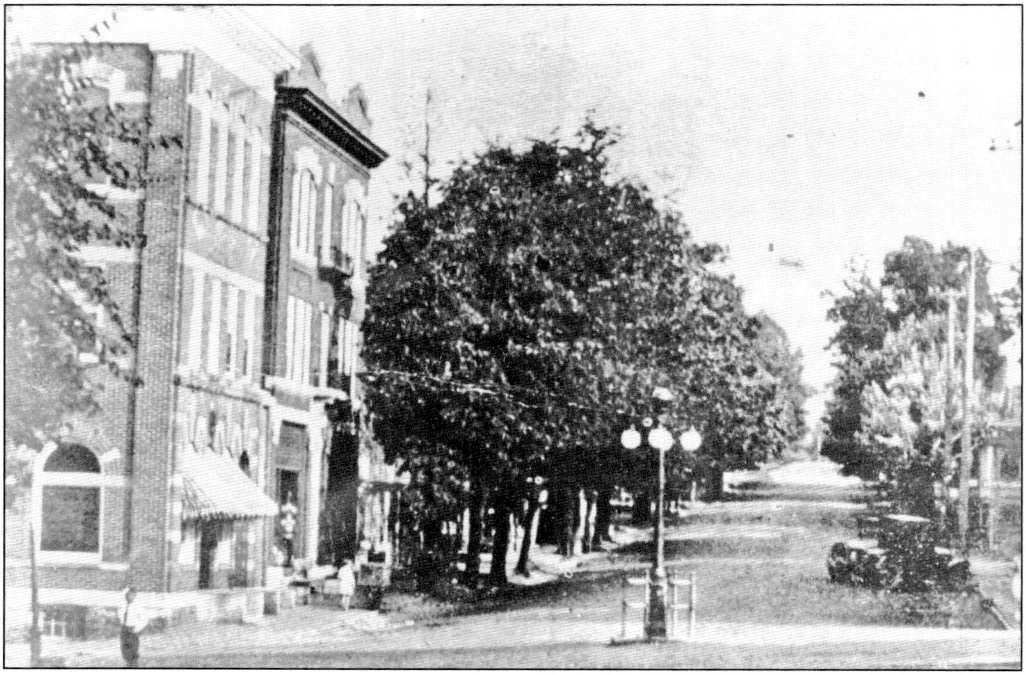

This photograph of the northwest corner of Smithsburg Square was taken in the early 1900s. At the center of the town square stands a streetlight. At left, 1–3 South Main Street was purchased by Lucien Brenner in 1881 to open a general store. The People's Banking Company purchased the property in 1910, and the old general store building was demolished. By 1923, the bank occupied the first floor of this building. (Courtesy of the Smithsburg Historical Society.)

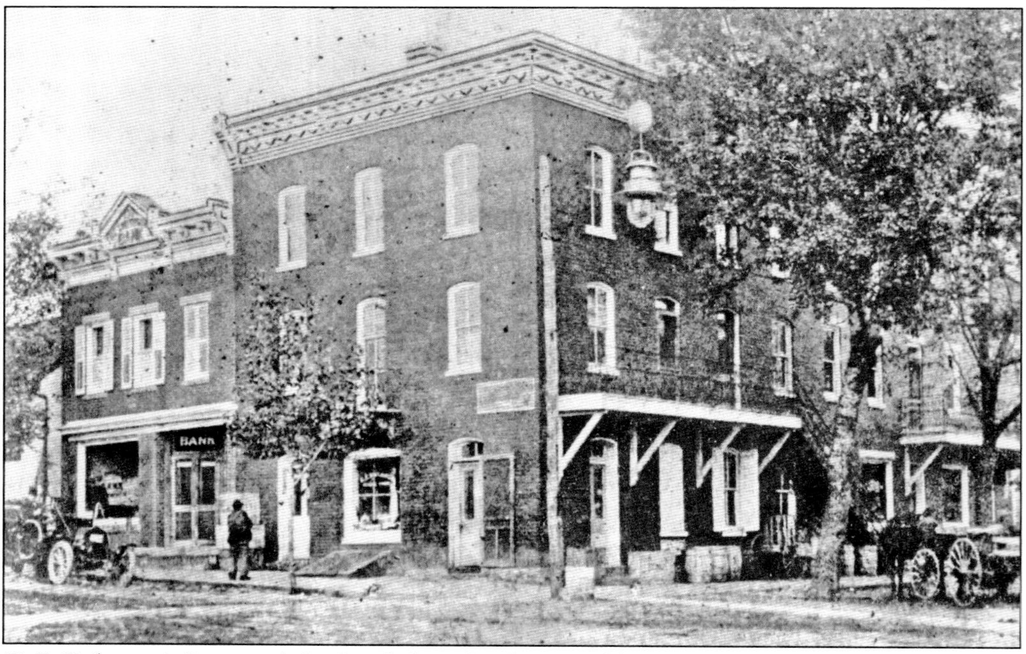

G. E. Ridenour's Store and the Smithsburg Bank are visible on Smithsburg Square. The bank is to the left of Ridenour's building. G. E. Ridenour published this photograph in the late 1800s. (Courtesy of the Smithsburg Historical Society.)

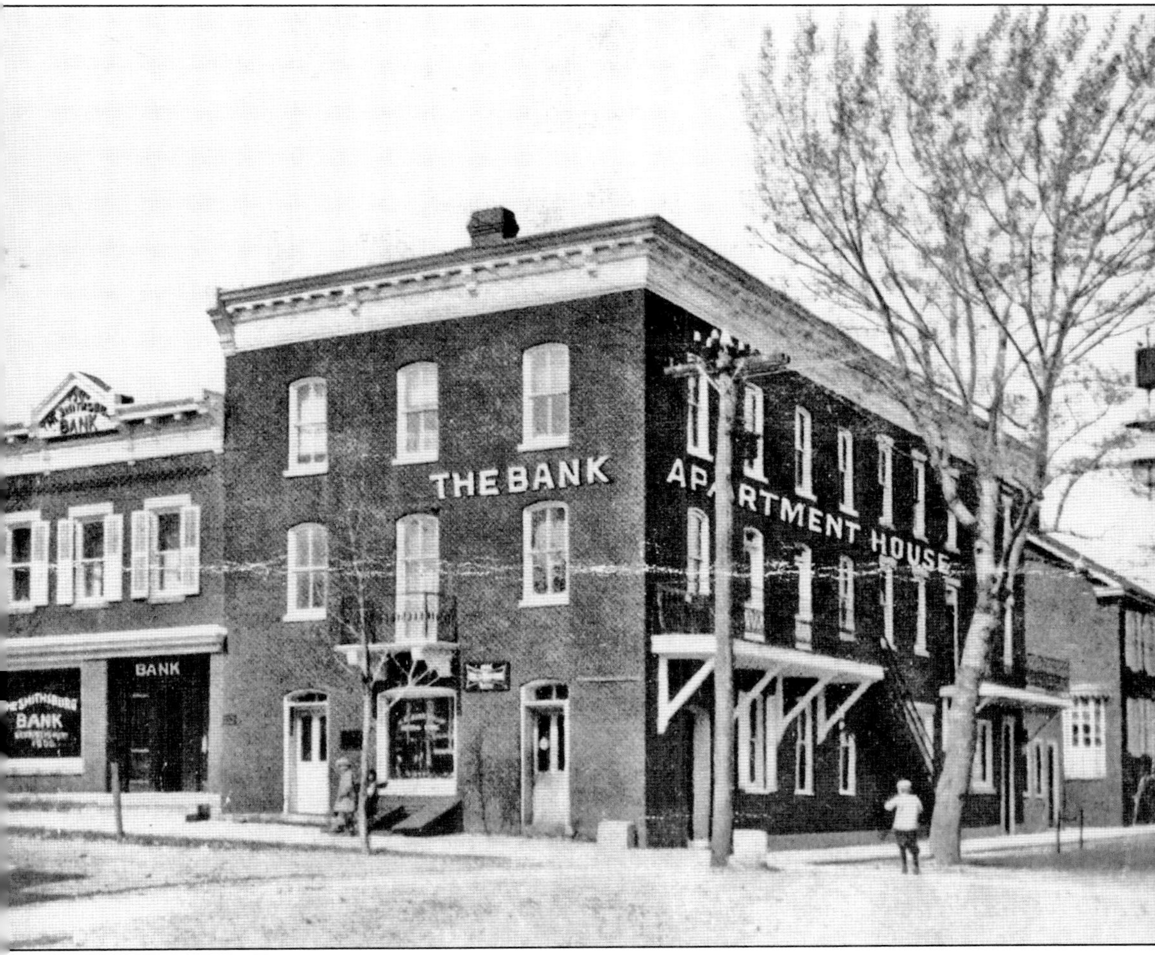

The building at 5–7 North Main Street was constructed in the first decade of the 20th century. The part of the building known as 1–3 North Main was constructed prior to 1866. The first known occupant was L. B. Brenner, who opened a general store in 1866. In 1904, the Smithsburg Bank moved into 4 West Water Street, shown in this photograph. (Courtesy of the Smithsburg Historical Society.)

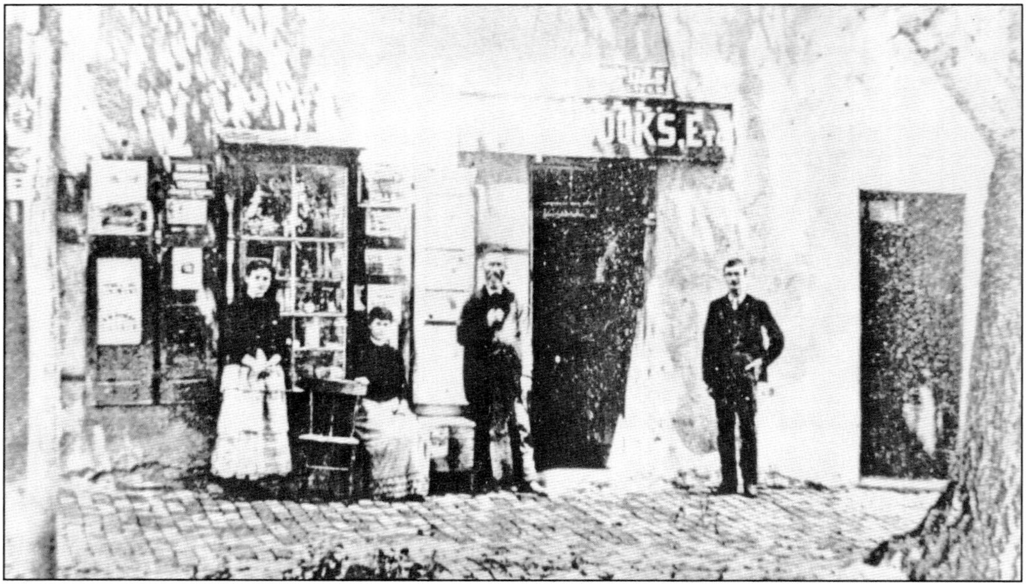

Area residents are pictured out in front of Brenner's general store on Main Street. The old poplar tree to the right in this photograph still stands today. (Courtesy of the Smithsburg Historical Society.)

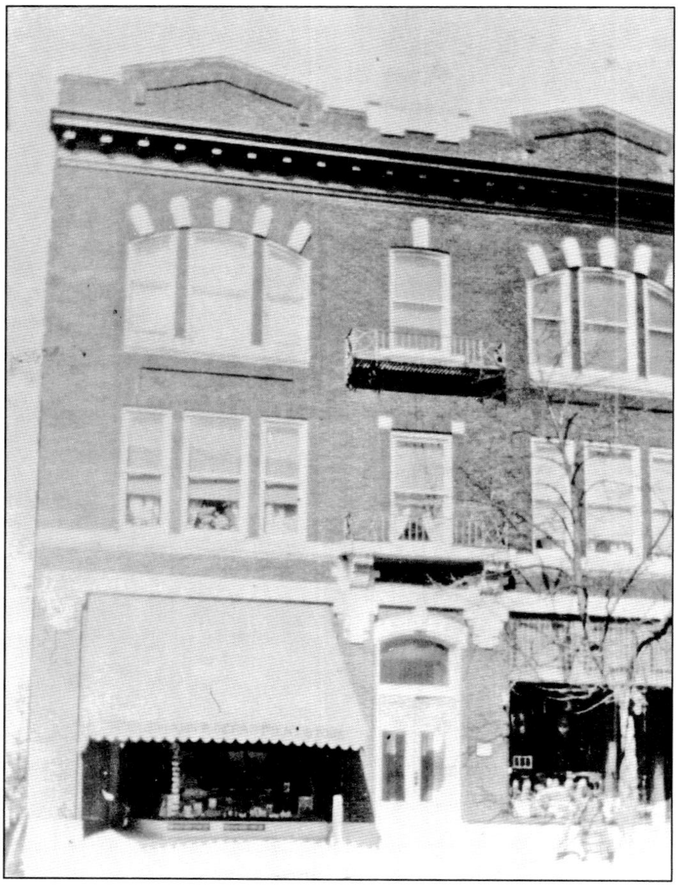

Feldman's Department Store is pictured on the left and Geiser and Wolfinger Hardware Store on the right on West Main Street around 1920. Today Vince's Italian Restaurant occupies the section of the building at right. (Courtesy of the Smithsburg Historical Society.)

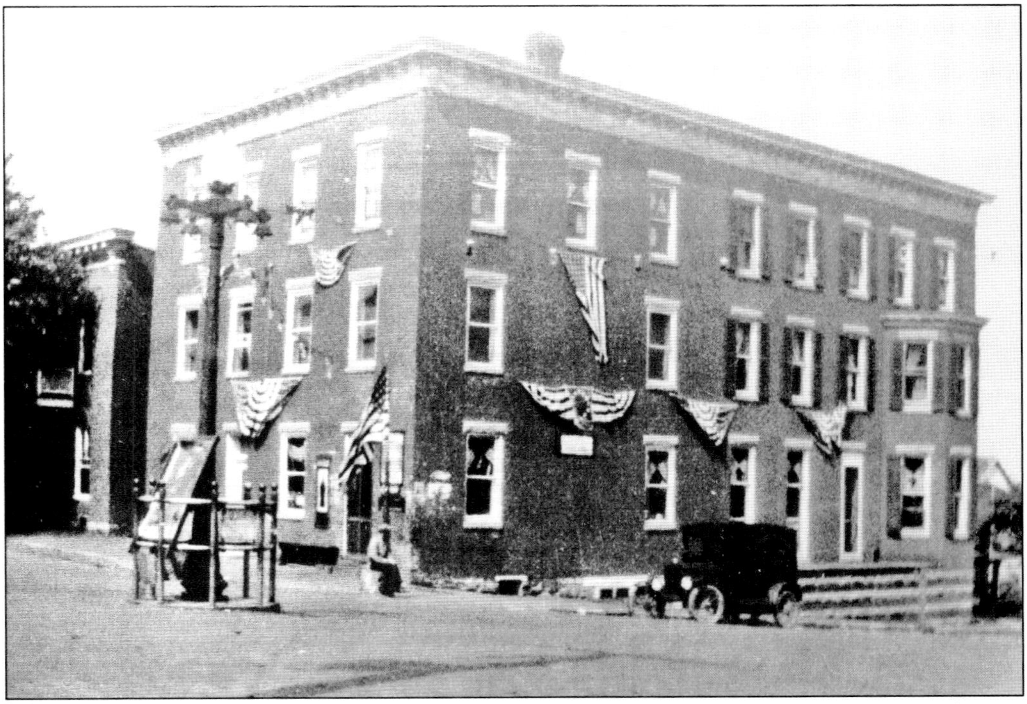

An early-1900s photograph shows Brenner's Store on the corner of East Water Street and Main Street. L. B. Brenner moved his store from the southeast corner of Main Street to the northeast corner after the original Brenner's Store was demolished in the early 1900s.

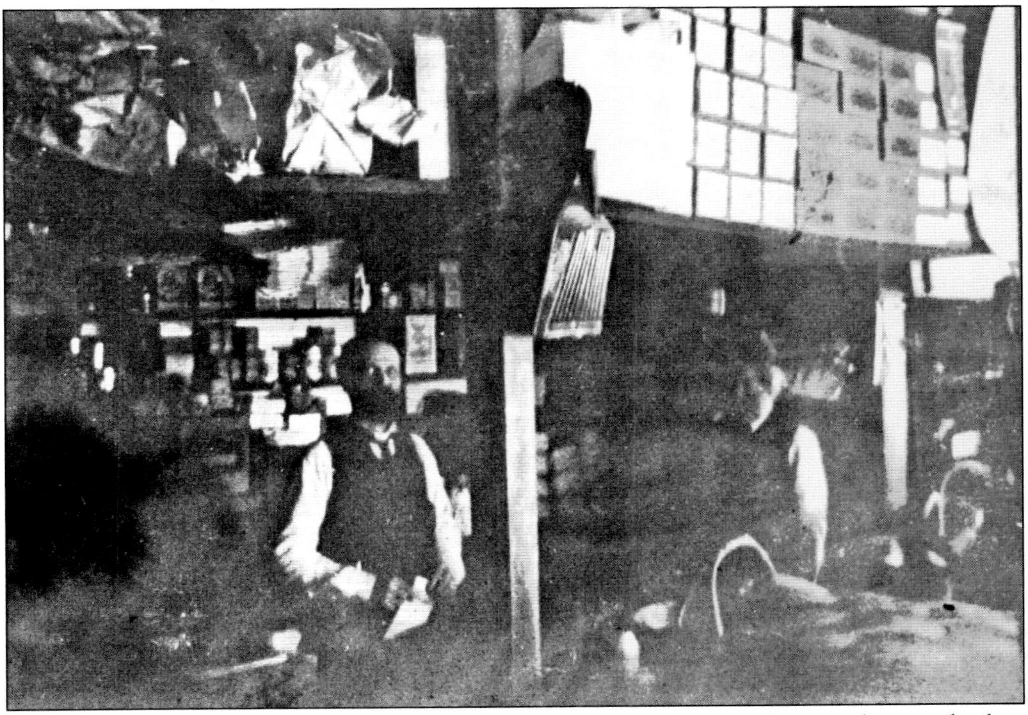

A rare glimpse inside Brenner's Store on Main Street, this photograph was taken in the late 1800s, prior to demolition. (Courtesy of the Smithsburg Historical Society.)

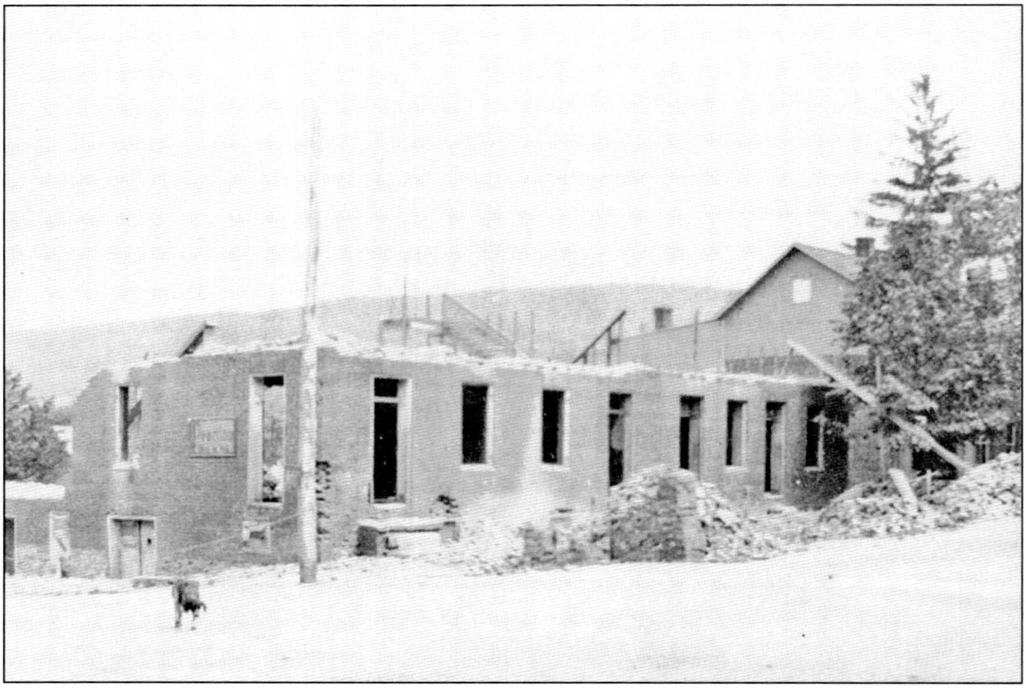

Old Brenner's Store was located on the southeast corner of Smithsburg Square until it was torn down in 1909. Brenner moved his store to the northeast corner of Main Street. (Courtesy of the Smithsburg Historical Society.)

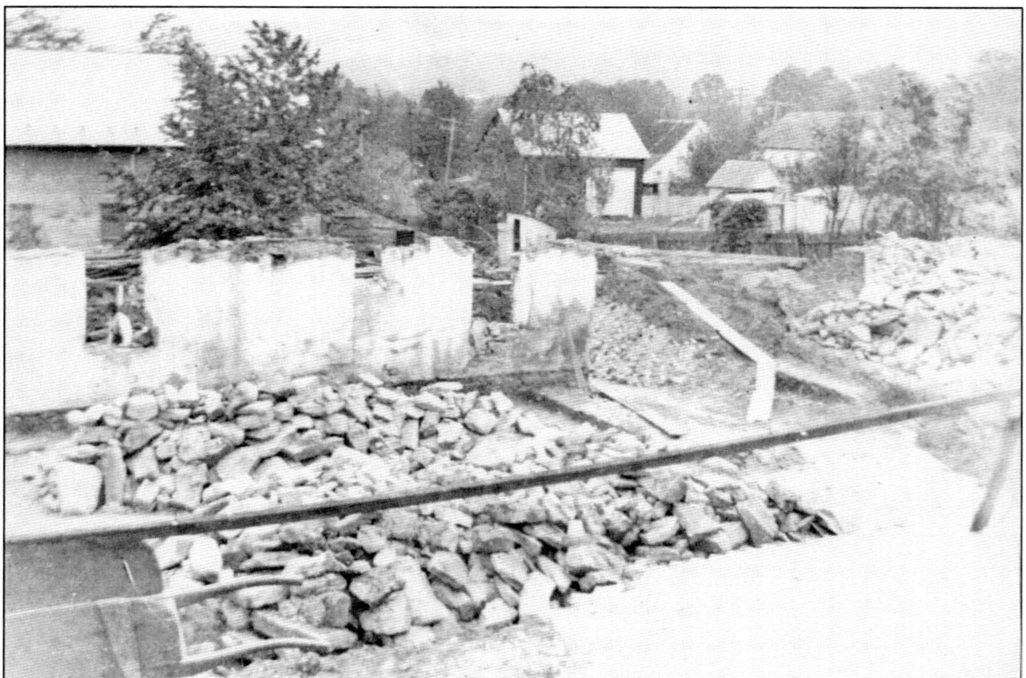

A different view of Brenner's Store shows the demolition in 1909. The piles of stones in this photograph were taken to the Cavetown quarry. (Courtesy of the Smithsburg Historical Society.)

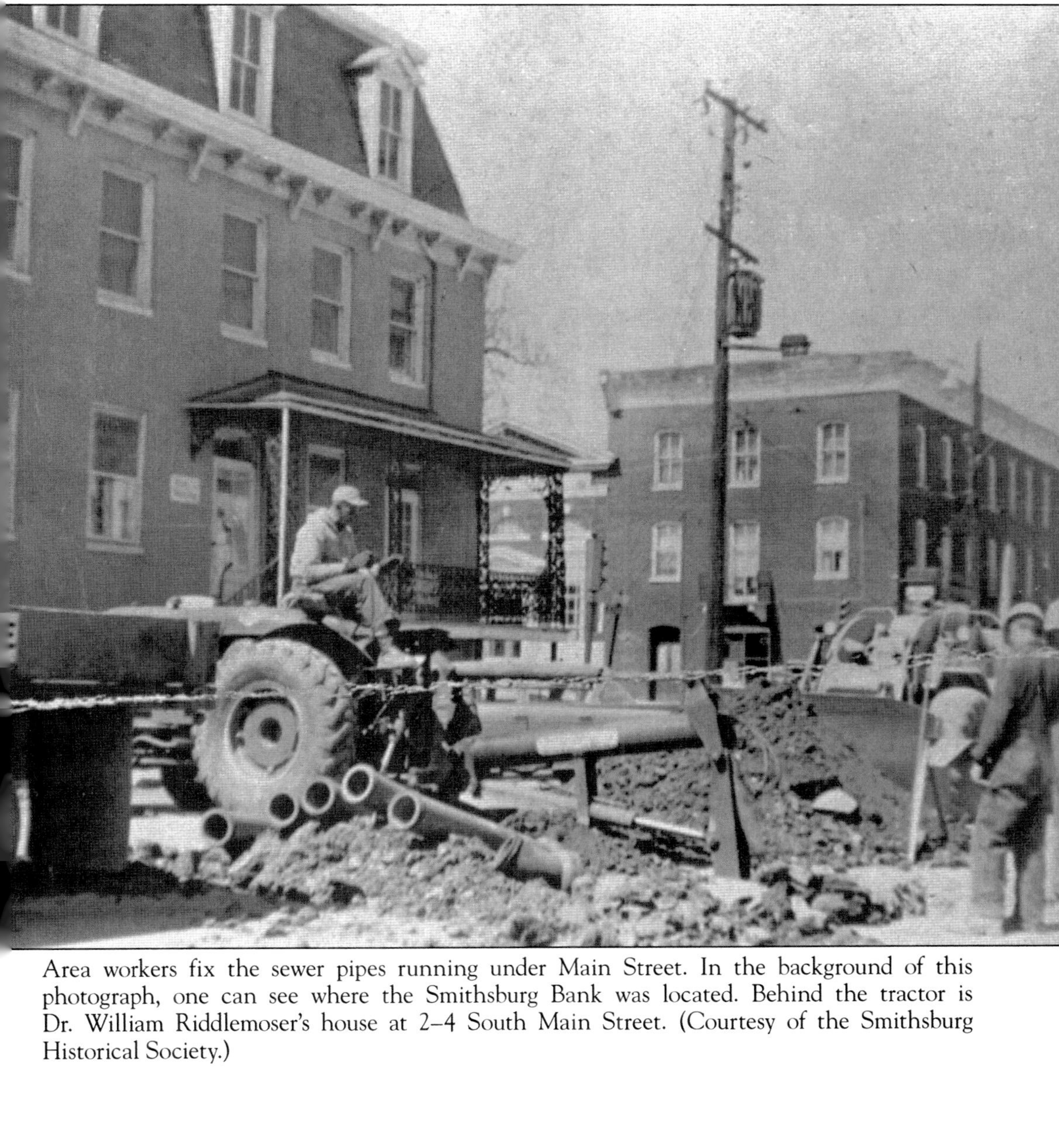

Area workers fix the sewer pipes running under Main Street. In the background of this photograph, one can see where the Smithsburg Bank was located. Behind the tractor is Dr. William Riddlemoser's house at 2–4 South Main Street. (Courtesy of the Smithsburg Historical Society.)

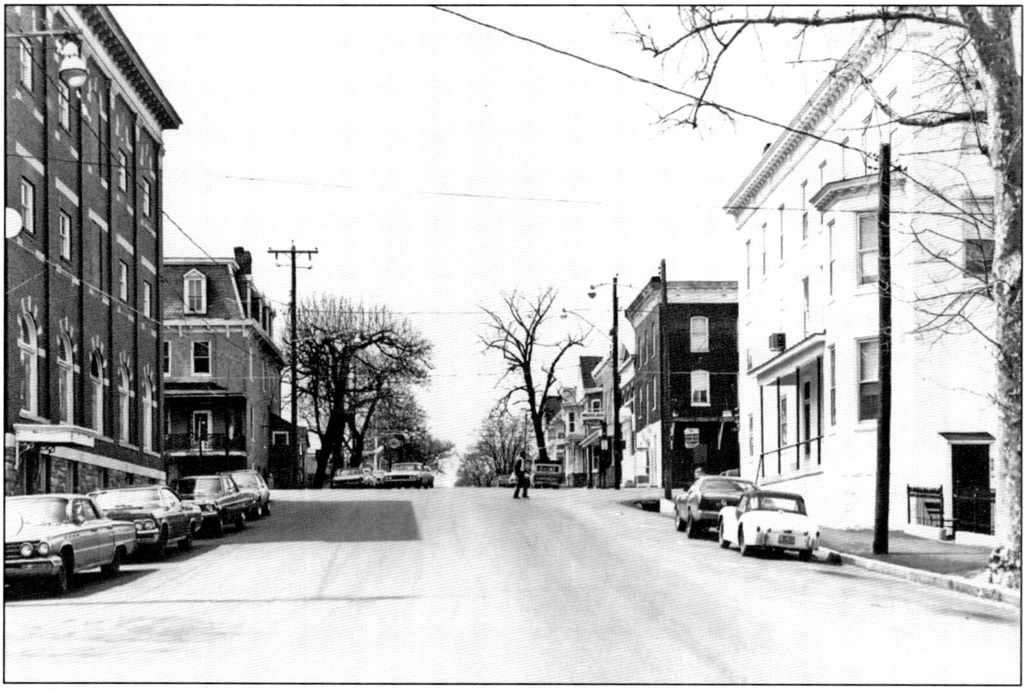

Looking along East Water Street toward the Main Street intersection, the white building directly to the right is a side view of where the general store used to be. (Courtesy of the Smithsburg Historical Society.)

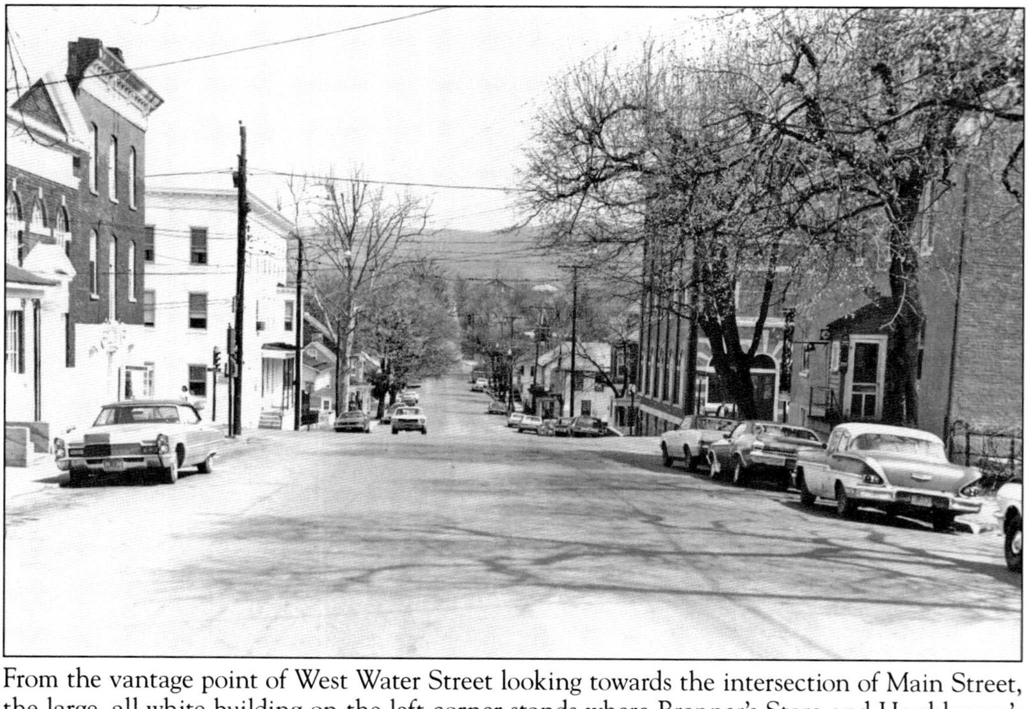

From the vantage point of West Water Street looking towards the intersection of Main Street, the large, all-white building on the left corner stands where Brenner's Store and Hershberger's general store used to stand. This photograph was taken in the early 1970s. (Courtesy of the Smithsburg Historical Society.)

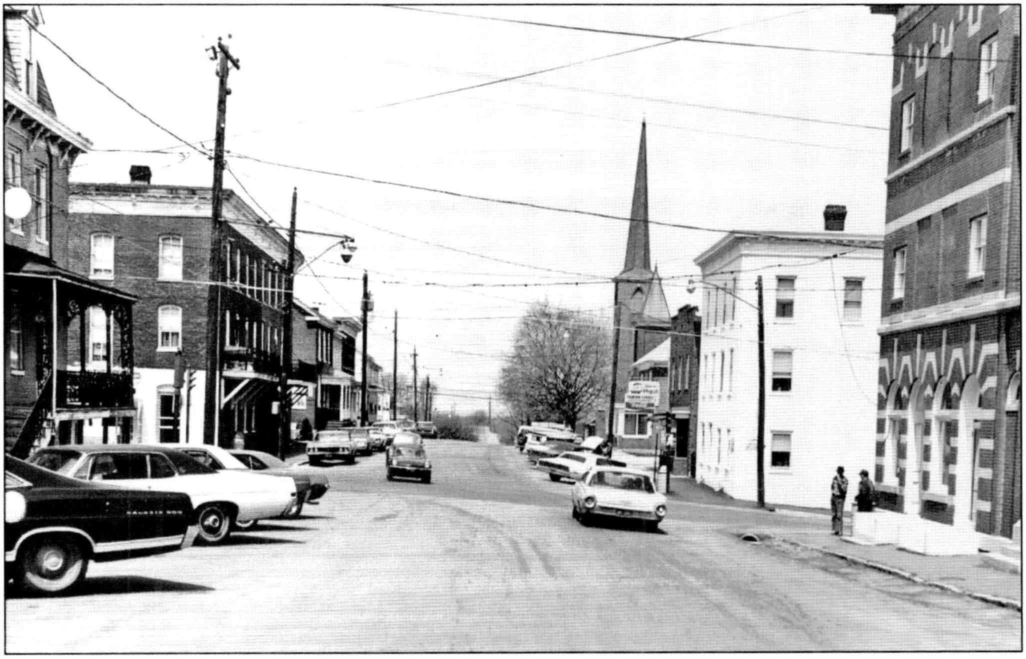

This 1974 photograph shows the Main Street and Water Street intersection looking towards West Main Street. In the background on the right is Trinity Lutheran Church. Just before the church is the Dixie Eatery, where many have had great food. (Courtesy of the Smithsburg Historical Society.)

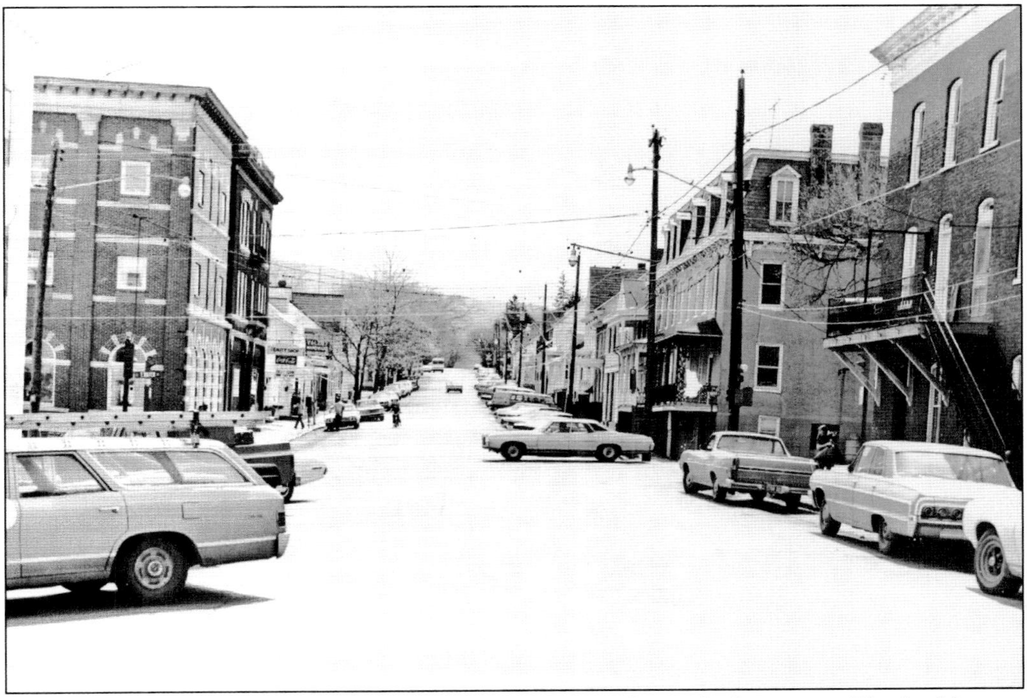

This perspective Smithsburg Square is from West Main Street looking east. The building to the right with the long staircase used to be the Smithsburg Bank. (Courtesy of the Smithsburg Historical Society.)

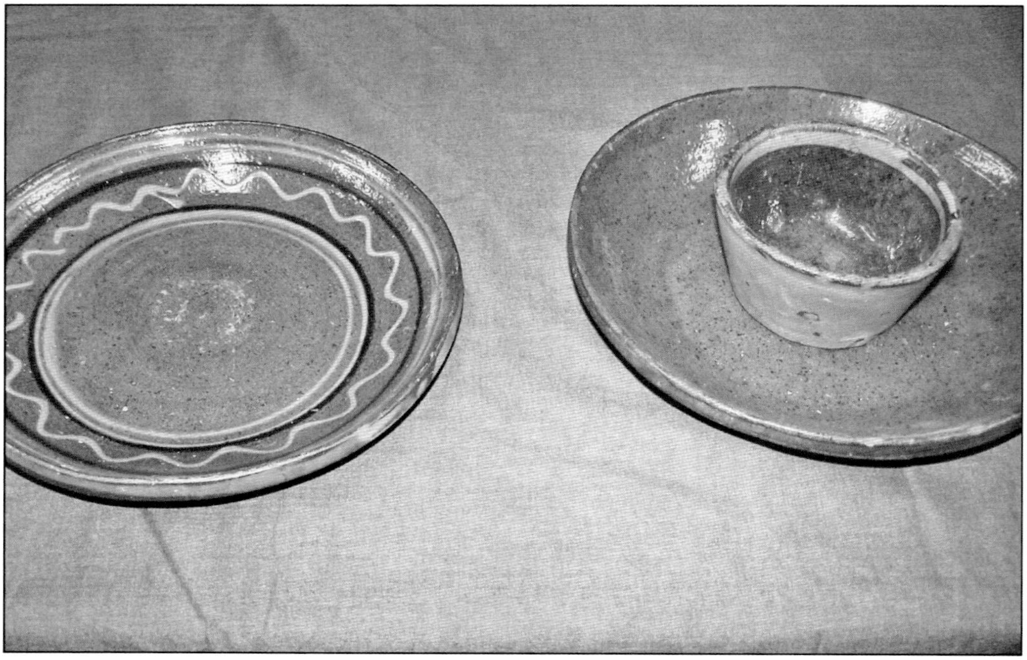

Pictured are two of the few pieces of Kimler Pottery still in existence. The Smithsburg Historical Society is lucky have a few pieces of this pottery. (Courtesy of the Smithsburg Historical Society.)

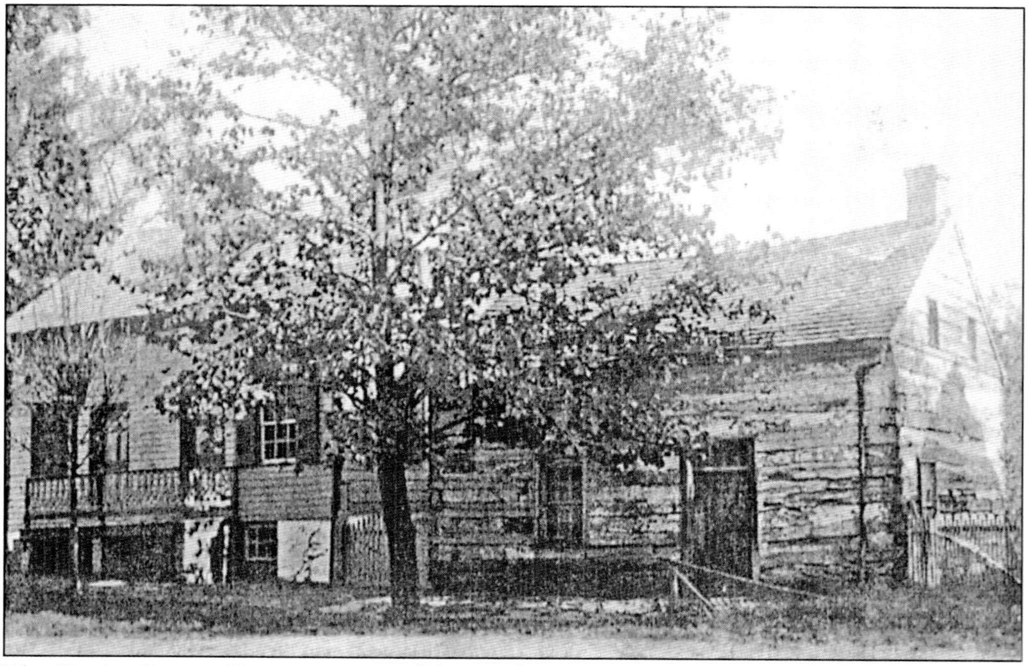

The Kimler Pottery House was named for Jacob Frederich Kimler, a German immigrant who settled in Smithsburg in 1832. Only a few pieces of Kimler pottery survive today. The house is located on East Water Street just steps away from the Smithsburg Historical Society. In the 1880s, the street was raised by 5 feet. The first floor of the house became the basement. William Kimler inherited the property in 1913. (Courtesy of the Smithsburg Historical Society.)

Three

People, Places, and Things

The Heart of a Town

As many people who come from a small town will say, it is the people who are the heart and soul of the town. The same can be said about Smithsburg. Since its inception, the town has produced many doctors, lawyers, educators, artists, and writers, as well as successful residents who have chosen to make Smithsburg their home. Some notable residents who have called Smithsburg their home include Christopher "Stuffle" Smith, Emily Clayton Bishop, Edgar Irving Brenner, Peter Geiser, Jacob Frederich Kimler, A. J. Harbaugh, George Pearson, George C. Pearson, Samuel Barkdoll, Dr. William Riddlemoser, and Luther B. Newcomer, among many others.

Emily Bishop, Young Scupltor, Dead.

Special to The New York Times.

PHILADELPHIA, March 2. — Miss Emily Clayton Bishop, one of the most promising graduates in last year's class at the Pennsylvania Academy of the Fine Arts, whose first works are on show in the current annual exhibition, died of heart disease last night at her home in Smithsburg, Md. Miss Bishop was regarded as one of the most promising of America's younger sculptors. She was but slightly more than 20 years old. Three of her recent works have a prominent place in the present exhibition. These are "Woman Knitting," "Portrait of Browning," and "John."

Obituary Notes.

BRAINARD RORISON of 800 Riverside Drive died suddenly yesterday of heart disease. Mr. Rorison was for many years a member of the A. L. Barber Asphalt Company of New York and Washington, and in company with A. L. Barber, the head of that company, went to California several years ago to develop California asphalt. He was a native of this State and was born at Waterloo 62 years ago.

The Rev. MICHAEL F. KELIHER, for the last five years assistant pastor of the Church of Our Lady of Solace, at White Plains Road and Van Nest Avenue, died after a brief illness on Friday. He was born in Oswego, N. Y., forty-six years ago, and was educated at Manhattan College and at St. Joseph's Seminary in Troy.

FREDERICK F. HASSAM, an antiquarian, died at the age of 86, on Thursday, at Needham, Mass. During the civil war he had a private recruiting station in the Old South Meeting House yard, and in 1863 President Lincoln appointed him censor of the local press. He retired from the hardware business in 1870. Mr. Hassam is survived by three sons.

ROBERT LAWRENCE VAN DEUSEN, a newspaper man of this city, died yesterday at Liberty, Sullivan County, N. Y., where he went two months ago in a last effort to fight off tuberculosis. Mr. Van Deusen was born in Great Barrington, Mass., 35 years ago, and started his newspaper work in New York on The Evening Sun. Later he was connected with The Evening World and The Evening Telegram, and for the last two years he was with The New York Herald.

JAMES J. WISEMAN, clerk in the office of Surrogate John P. Egan of Hudson County, died yesterday at 82 Wayne Street, Jersey City. He served as clerk of the Jersey City Board of Education from 1890 to 1892, and again from 1897 until 1905. Mr. Wiseman was 52 years old.

Mrs. MAGDALENE VAN BRUNT, widow of J. Holmes Van Brunt, died on Thursday in her apartment at the Hotel Mohawk, Washington Avenue, Brooklyn. Mrs. Van Brunt, who was born in 1834, the daughter of Charles B. Vanderveer, was a member of the Van Siclen family, who were of the earliest settlers of Kings County. Her son, Charles Van Brunt, and her daughter, Mrs. V. B. McKeever, survive her.

ANNE FITZHUGH MILLER, a granddaughter of Gerrit Smith, and a prominent woman suffragist, died on Friday at the Abbotsford in Boston. She was a daughter of the late Col. Charles Dudley Miller and Mrs. Elizabeth Smith Miller.

EUGENE ANDERSON died on Friday at his home in Amityville, L. I. He is survived by Mrs. Anderson, to whom he was married in 1894. She is a daughter of the late Hippolite Mali and a niece of the late Charles Mali, Consul General of Belgium in New York. Mr. Anderson was the greatgrandson of Caspar Samlar, a farmer of Dutch descent who lived in the first decade of the last century in a frame house on the site of the Gilsey House.

HENRY A. BARTLETT, for many years a member of the paper manufacturing firm of Darickson & Co., died on Friday at his home, 578 Bedford Avenue, Brooklyn. He was a member of the old Union Club of Williamsburg and of the baseball team of former years that was known as the Eckfords. Mr. Bartlett was 72 years of age.

Mrs. MABEL TAYLOR PIERCE, widow of Lieut. Earl C. Pierce, U. S. A., died on Fri-

This obituary for Emily Clayton Bishop ran in the *New York Times* on Sunday, March 3, 1912, on page 15. Her obituary states the cause of death as heart disease; however, it is debatable whether Bishop died from heart disease or tuberculosis. (Courtesy of the Smithsburg Historical Society.)

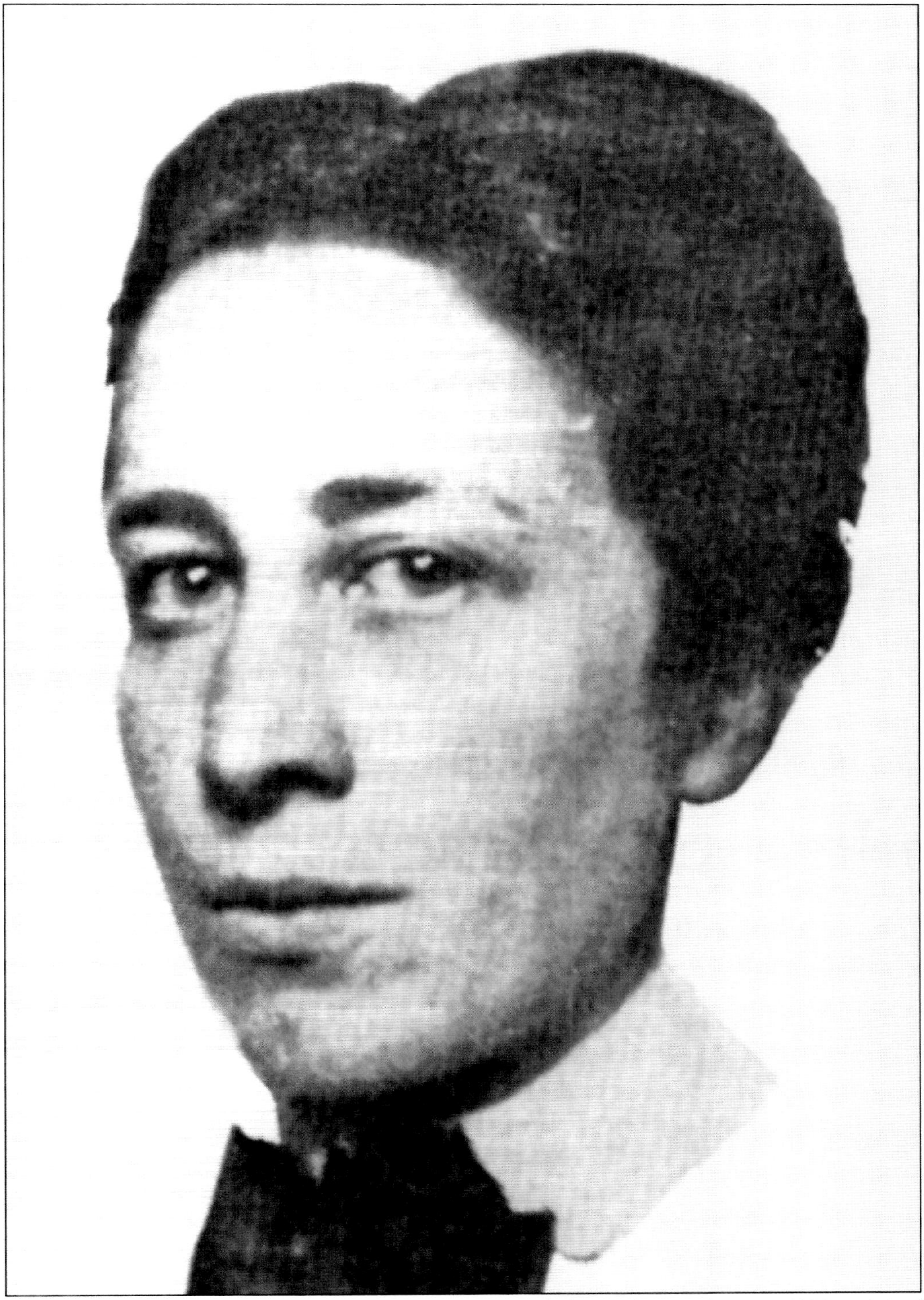

Emily Clayton Bishop was a prominent artist from Smithsburg. She was born in 1883 and died in 1912 of either heart disease or tuberculosis. Having traveled to foreign lands, Bishop studied her art extensively by earning scholarships to prestigious schools. (Courtesy of the Smithsburg Historical Society.)

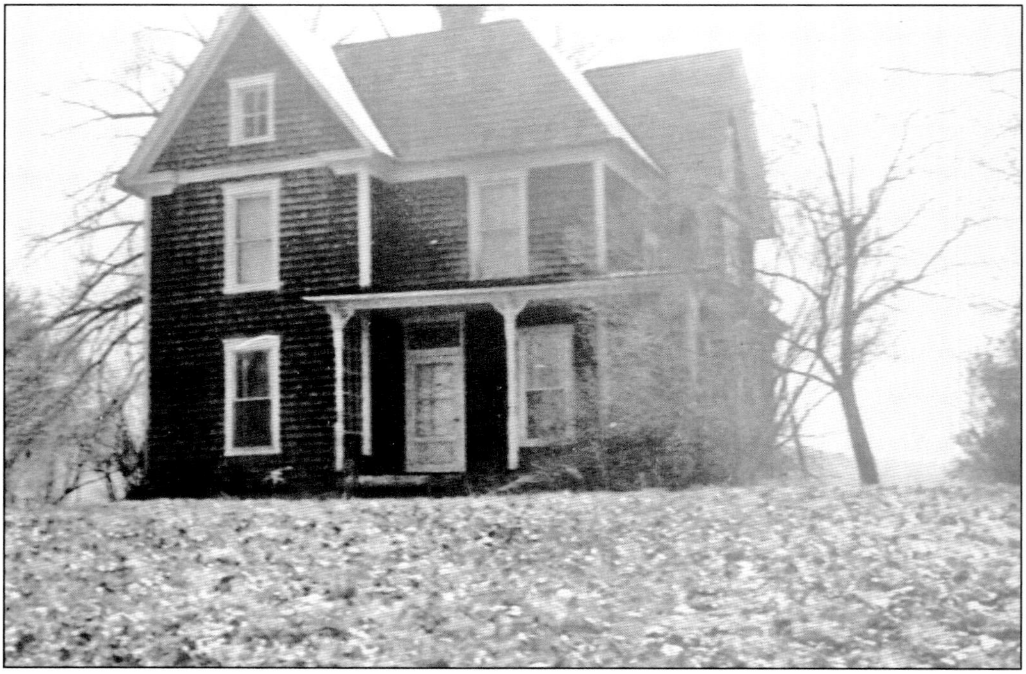

This was the home of Benjamin, Susanne, Emily, and Lucy Bishop. Dedicated Episcopalians, the Bishop family attended St. Ann's Episcopal Church in Smithsburg. Unfortunately the house was torn down in 1968. (Courtesy of the Smithsburg Historical Society.)

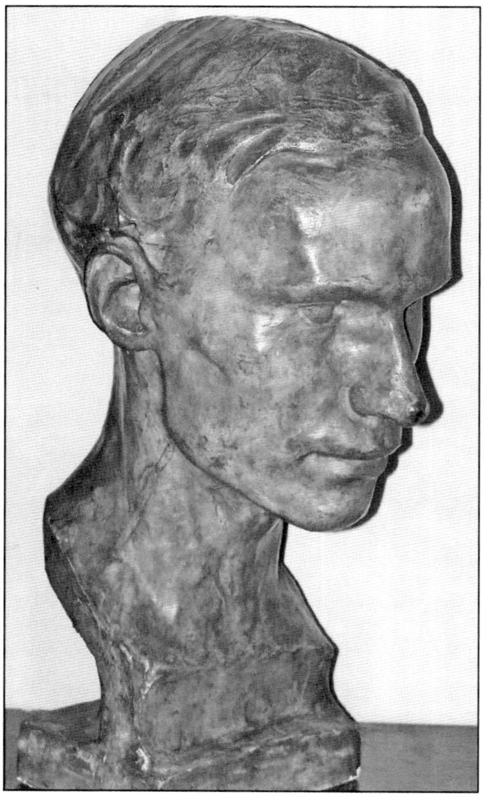

Emily Clayton Bishop created this statue. While many of her works are displayed at museums throughout the United States, including the Smithsonian in Washington, D.C., some of her works are on display at the Smithsburg Historical Society. (Courtesy of the Smithsburg Historical Society.)

This is another sculpture by Emily Clayton Bishop. A generous portion of Bishop's works is on display at the Smithsburg Historical Society. (Courtesy of the Smithsburg Historical Society.)

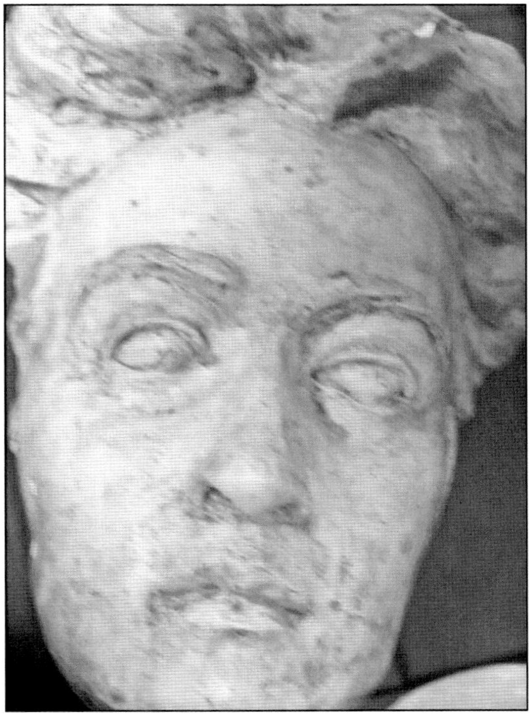

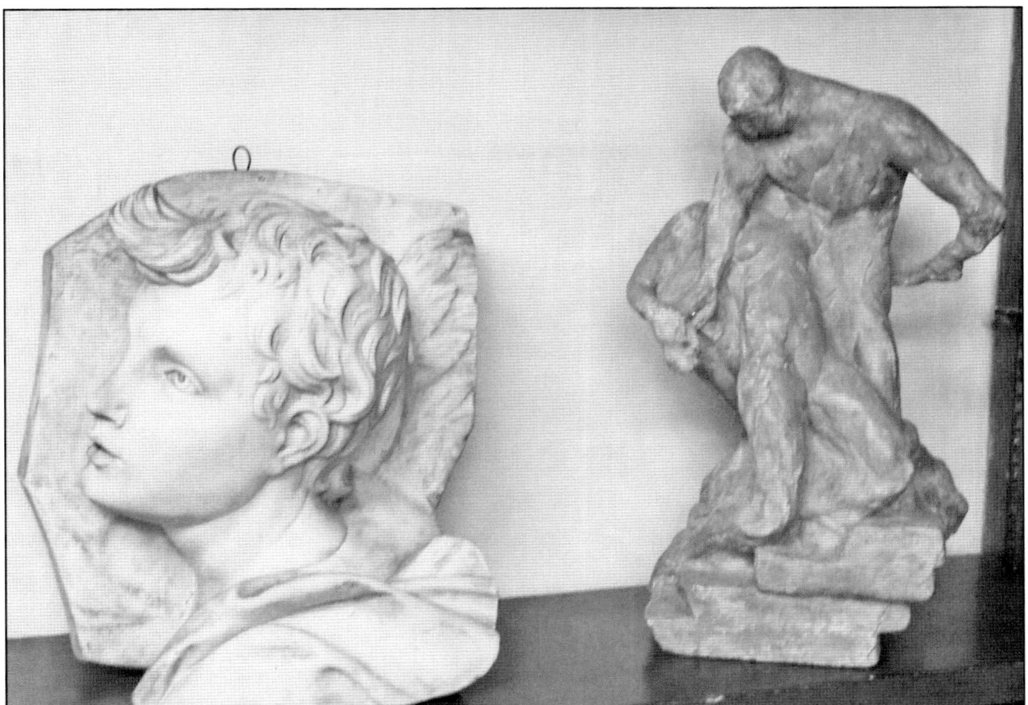

Emily Clayton Bishop's artwork is displayed in the town historical society. Bishop attended the Maryland Institute School of Art in Baltimore at age 16. As a prominent artist, Bishop traveled to England, Holland, Paris, Italy, and Greece on scholarship. (Courtesy of the Smithsburg Historical Society.)

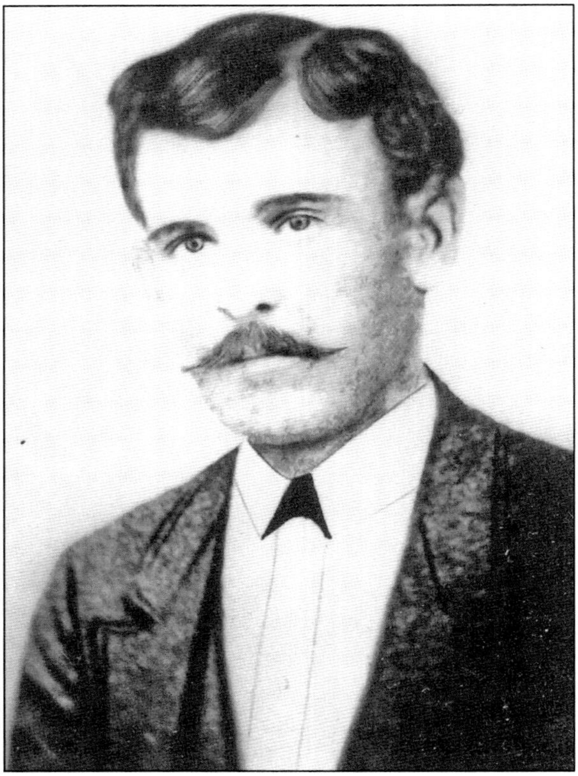

William Tilden Slick is pictured after his death. Whiskers have been drawn on his face, and other features, such as the eyes, are enhanced by pen. (Courtesy of Sari Slick Kilheffer.)

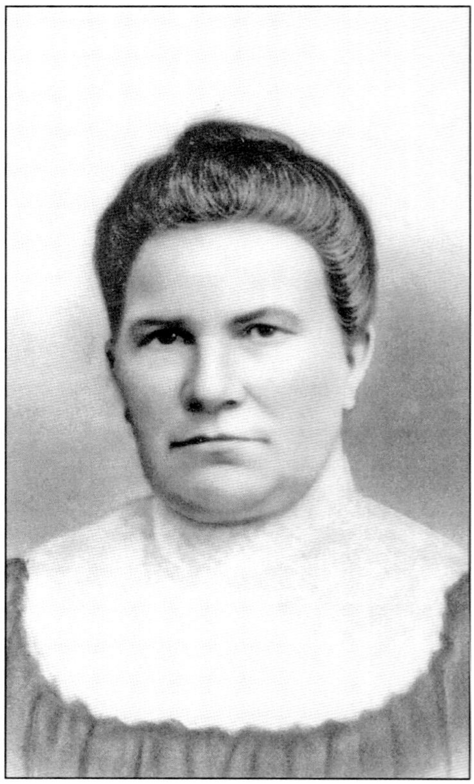

This charcoal drawing is of Anna Masters. Such portraits were a common way of documenting history from the late 1800s to early 1900s. (Courtesy of Sari Slick Kilheffer.)

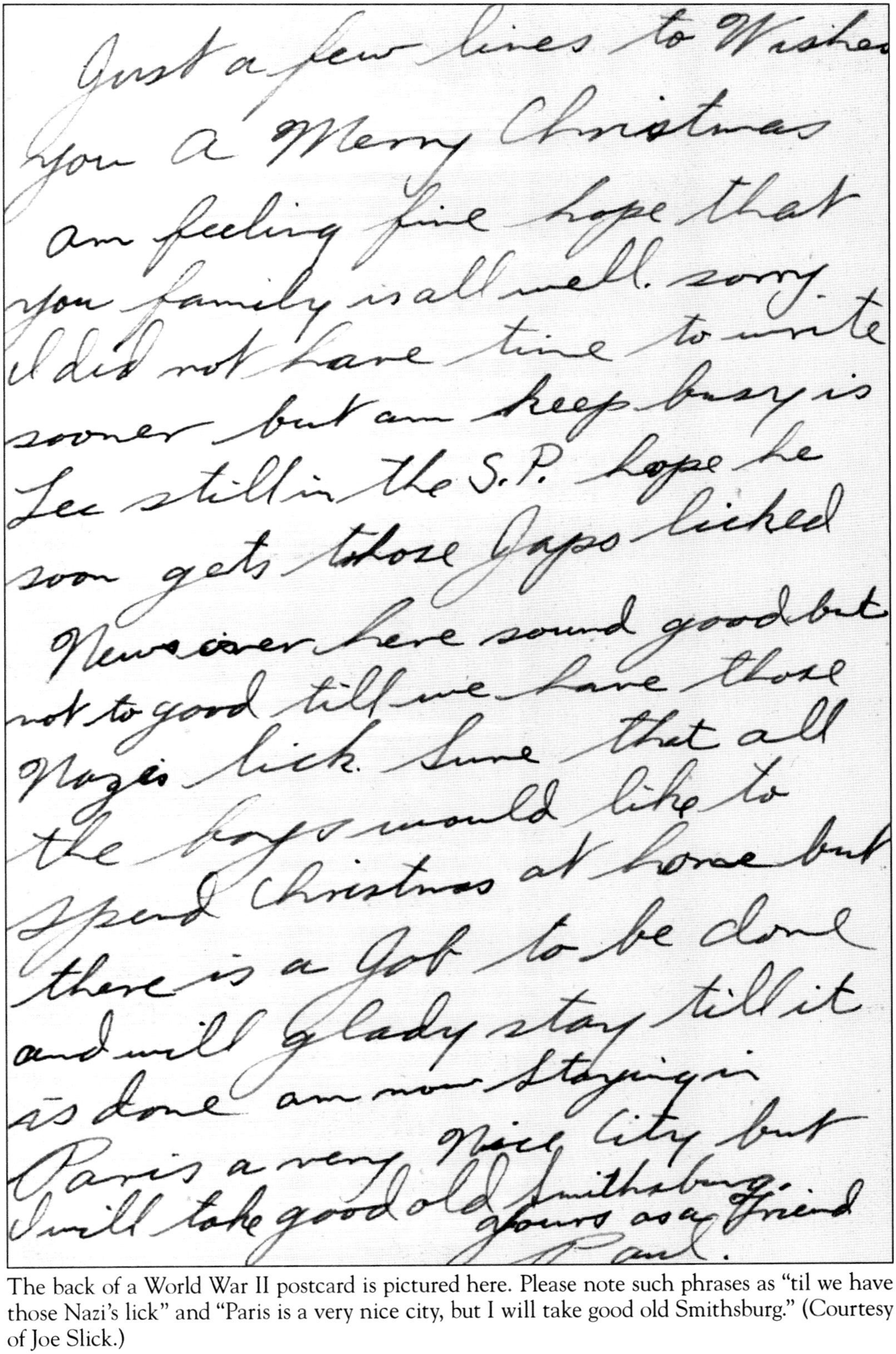

Just a few lines to Wishes
you a Merry Christmas
am feeling fine hope that
you family is all well. sorry
I did not have time to write
sooner but am keep busy is
Lee still in the S.P. hope he
soon gets those Japs licked
News over here sound good but
not to good till we have those
Nazi's lick. Sure that all
the boys would like to
spend Christmas at home but
there is a Job to be done
and will glady stay till it
is done am now Staying in
Paris a very Nice City but
I will take good old Smithsburg.
yours as a Friend
Paul.

The back of a World War II postcard is pictured here. Please note such phrases as "til we have those Nazi's lick" and "Paris is a very nice city, but I will take good old Smithsburg." (Courtesy of Joe Slick.)

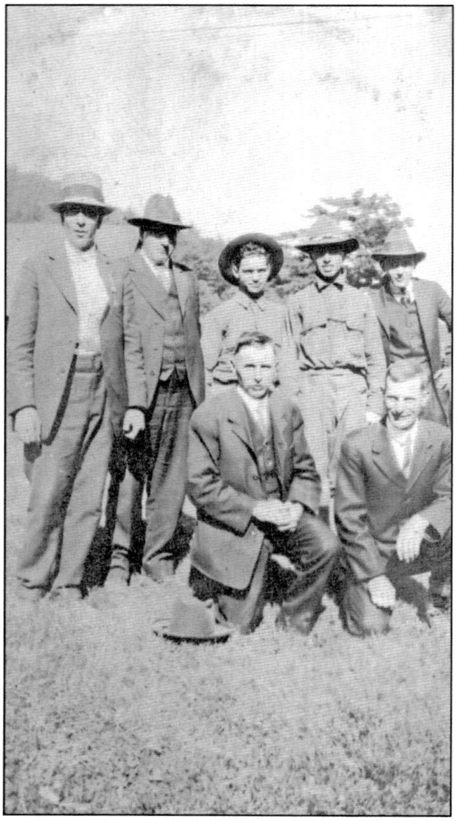

A group of mostly unidentified men (Charles Slick Sr. is in the bottom right corner) stands in a Smithsburg backyard for this photograph taken early 1900s. (Courtesy of Sari Slick Kilheffer.)

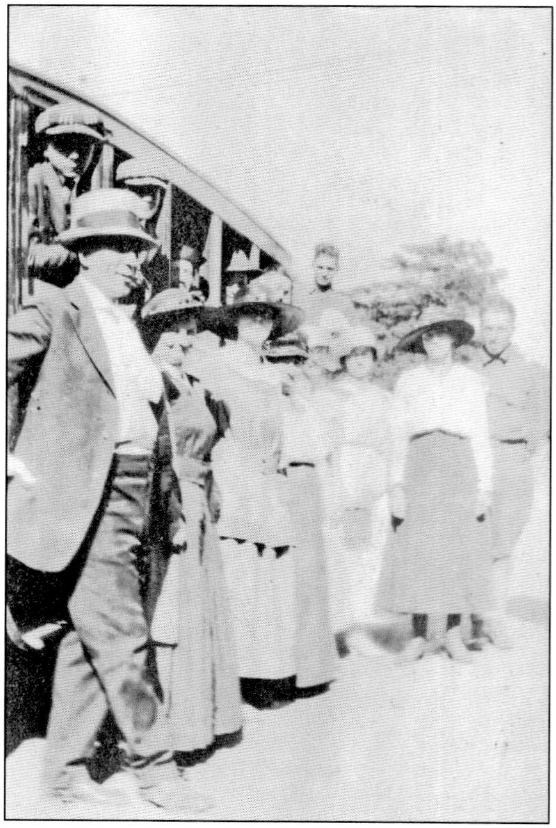

A bus ride to Pen Mar, not terribly far from Smithsburg, provides an opportunity to get away from town for a few hours. (Courtesy of Joe Slick.)

Maurice Slick is pictured in his grandmother's backyard around 1917. The house, located in Smithsburg, still stands today. (Courtesy of Sari Slick Kilheffer.)

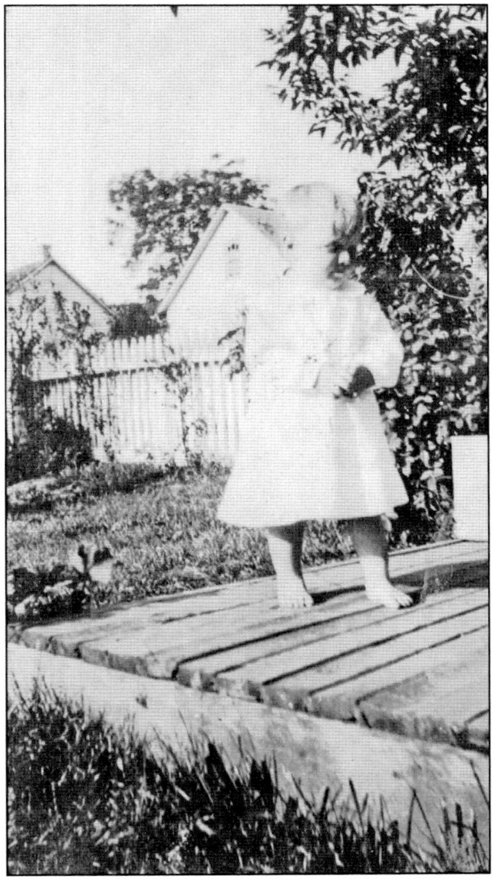

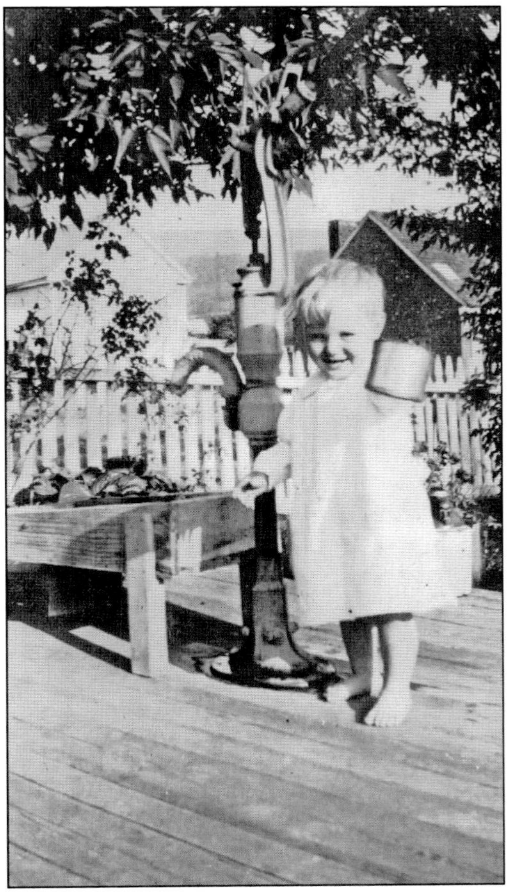

Maurice Slick is at the well getting ready for a drink around 1917. Most of the residents had well water with these pumps attached. (Courtesy of Sari Slick Kilheffer.)

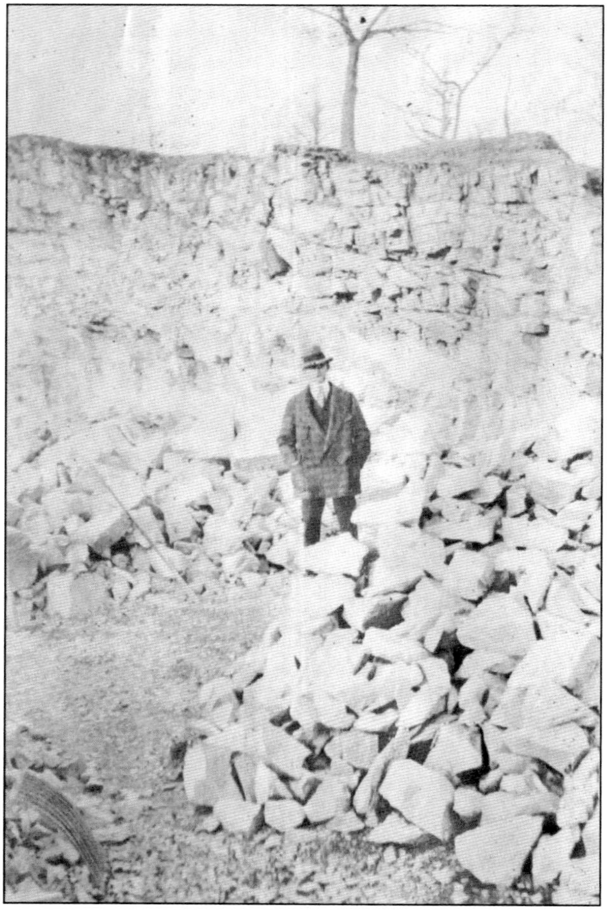

An unidentified man is pictured at the Cavetown Quarry. The quarry provided many townspeople with the materials to build their homes. (Courtesy of Sari Slick Kilheffer.)

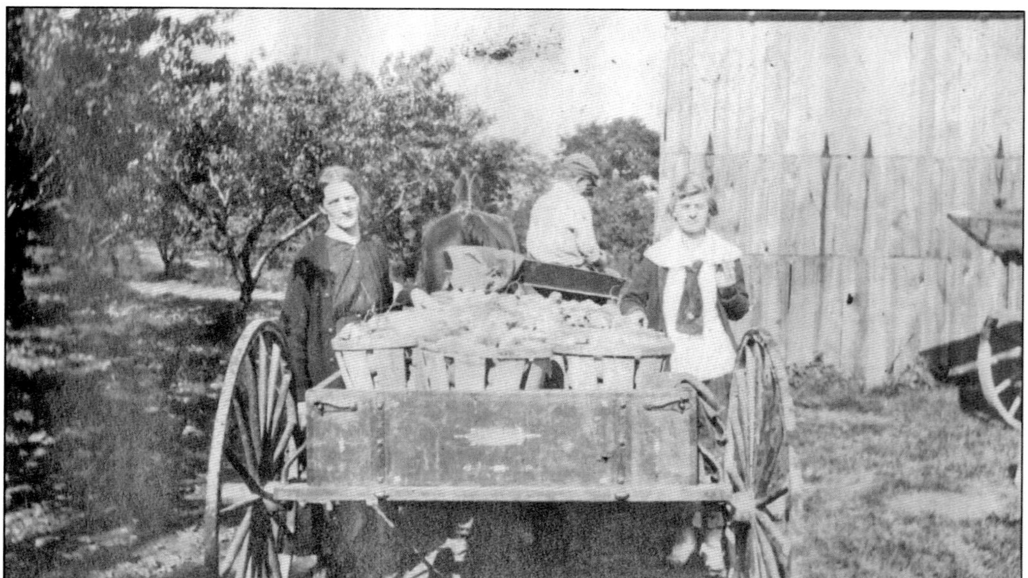

Gertrude Hessong Smith, left, gathers the harvest on her property. The photograph was taken around 1900. (Courtesy of Joe Slick.)

On July 28, 1918, these unidentified people had to change the tire on their car. (Courtesy of Sari Slick Kilheffer.)

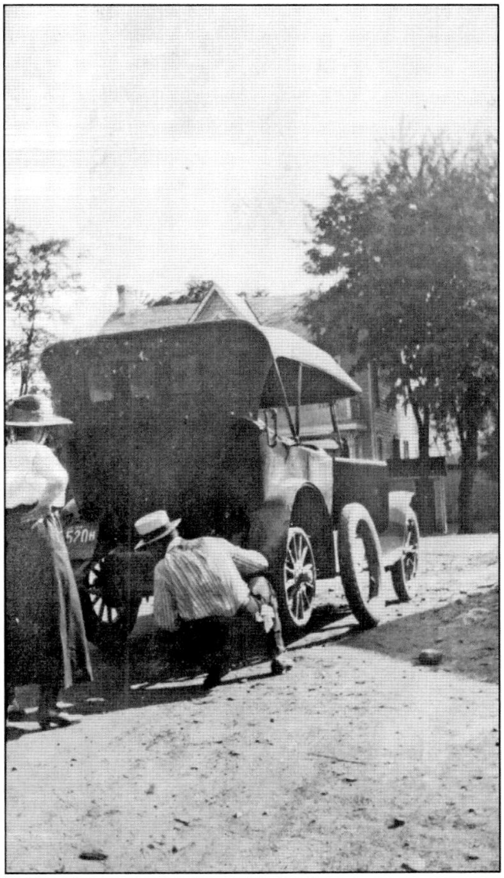

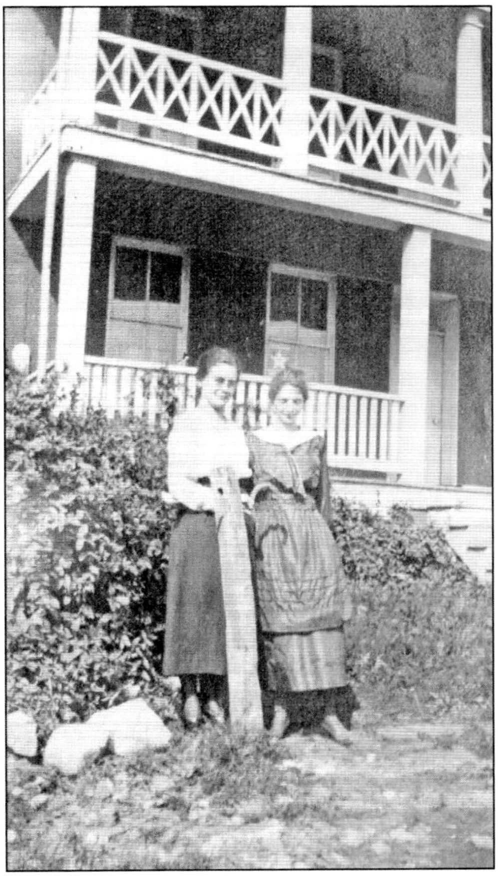

Matilda Smith Harris is pictured at right with an unidentified woman at left in front of a Smithsburg home. (Courtesy of Joe Slick.)

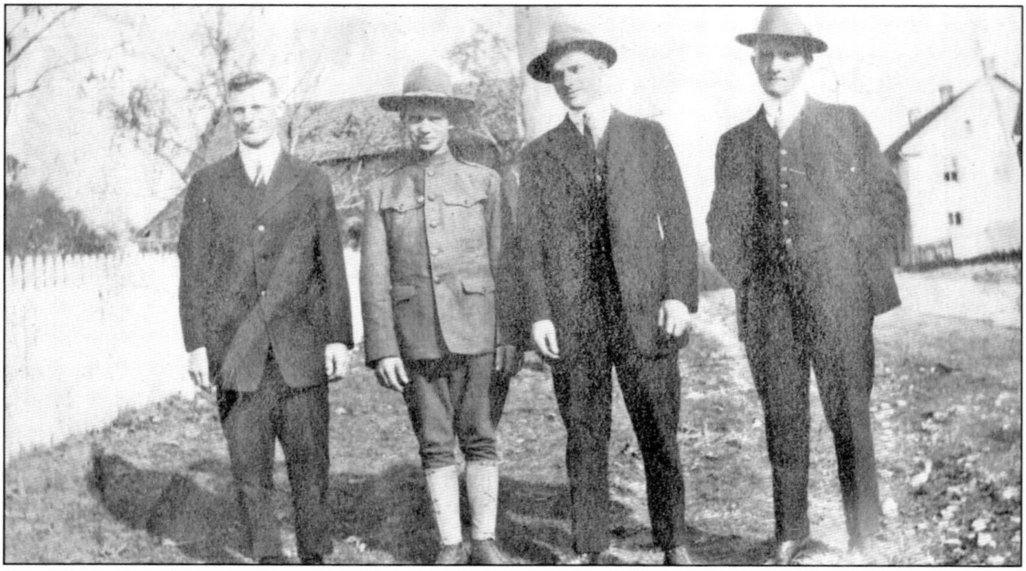

From left to right are Charles Slick Sr., Paul Smith, and two unidentified men in Cavetown. (Courtesy of Joe Slick.)

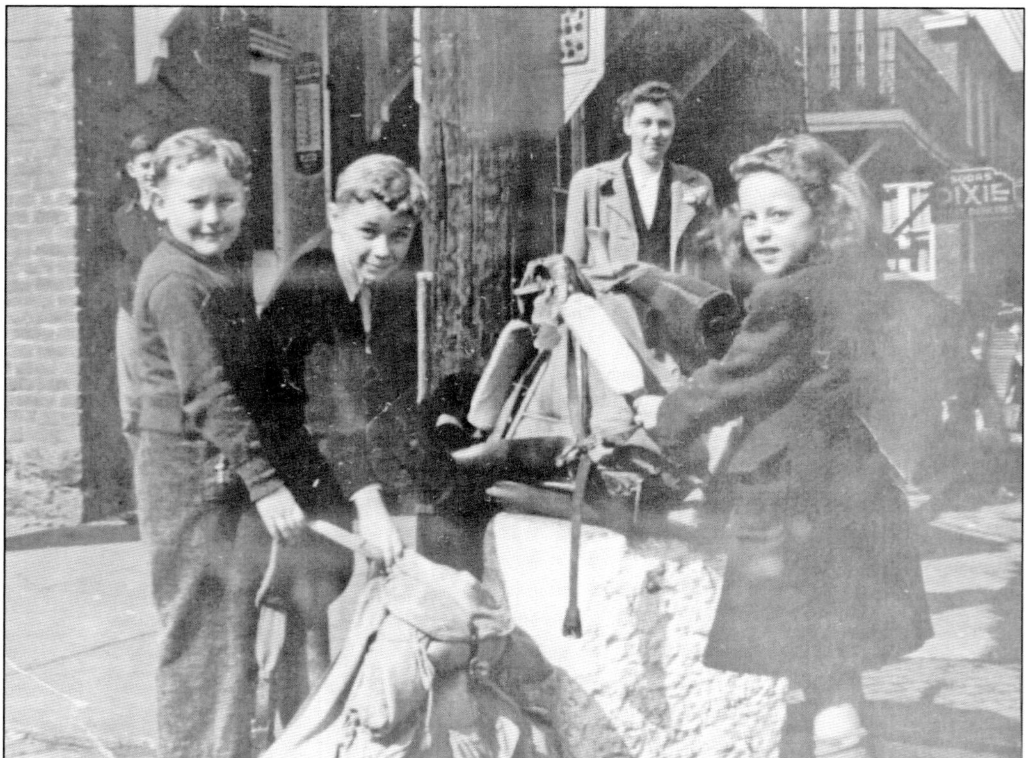

This photograph captures schoolchildren waiting on Main Street. The Dixie Eatery is present in the background. (Courtesy of Joe Slick.)

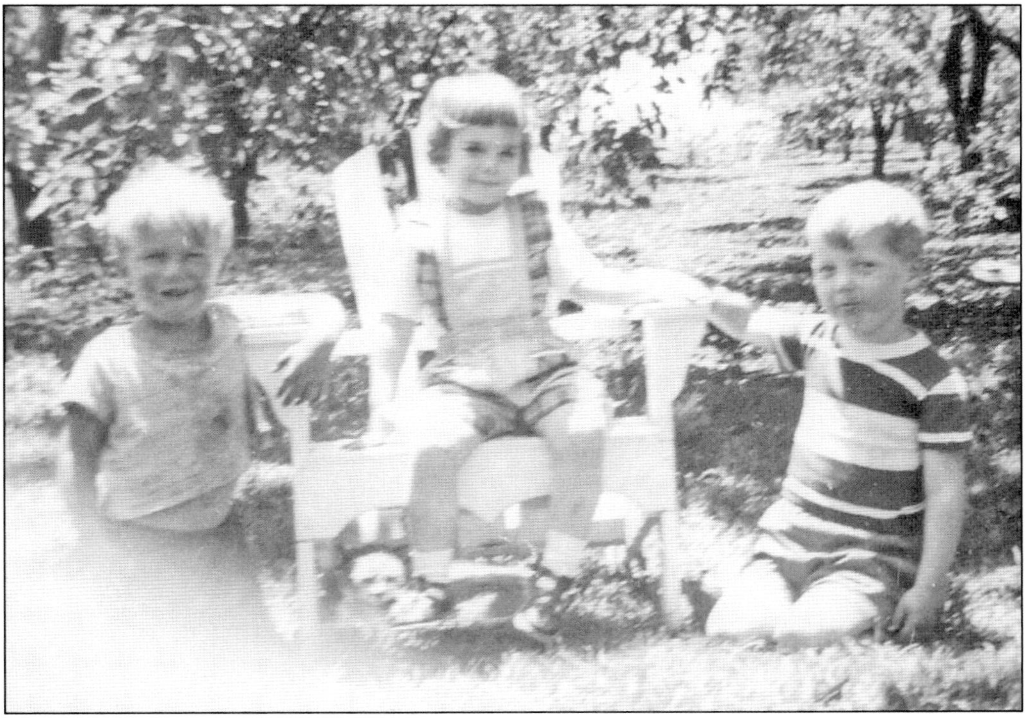

From left to right are Dick Kuhn, Barbara Boyle, and Tommy Kline having fun in a plum orchard around 1955. (Courtesy of Sari Slick Kilheffer.)

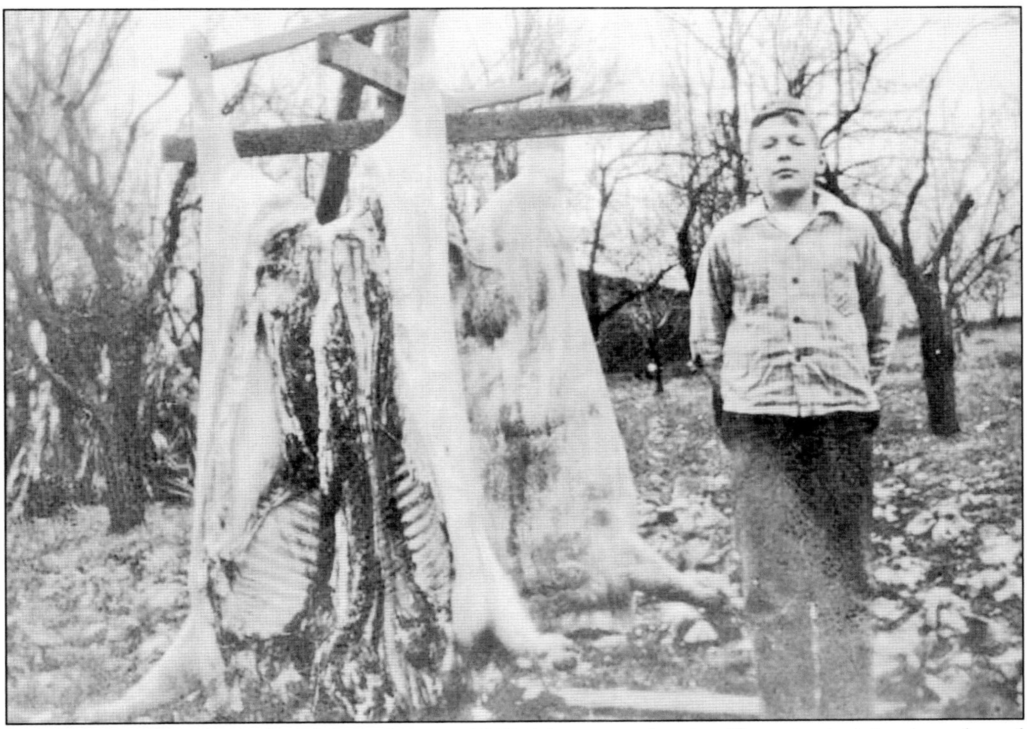

Raymond Slick is shown butchering hogs in 1948. Many people raised hogs in their backyards and held butchering parties during the day while they cooked. (Courtesy of Sari Slick Kilheffer.)

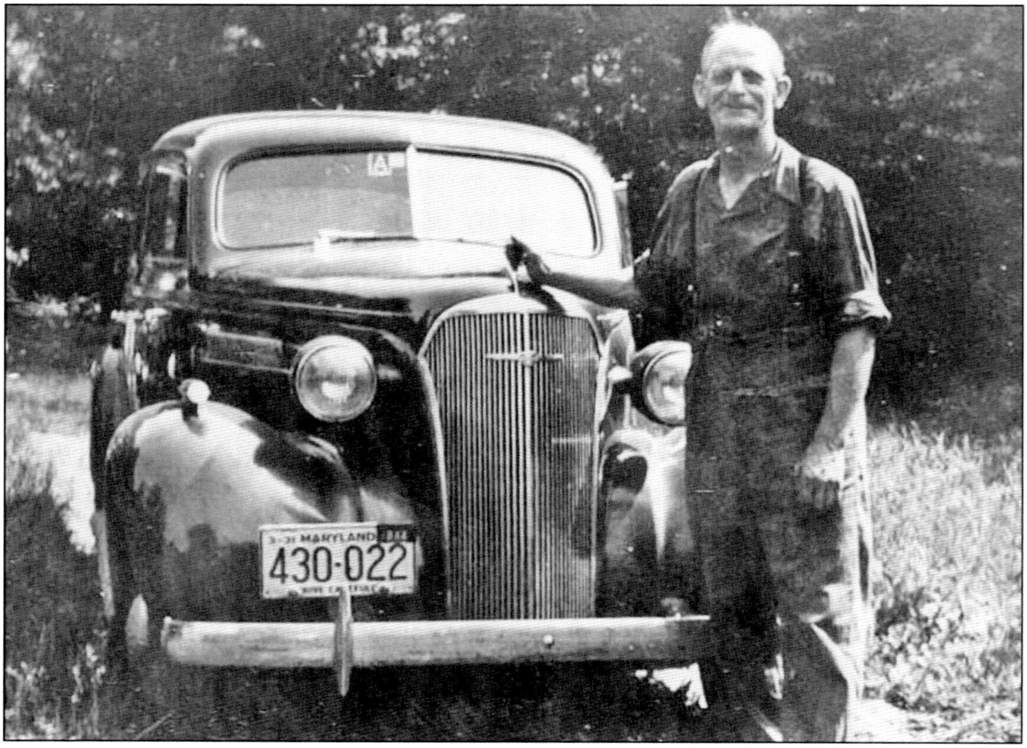

Charles Slick Sr. literally bought this 1937 Chevrolet with $700 worth of pennies. (Courtesy of Sari Slick Kilheffer.)

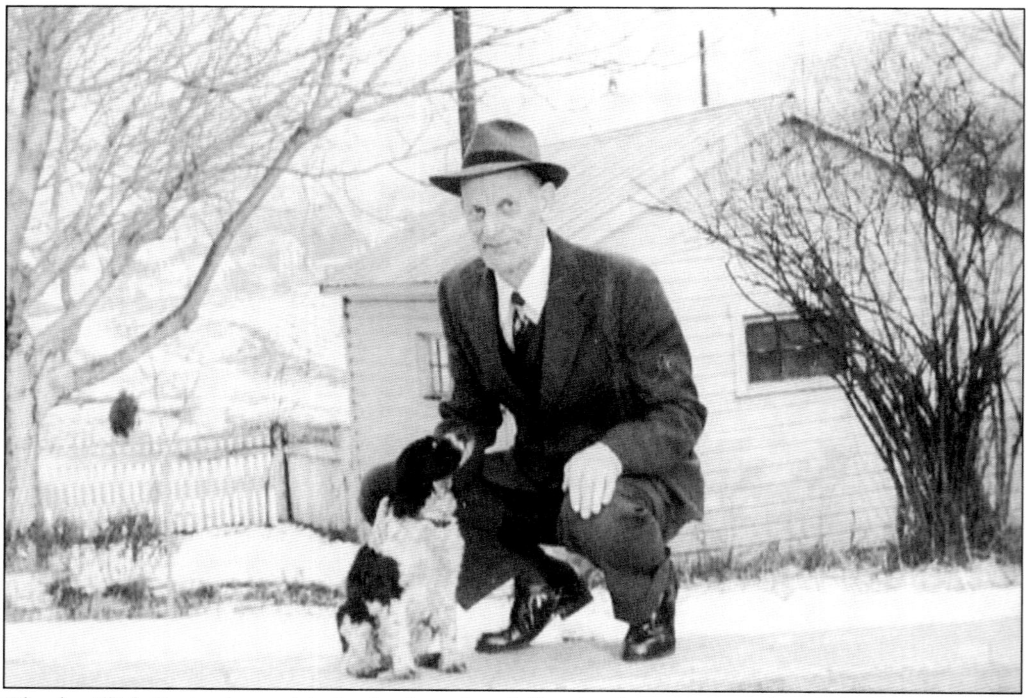
Charles Slick Sr. is pictured in his backyard with Ike the dog in 1946. The Slicks lived off Main Street. (Courtesy of Sari Slick Kilheffer.)

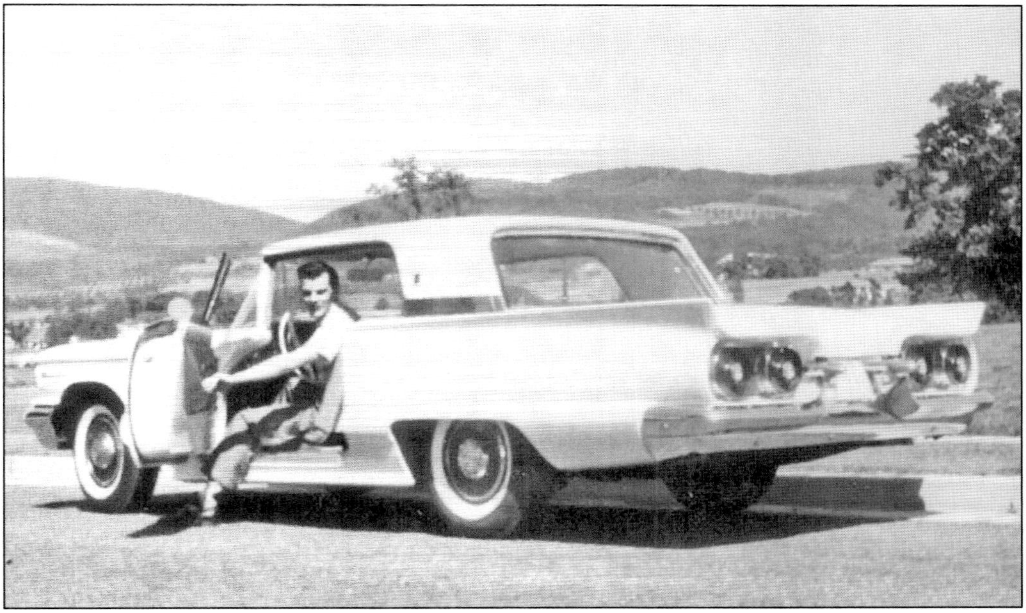

Charlie Slick Jr. in shown in this 1959 photograph taken at the top of the hill where Smithsburg Elementary School is located. In the background are the rolling hills of Smithsburg. (Courtesy of Joe Slick.)

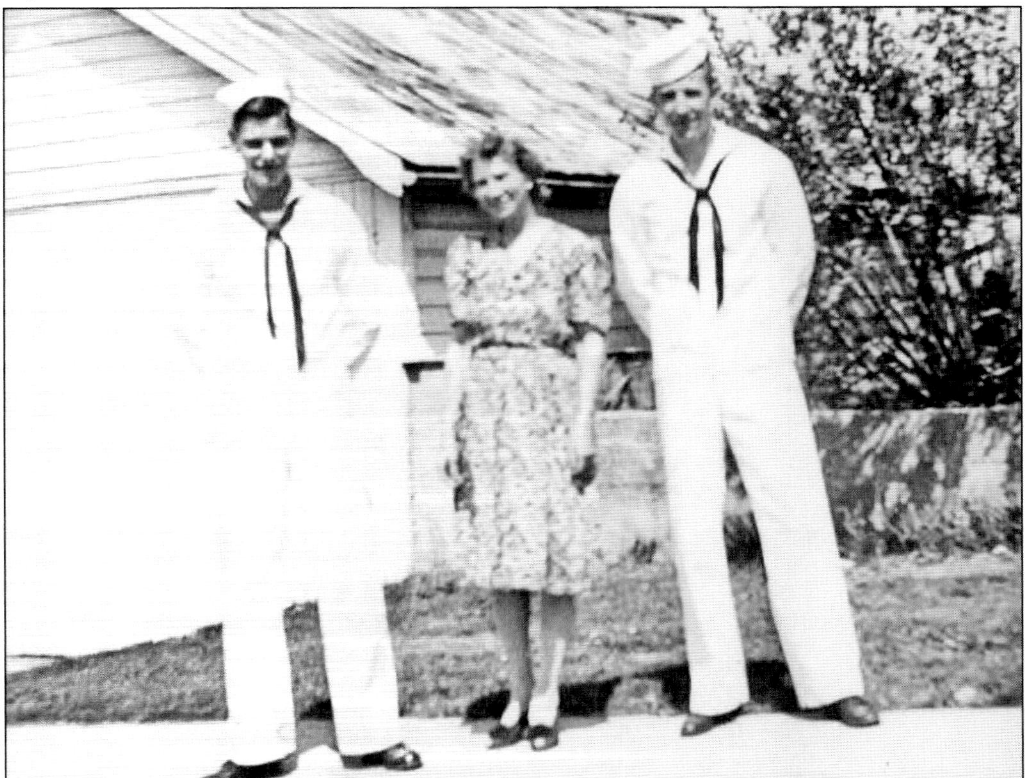

Rose Schauer is shown in 1947 with her grandson Carl Shaffer on the right and Joe Slick on the left. (Courtesy of Joe Slick.)

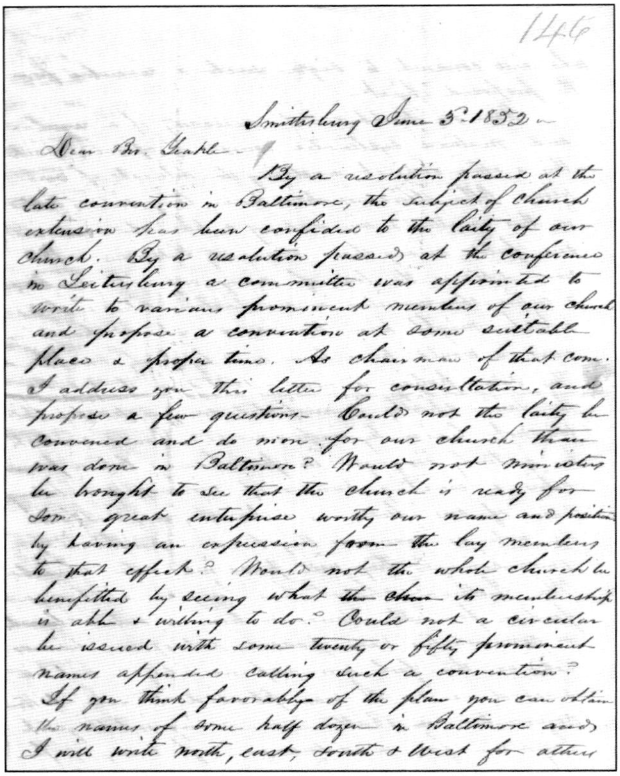

146

Smithsburg June 3. 1852

Dear Br. Geahle

By a resolution passed at the late convention in Baltimore, the subject of Church extension has been confided to the laity of our church. By a resolution passed at the conference in Leitersburg a committee was appointed to write to various prominent members of our church and propose a convention at some suitable place & proper time. As chairman of that com. I address you this letter for consultation, and propose a few questions. Could not the laity be convened and do more for our church than was done in Baltimore? Would not ministers be brought to see that the church is ready for some great enterprise worthy our name and position by having an expression from the lay members to that effect? Would not the whole church be benefitted by seeing what ~~the chur~~ its membership is able & willing to do? Could not a circular be issued with some twenty or fifty prominent names appended calling such a convention?

If you think favorably of the plan you can obtain the names of some half dozen in Baltimore and I will write north, east, south & West for others

This letter, dated June 3, 1852, shows such beautiful penmanship. It addresses the needs of a church and compares their church to one in Baltimore. (Courtesy of Joe Slick.)

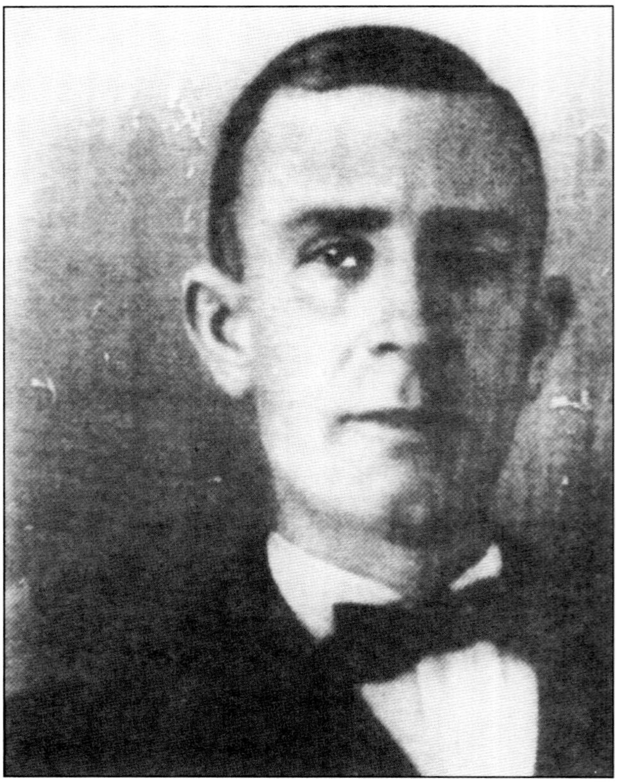

Albert J. Harbaugh served as principal of the Smithsburg School from 1885 to 1889. The school, located just beyond the limits of South Main Street, educated all grades in the same building. (Courtesy of the Smithsburg Historical Society.)

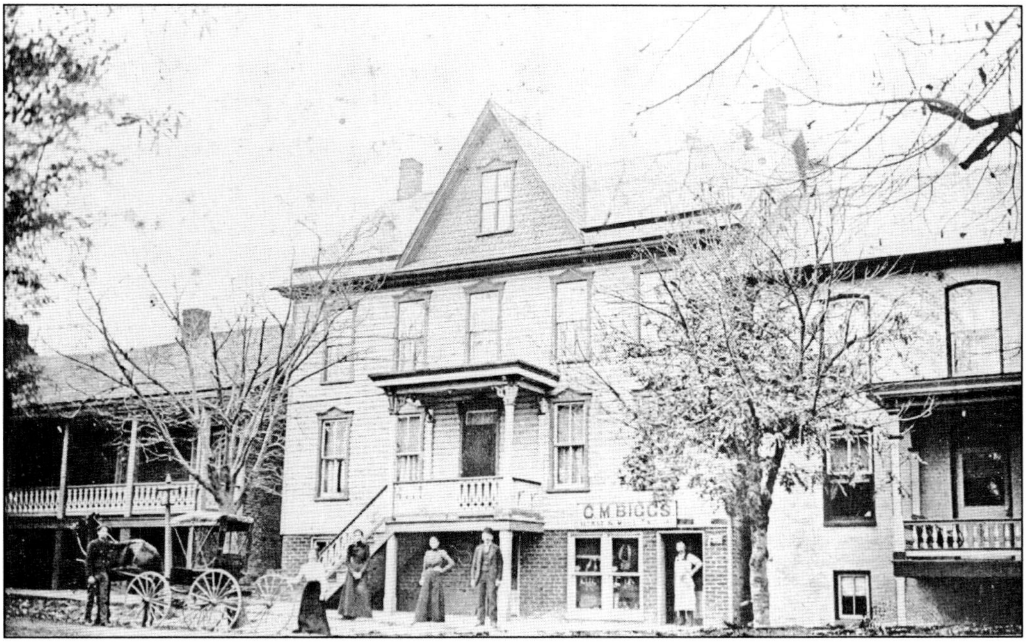

This photograph from the early 1900s shows the home of Samuel Barkdoll and the C. M. Biggs Horse and Mule Tailor shop at 22 South Main Street. Also pictured are the Hollingsworth and Hershberger homes. (Courtesy of the Smithsburg Historical Society.)

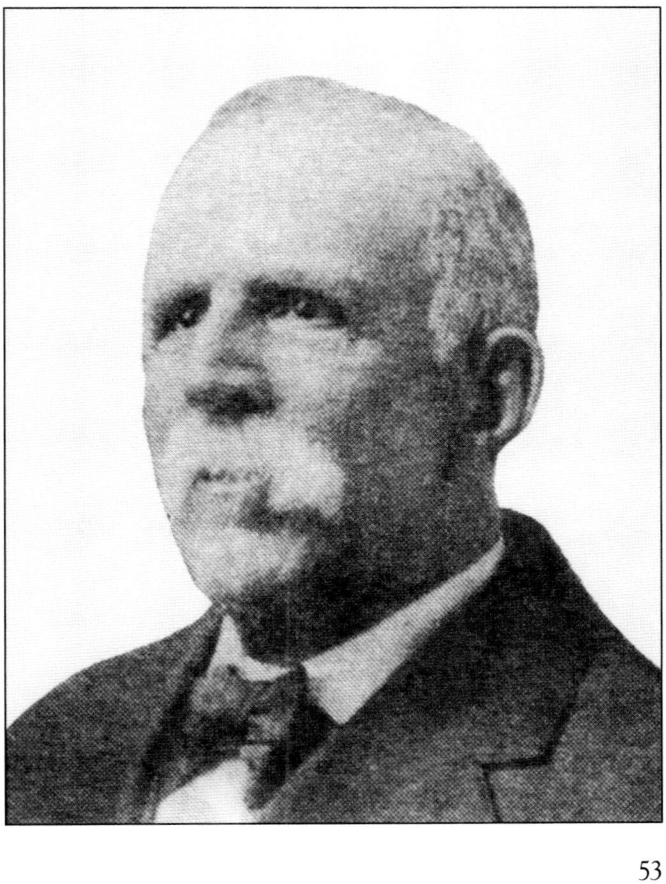

George C. Pearson was the son of George Pearson. The younger Pearson taught at Smithsburg School under his father until matriculating at Franklin and Marshall College in Lancaster, Pennsylvania. After his return, he took over his father's position as principal at Smithsburg School. (Courtesy of the Smithsburg Historical Society.)

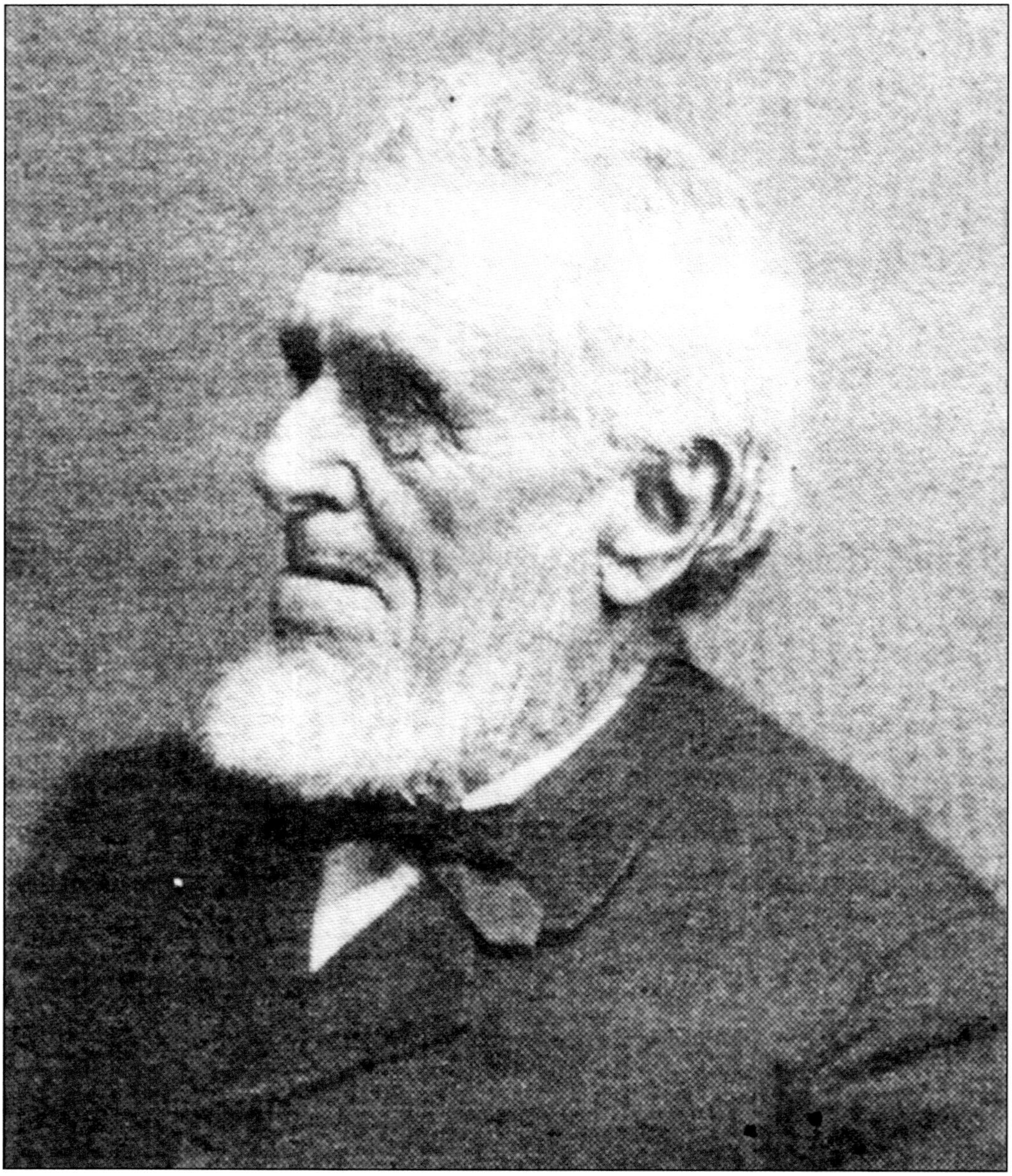

George Pearson was appointed schoolmaster of Smithsburg School. Pearson was a devoted teacher and earned a loyal following of students. (Courtesy of the Smithsburg Historical Society.)

Catherine Fiery Brenner was the mother of poet Edgar Irving Brenner. Catherine and her husband, Lucien, had nine children. This photograph is courtesy of the Brenner family. (Courtesy of the Smithsburg Historical Society.)

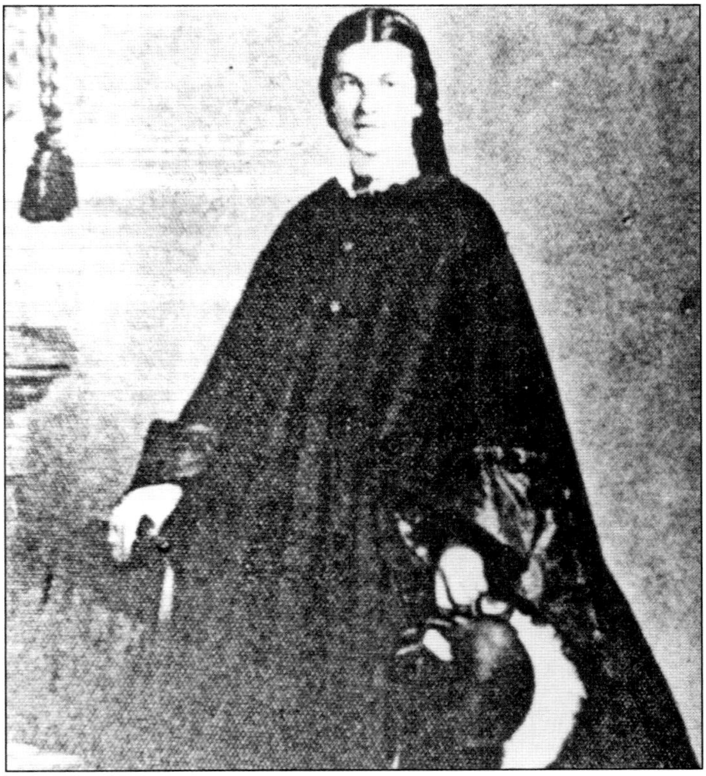

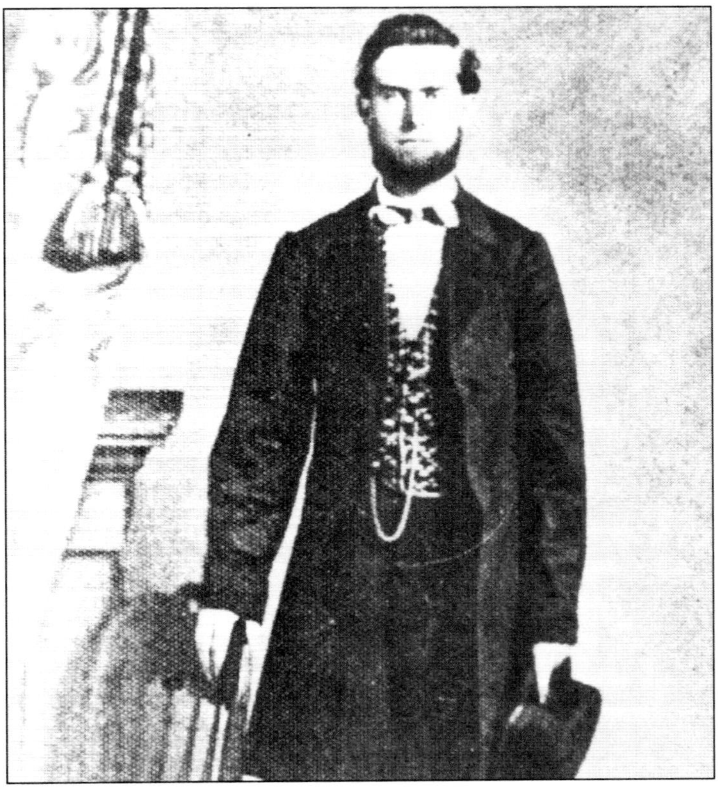

Lucien B. Brenner, pictured at left, was the father of Edgar Irving Brenner. This photograph is courtesy of the Brenner family. (Courtesy of the Smithsburg Historical Society.)

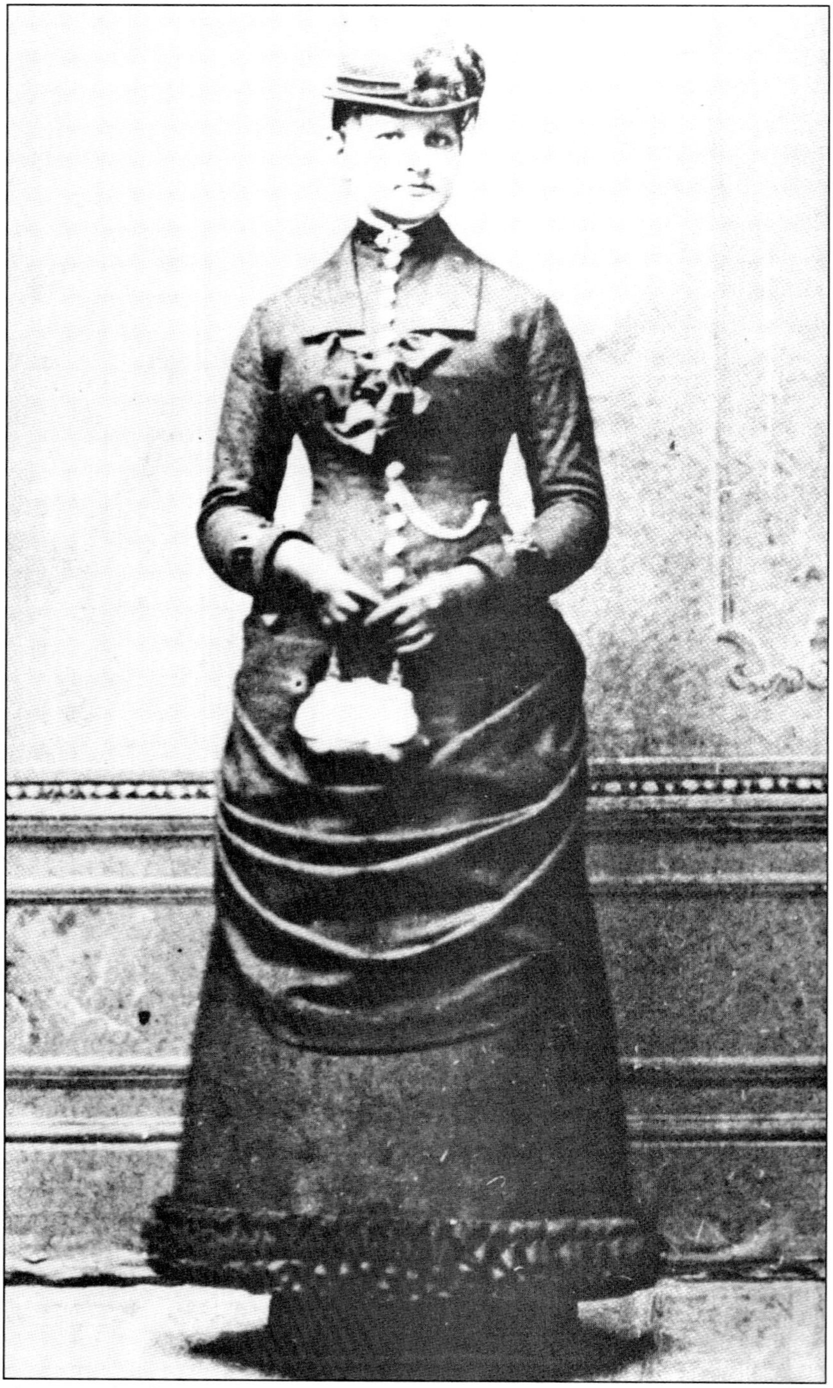

This is a photograph of Margaret McLean. She is the subject of Edgar Irving Brenner's poem on the following page entitled "Margaret." Brenner, a young and gifted artist and poet, enrolled at Yale Divinity School in New Haven, Connecticut. Brenner died tragically when he drowned in an ice-skating incident in December 1886 in the icy waters of New Haven's Lake Whitney. *The Poetical Works of Edgar Irving Brenner* was published by the Smithsburg Historical Society and is available there for purchase. (Courtesy of the Smithsburg Historical Society.)

EDGAR IRVING BRENNER

Margaret

'Tis peaceful now:
A holy glad sereneness fills the earth
And yet, I know not why nor how
Myriads of fairy voices falling, falling
From the great otherwhere, give joyous birth
To music so divine, so sweet, so thrilling
I faint to hear these glorious voices filling
The air with one grand madrigal of Love!
I wake, and, lo! they're calling, calling, calling
From far ethereal balconies above
The name of one whose gentle, tender presence
Hovering forever near me in the busy mart
Of worldly selfishness, doth bid all else depart
Save Love and Hope and Peace. E'en dull Care lessons
And Misery smiles at sight of her sweet face--
Ah! They're already going. Fainter and fainter still--
As if they go swayed by some stronger will
And much against their own, --the airy space
Echoes their tremulous bliss. And now they're gone!

They're gone. And yet, and yet,
Earth, air, trees, rocks, glens, rivers, dales,
All Nature's volumes of all nature's tales
Echo the story of the days we met
And ring into my dazed ears the sound
Of one dear name, pure as its emblem found
In deep blue depths of ocean. Where'er I go,
They breathe it lovingly, they breathe it low,
The name, sweetest of all names as yet,
The name of -- Margaret.

August 3, 1884

Brenner's poem "Margaret" was dedicated to Brenner's love with the same name. Although her last name is unknown, what is clear is Brenner's gift for poetry. (Courtesy of the Smithsburg Historical Society.)

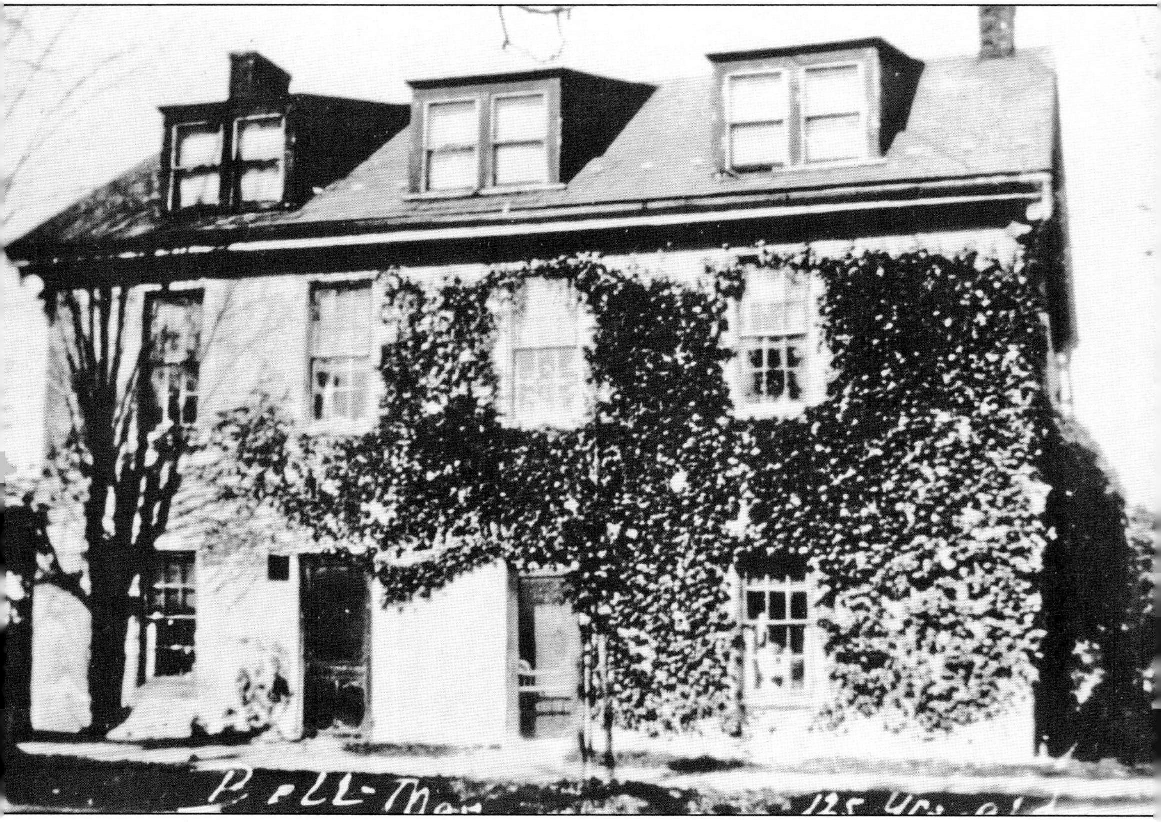

Located at 13–15 East Water Street, the Bell-Mar House was constructed by Christopher Smith, founder of Smithsburg, as a distillery. Smith would become destitute as a result of pouring his money into the distillery. The house was used as a hospital during the Civil War. (Courtesy of the Smithsburg Historical Society.)

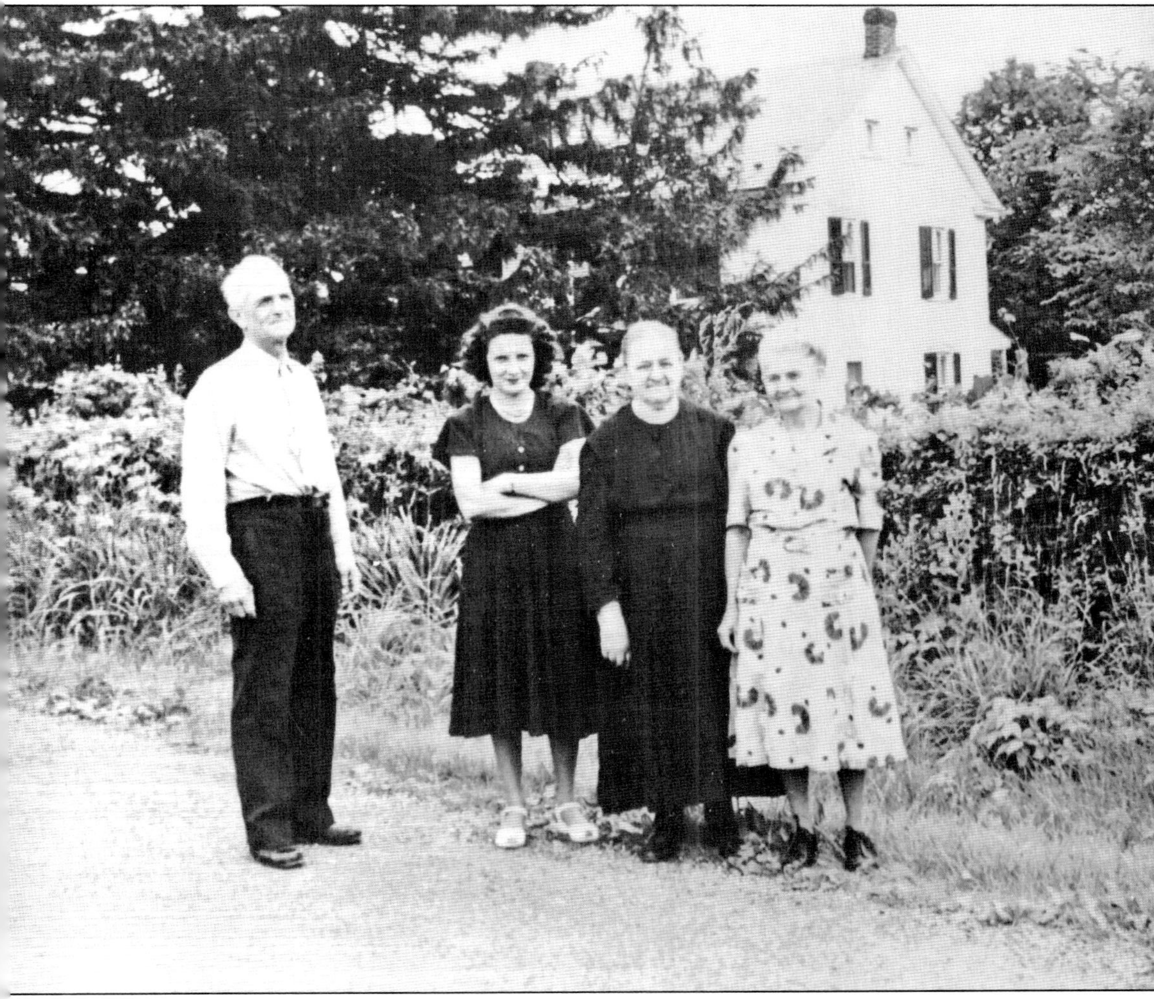

Luther B. Newcomer, left, and friends stand in front of his farmhouse in Smithsburg. A promising artist, Newcomer was born in 1883 and had nine brothers and sisters. (Courtesy of the Smithsburg Historical Society.)

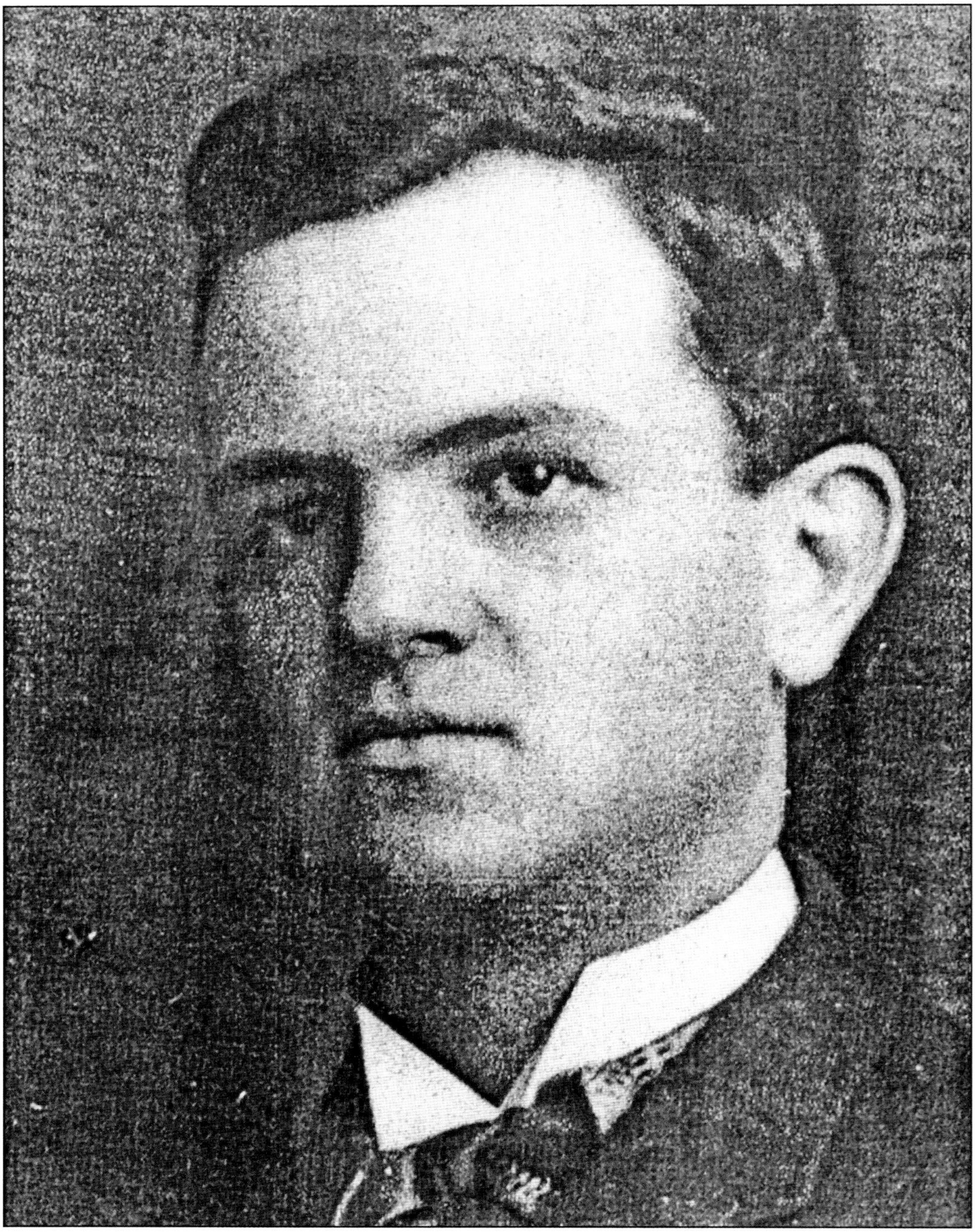

Luther B. Newcomer grew up on a farm in Leitersburg. Luther went to New York and studied art with some of the same teachers as Emily C. Bishop. He abandoned his art career to return home to take care of his ailing mother. Newcomer died in 1972. (Courtesy of the Smithsburg Historical Society.)

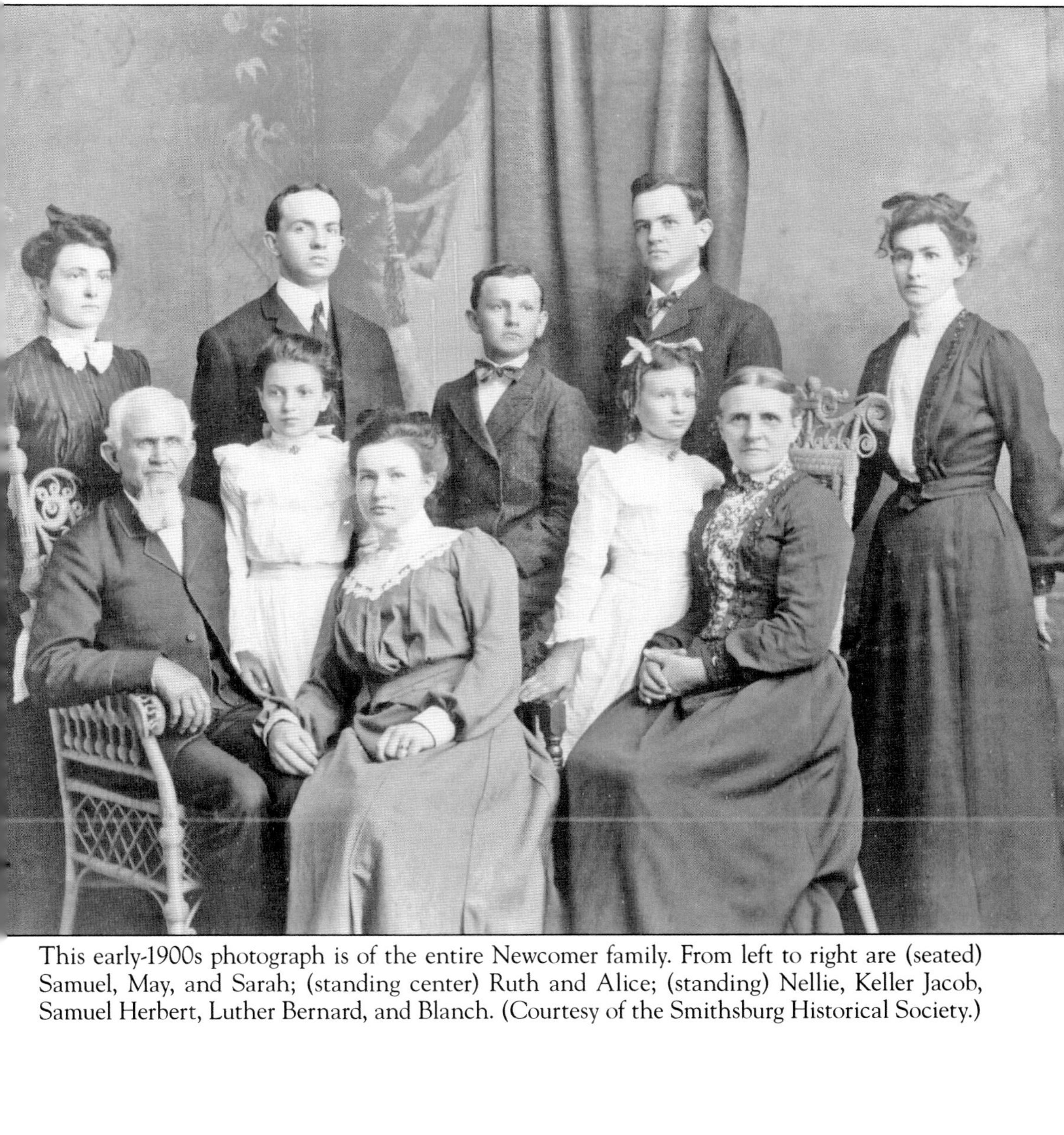

This early-1900s photograph is of the entire Newcomer family. From left to right are (seated) Samuel, May, and Sarah; (standing center) Ruth and Alice; (standing) Nellie, Keller Jacob, Samuel Herbert, Luther Bernard, and Blanch. (Courtesy of the Smithsburg Historical Society.)

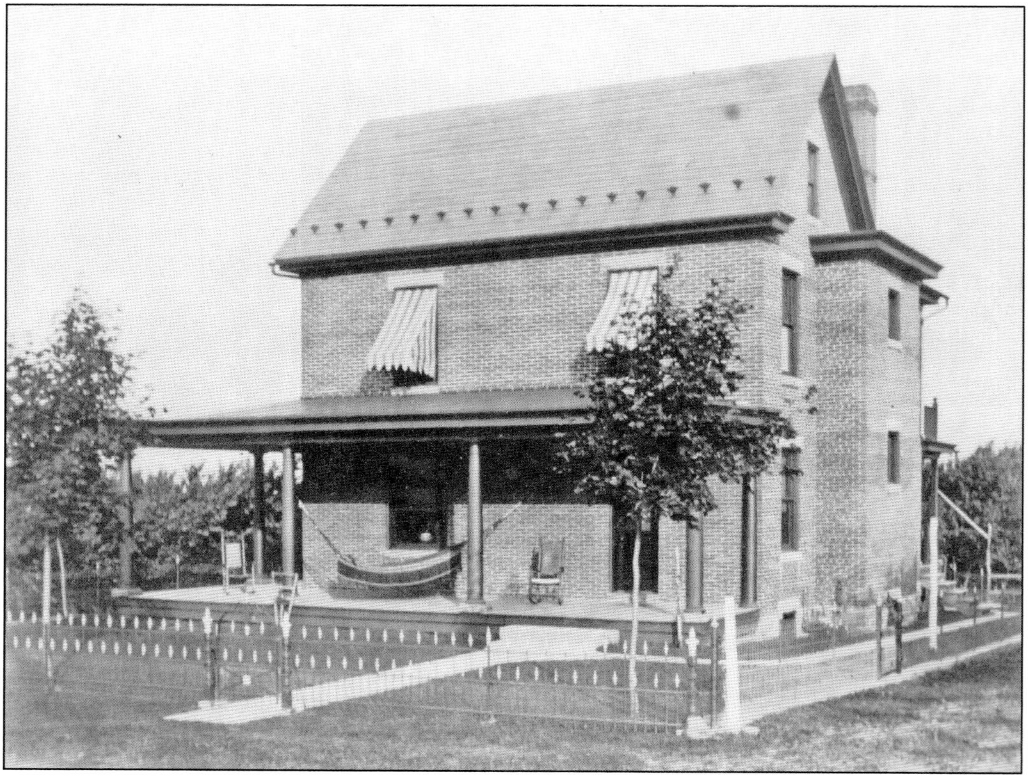

The home of Keller J. Newcomer, located on East Water Street, is shown in the early 1900s. The house still stands today. (Courtesy of the Smithsburg Historical Society.)

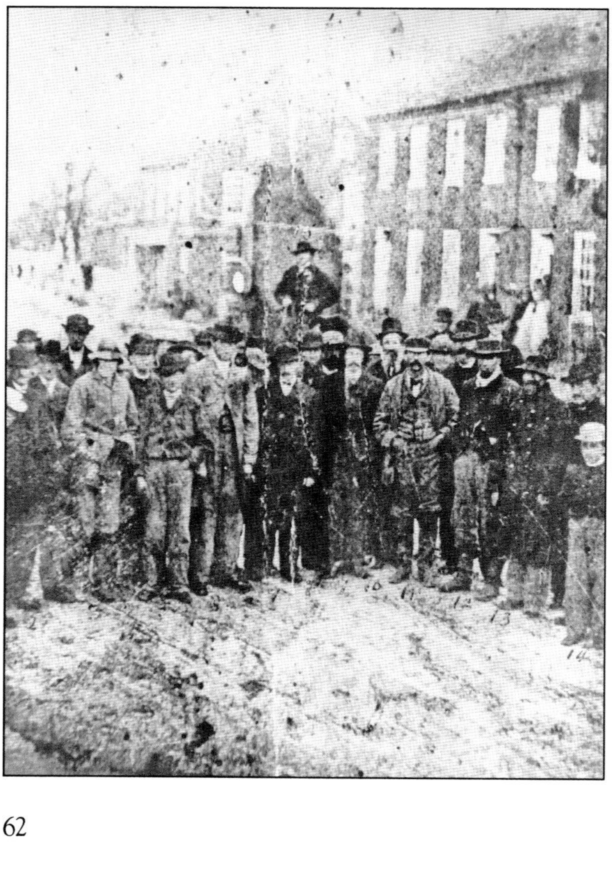

This photograph was taken on Christmas Day 1865. Though it is quite worn, one can see that everyone in the photograph is male with the exception of one female to the left of center. (Courtesy of the Smithsburg Historical Society.)

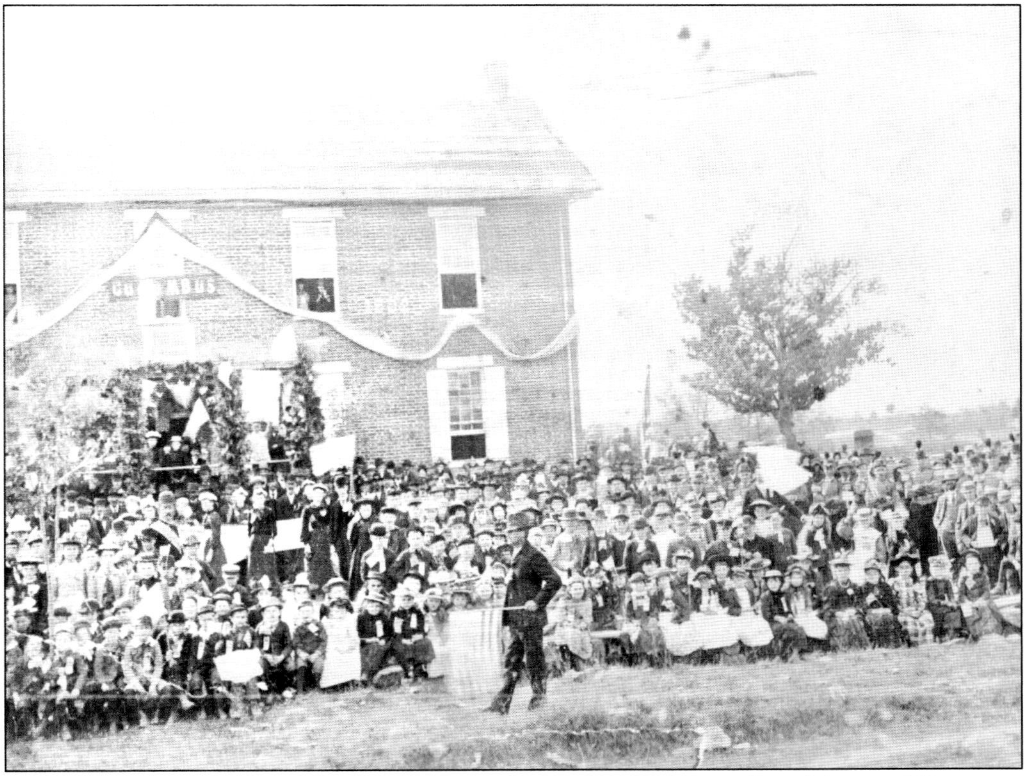

Townspeople celebrate Memorial Day in the late 1800s. Events such as Memorial Day were important celebrations in Smithsburg. (Courtesy of the Smithsburg Historical Society.)

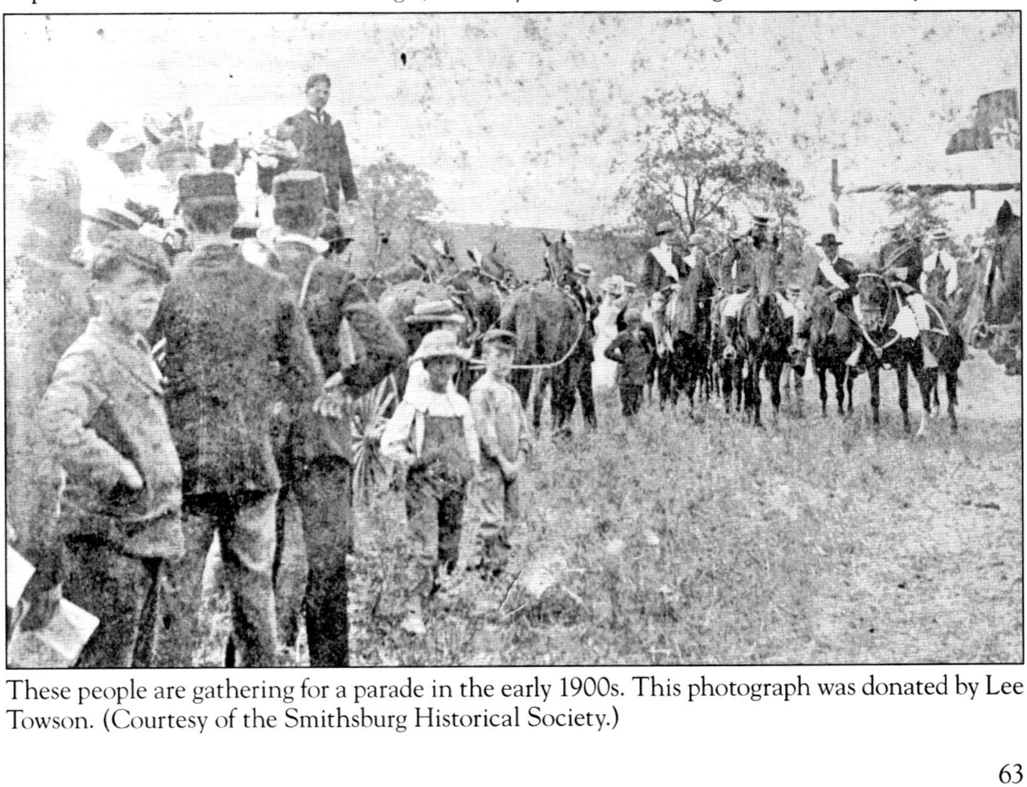

These people are gathering for a parade in the early 1900s. This photograph was donated by Lee Towson. (Courtesy of the Smithsburg Historical Society.)

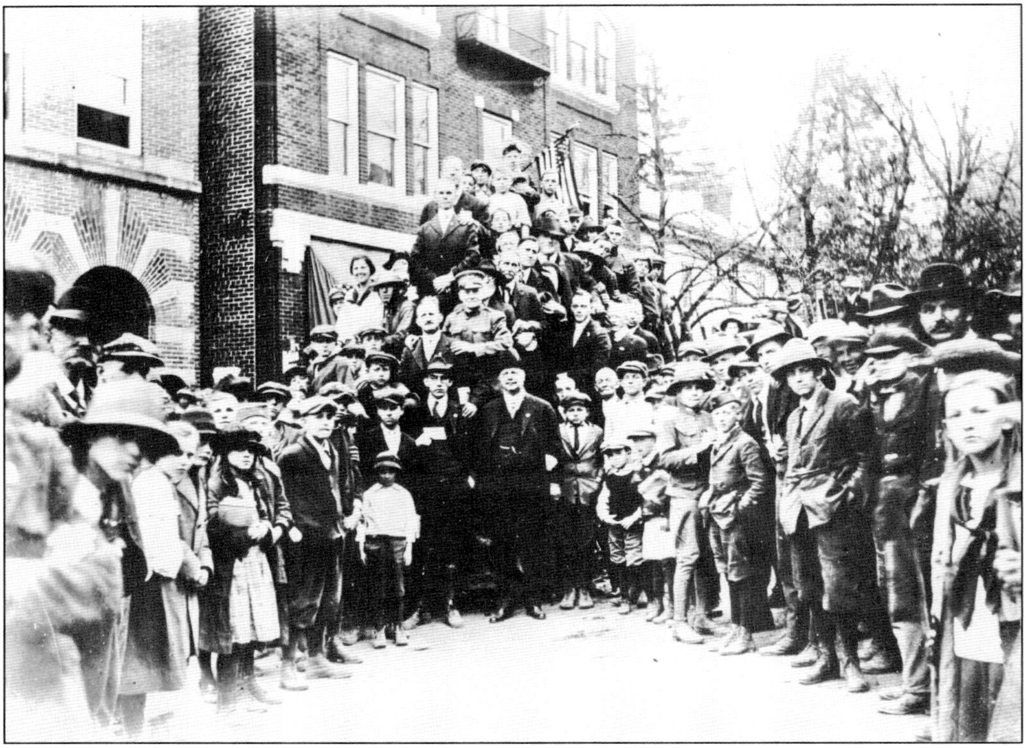

In the midst of World War I, a Liberty Bond rally took place on Main Street in Smithsburg in 1916. At the very top of the crowd, the American flag is visible. (Courtesy of the Smithsburg Historical Society.)

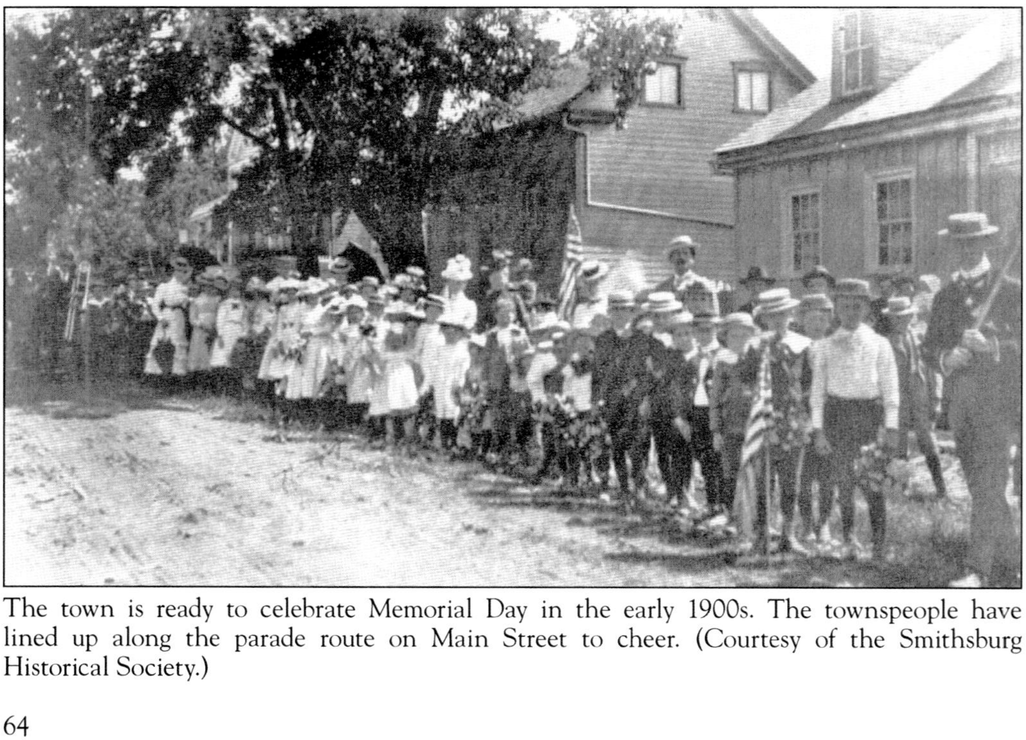

The town is ready to celebrate Memorial Day in the early 1900s. The townspeople have lined up along the parade route on Main Street to cheer. (Courtesy of the Smithsburg Historical Society.)

The post office was organized in 1829, 16 years after the town was founded. Lancelot Jacques served as postmaster from 1897 to 1914. The post office was located in the basement of the People's Banking Company Building on East Water Street. (Courtesy of the Smithsburg Historical Society.)

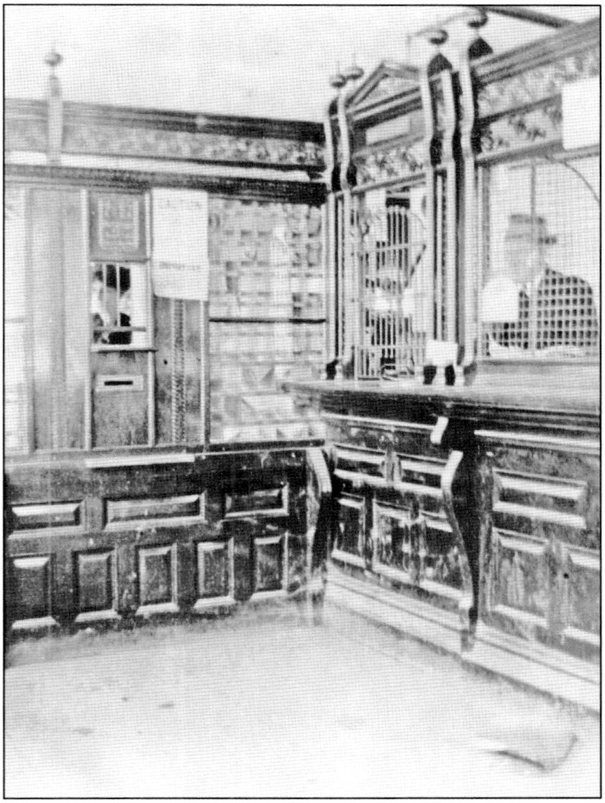

Postal carriers in 1910 are, from left to right, Frank Shank, Samuel D. Newman, John Welty, Sam Welty, and Max Newman. (Courtesy of the Smithsburg Historical Society.)

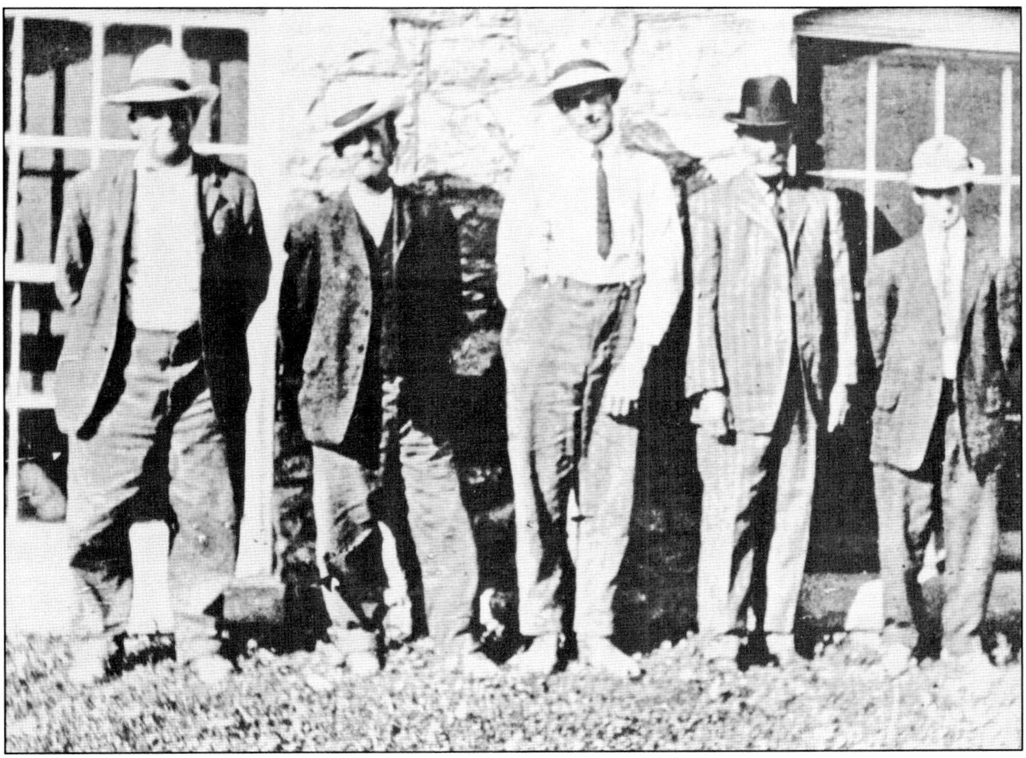

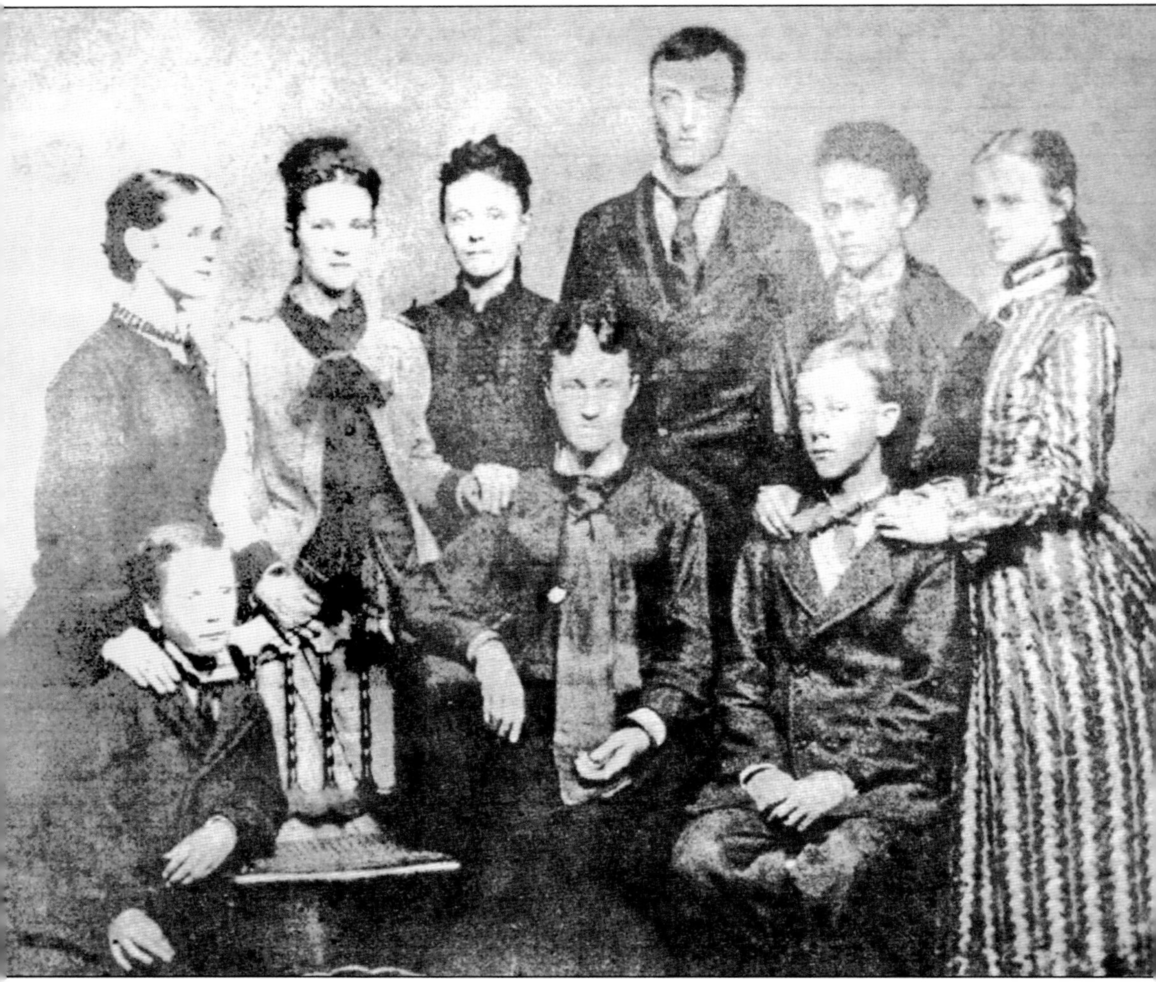

This photograph of an unidentified family has one chair left empty. Usually the empty chair signified a father or brother who has left for war or has died. The photograph was provided by Frank Greenwalt, a descendent of a 6th Maryland Infantry veteran. (Courtesy of the Smithsburg Historical Society.)

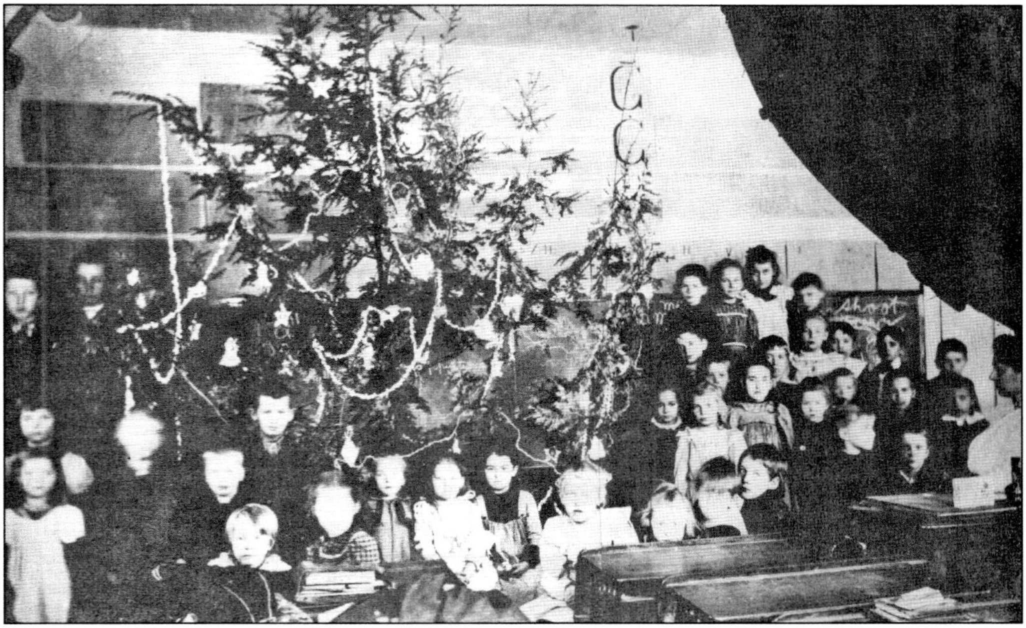

Smithsburg's school-aged children gear up for the holiday season in 1901. Popcorn is strung across the giant tree in the background. (Courtesy of *Maryland Cracker Barrel.*)

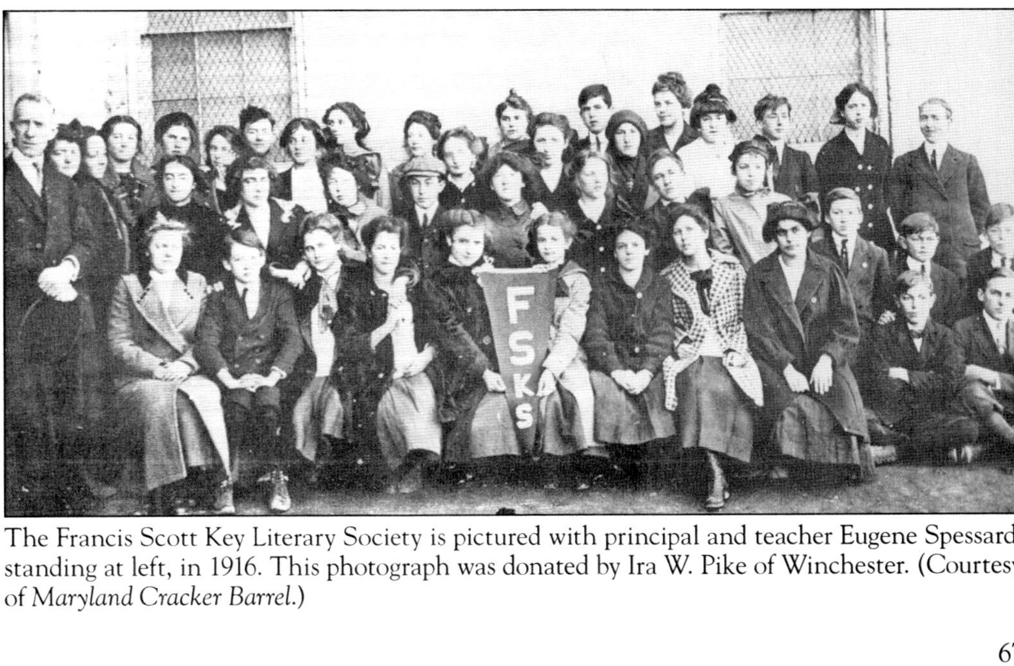

The Francis Scott Key Literary Society is pictured with principal and teacher Eugene Spessard, standing at left, in 1916. This photograph was donated by Ira W. Pike of Winchester. (Courtesy of *Maryland Cracker Barrel.*)

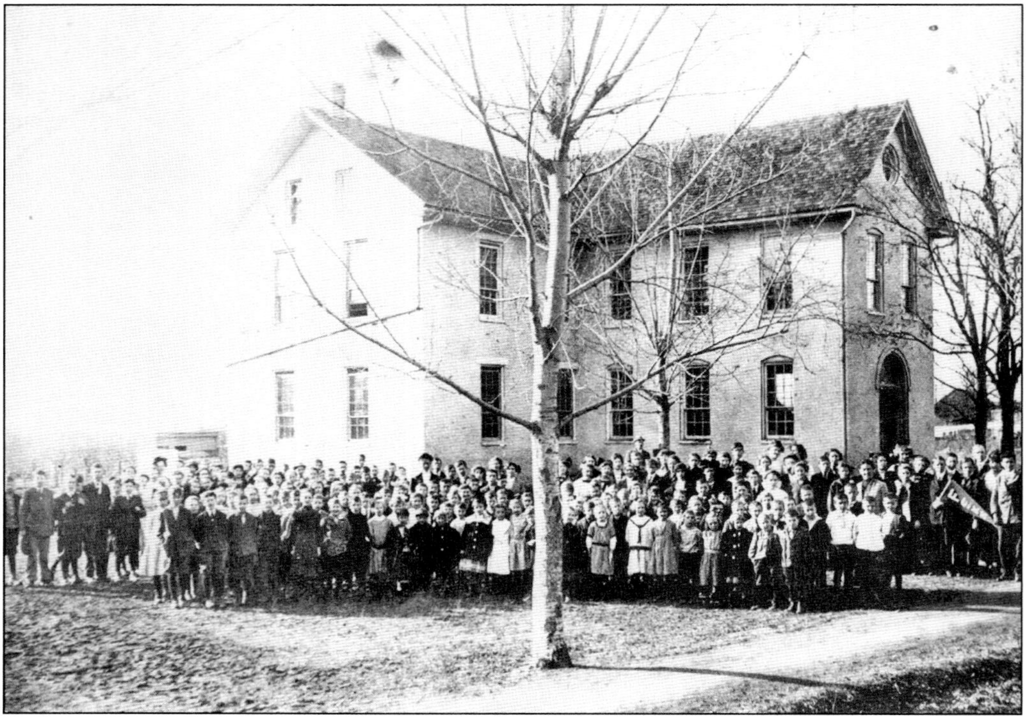

Ira W. Pike donated this photograph as well. The old Smithsburg School is pictured in 1905. This school held all grades in this two-story building. (Courtesy of *Maryland Cracker Barrel.*)

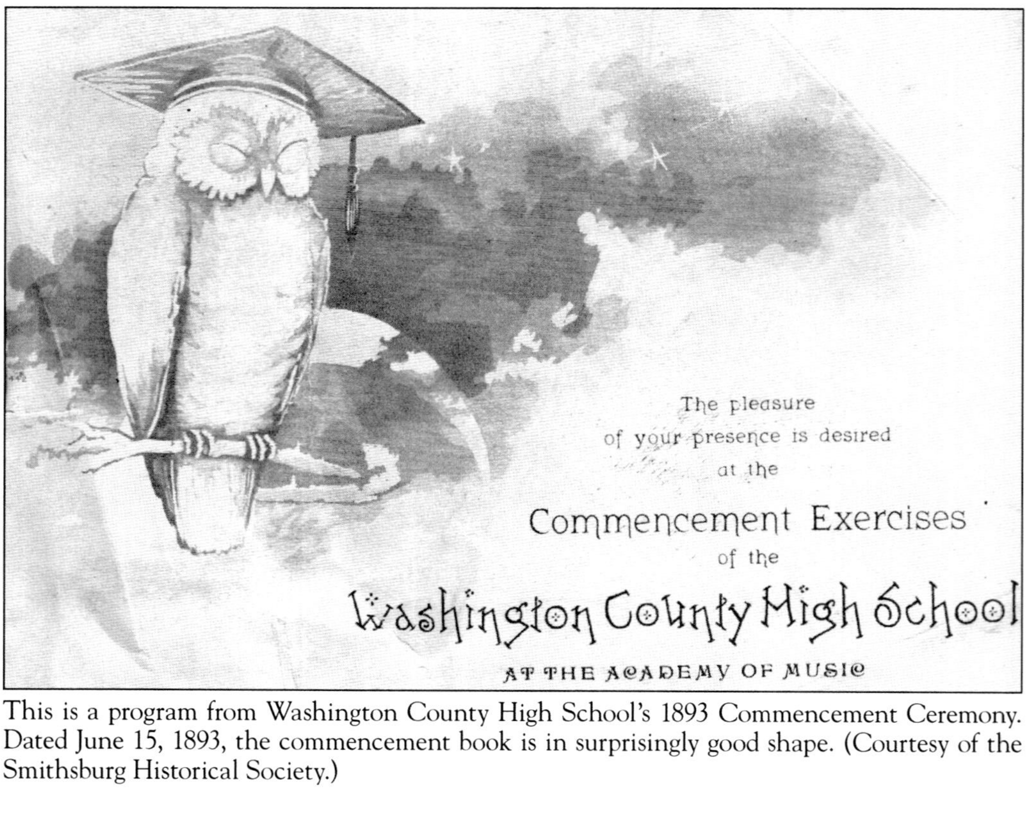

This is a program from Washington County High School's 1893 Commencement Ceremony. Dated June 15, 1893, the commencement book is in surprisingly good shape. (Courtesy of the Smithsburg Historical Society.)

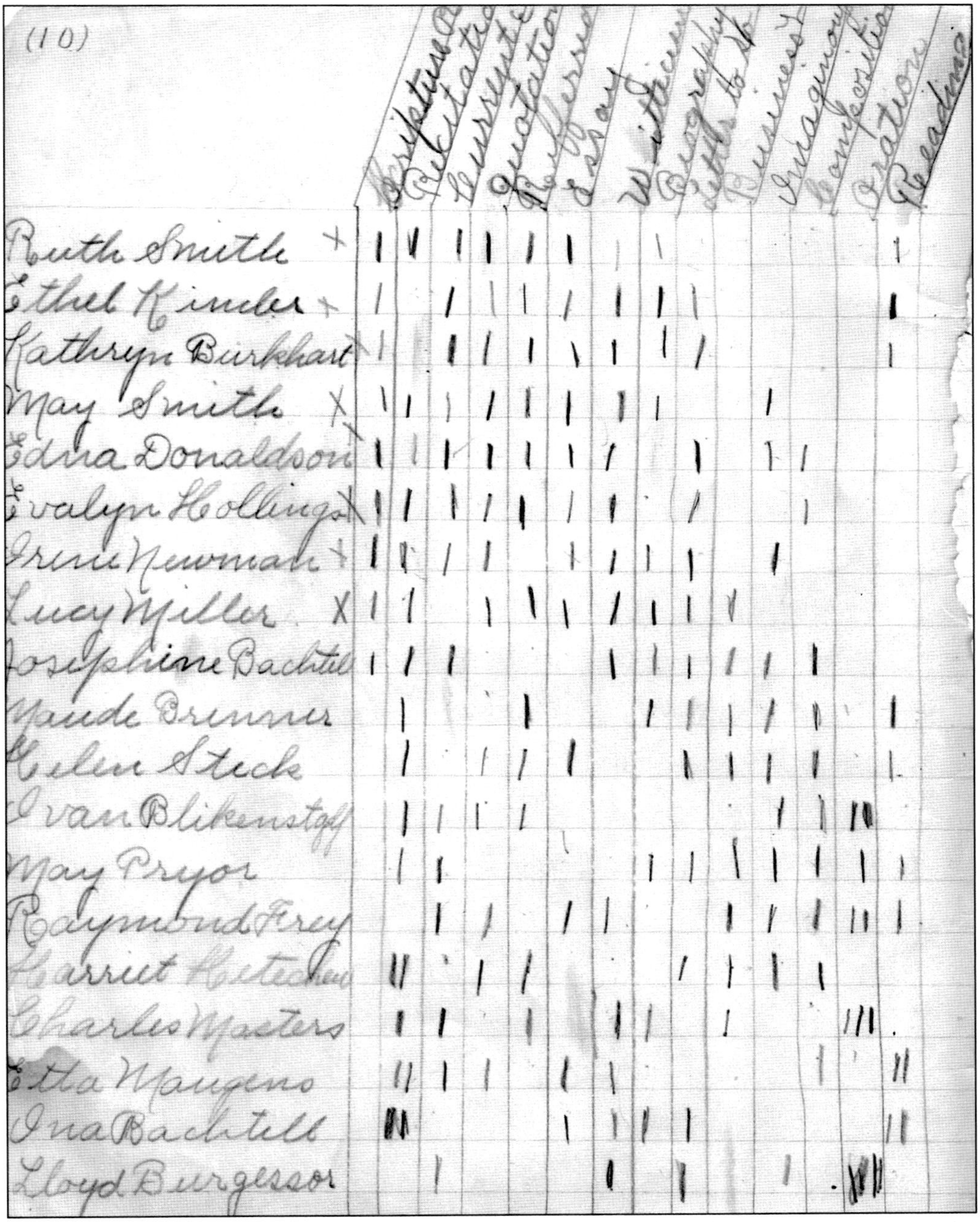

A page out of Ethel L. Kimler's composition book is dated April 26, 1910. As a teacher, Kimler graded students on various subjects, such as scripture, quotation, oration, and imaginary. (Courtesy of the Smithsburg Historical Society.)

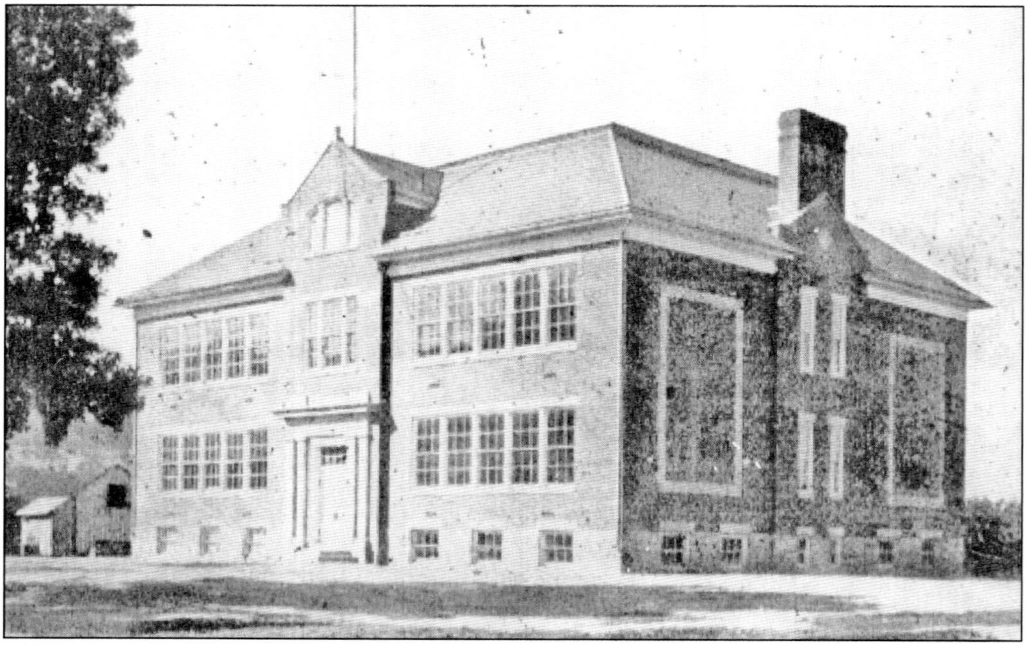

The "newer" Smithsburg School, located on South Main Street and shown before additions were made, served grades K-12 until 1954 when Smithsburg Elementary School became a separate school. Blue Mountain Estates, a senior living community, stands on the site where the old school stood. The class of 1965 was the last class to graduate from this school. Smithsburg High School, at the top of West Main Street, opened in 1966 and still operates today. (Courtesy of the Smithsburg Historical Society.)

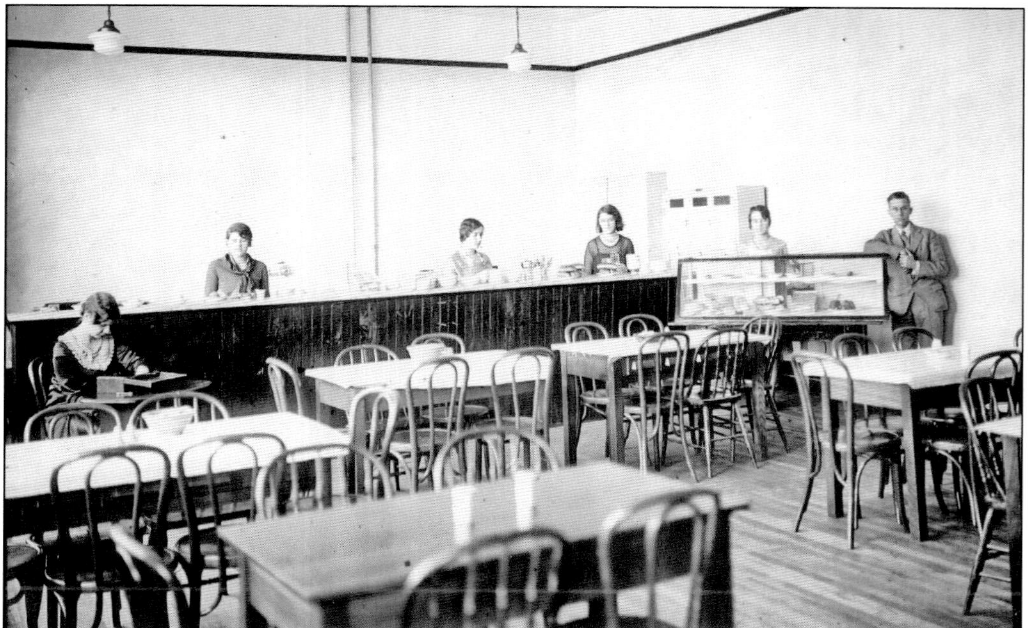

The cafeteria, located on the second floor of the Smithsburg School, had wooden floors that needed special oil in order to clean them. The principal is shown in the right corner of the photograph. (Courtesy of the Smithsburg Historical Society.)

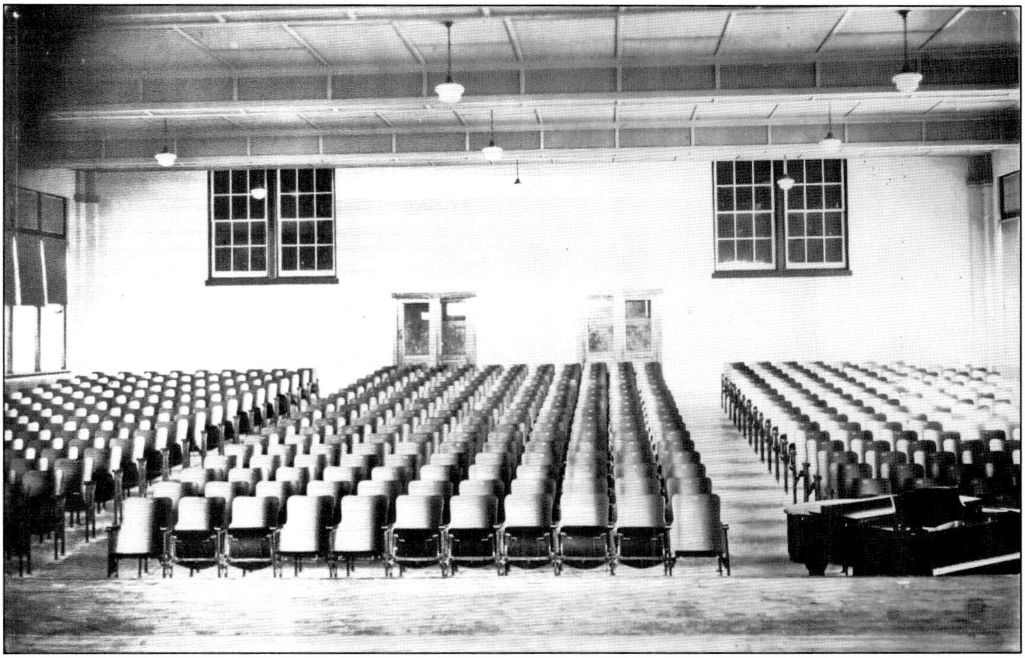

This is a photograph of the Smithsburg School auditorium. The upper left window would later become the principal's office. Class assemblies, plays, and pep rallies were held in this section of the school. (Courtesy of the Smithsburg Historical Society.)

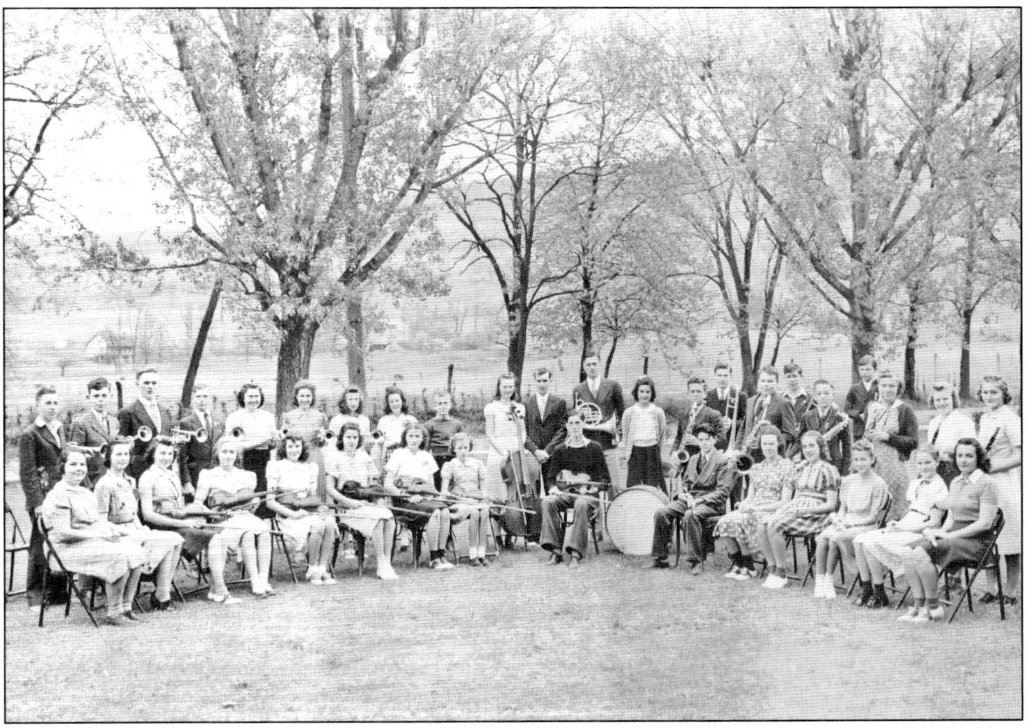

Smithsburg School's class of 1940 orchestra is shown outside the school on the lawn. The land behind the trees would soon be developed into neighborhoods of Smithsburg. (Courtesy of the Smithsburg Historical Society.)

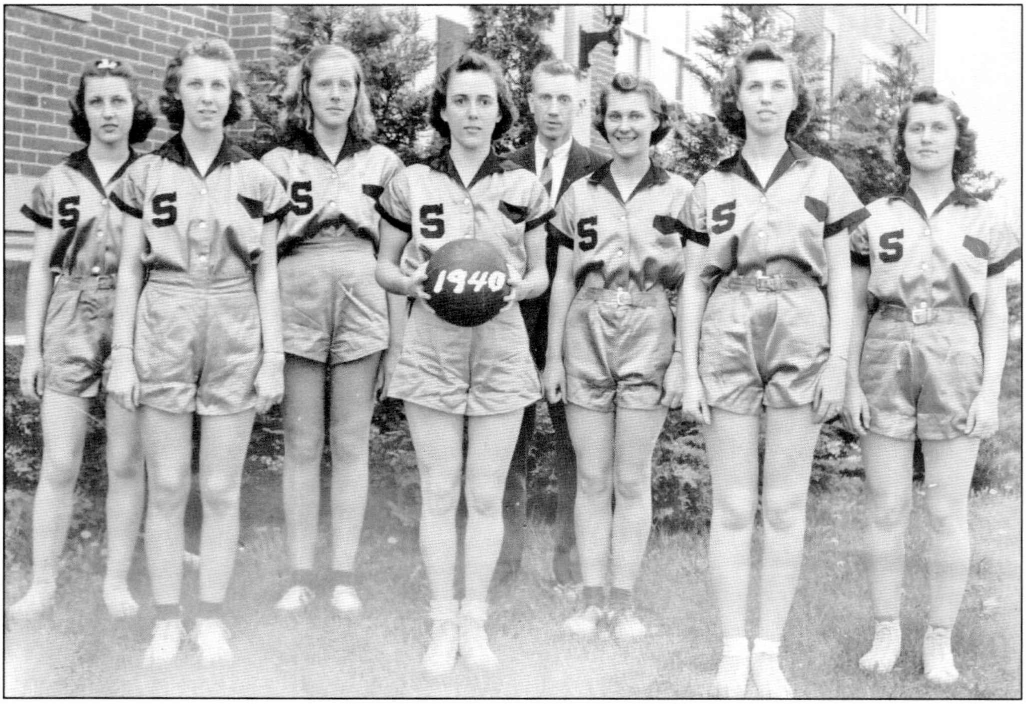

Although much information is not supplied, this picture is of the 1940s basketball or field ball team. While the uniforms may have changed, Smithsburg's love of sports has remained throughout the years. (Courtesy of the Smithsburg Historical Society.)

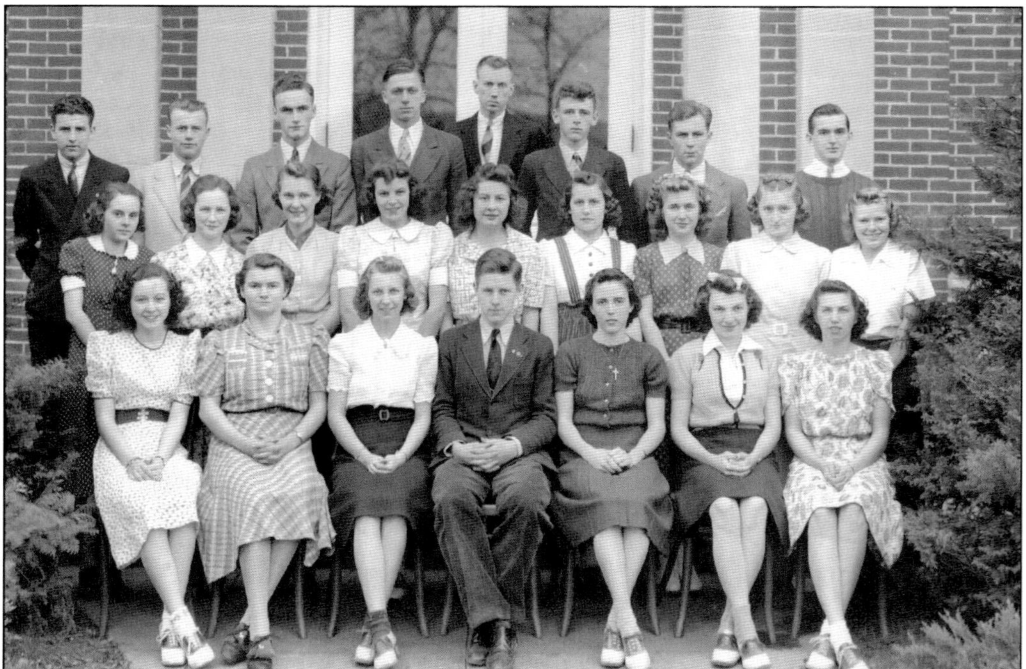

Smithsburg School's graduating class of 1940 is captured in this photograph with the school principal in the center of the back row. (Courtesy of the Smithsburg Historical Society.)

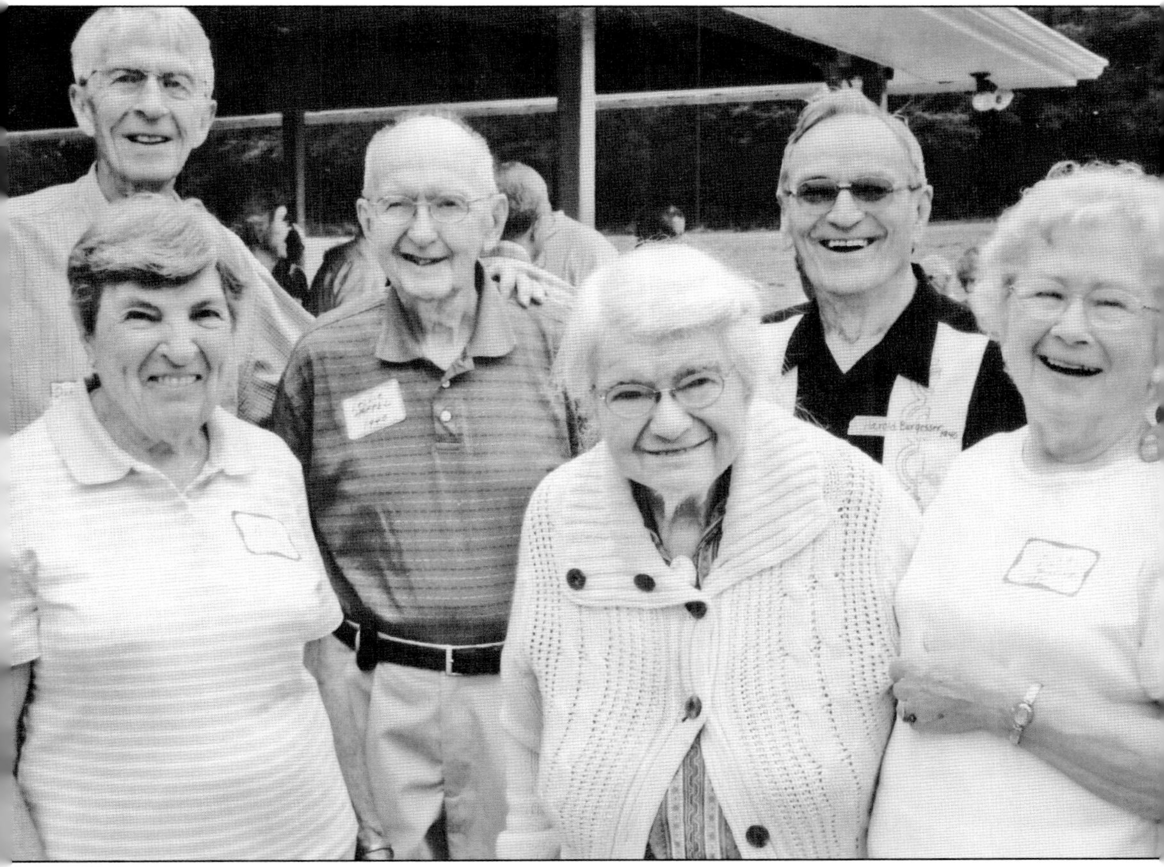

The class of 1940's reunion took place on August 5, 2007. Pictured are, from left to right, (first row) June Frey Bachtell, Mary Katherine Newcomer, and Virginia Laspe Bruneske; (second row) Richard Winters, Leslie Happel, and Harold Burgessor. (Photograph courtesy of Ed Distad.)

Class Will

We, the members of the graduating class of 1940 of Smithsburg High School, as a token of our appreciation of favors shown us in the past, graciously make this our last will and testament.

To the faculty members we will our thanks and appreciation for their guidance through our four years of high school life.

To the Junior Class we will our co-operation in school activities and the right to be called Seniors after ten o'clock, June 7.

To the Sophomores we will our great success in planning the Junior Prom and our very studious abilities.

To the Freshmen we leave our ability to stay in school and work hard for four years.

As individuals we wish to dispose of our personal belongings as follows:

Richard Myers leaves his position as president of the Senior Class to Betty Jane Oller.

Betty Fager, vice president, wills her singing abilites to the blond Freshman girl, La Nona Hahn. Music and athletics mix well, La Nona.

Virginia Harp, secretary-treasurer of the class, bequeaths her forward position on the basketball team to none other than her sister, Betty. A little exercise or hard work won't hurt you, Betty.

Wilbur Clark, our Hindu actor in the Senior play, "Tiger House," wills his curly black hair to Richard Olsen.

Virginia Blickenstaff leaves her sewing accomplishments to Louise Wolf. It may be of use to you some day, Louise.

Mable Kuhn wills her talkativeness to none other than that very quiet Junior, Betty Frazer.

Paul Moore, an agriculture student, leaves his deep voice to Roswell Werdebaugh.

Mary Katharine Newcomer, a very studious member of the class, leaves her position as editor-in-chief of the "High News" to her assistant, Mary Datillio.

Delbert Biser wills his slyness at playing "hookey" without getting caught to Quinn Fogle.

Violet Boswell very generously gives all her acting skill to Nellie Decker.

June Frey bequeaths to Donald Bollinger her reputation as a Rubinoff imitator.

Emerson Ridenour, a very bashful Senior (around girls), leaves this trait to Clifton Harbaugh. After all, Clifton, the girls like a rest, too.

Anna Belle Smith wills her slimness and quietness to Doris Wiles.

Mary Stottlemyer bequeaths to Ruth Hayes her position as Mr. Hartle's office "keeper" and secretary.

Richard Winters, known around Smithsburg High School as "Dick", leaves his bass voice to Joseph Newcomer.

Miriam Kline gives her dancing ability to Dorothy Smith. It's a great pastime and lots of fun, Dorothy.

Leslie Happel bequeaths his good looks and winning ways with the faculty to that "Jolly Junior," Jesse Garrison.

Virginia Laspe leaves her blond hair to Joyce Dayhoff. I think you'll like the change, Joyce.

Honora Wolf bequeaths her individual walk to Betty Stottlemyer. Don't walk the halls too much, Betty.

Helen Kline wills her blue eyes and fair complexion to Frances Green.

Catherine Deal, better known as "Cass," bequeaths her way with the boys to Rachel Gearhart. After all, Rachel, we may as well make use of leap year.

Edgar Myers leaves his artist's accomplishments to Helen Needy.

Buelah Walter gives her ability to obtain "ads" for the "High News" from Waynesboro to Edward Bachtell.

The Smithsburg School's graduating class of 1940 left their "Class Will" for the underclassmen to follow. "To the Freshman we leave our ability to stay in school and work hard for four years." Anna Belle Smith willed her slimness and quietness to Doris Wiles. (Courtesy of the Smithsburg Historical Society.)

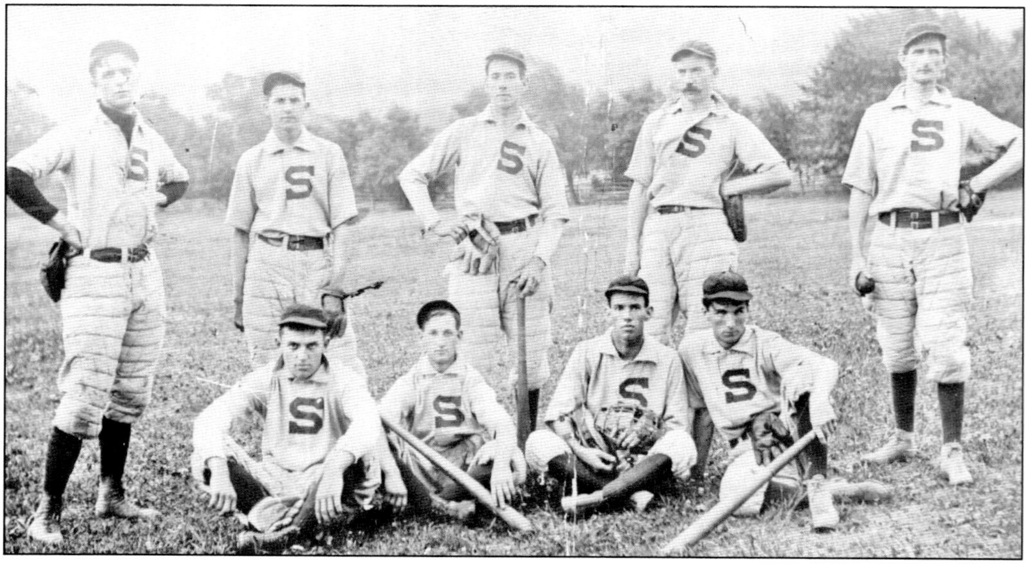

Smithsburg School's baseball team is pictured in 1903. From left to right are (seated) Dan Steck, Max Newman, Allen Geiser, and Bob Ferguson; (standing) Doc Sheely, John Phetterplace, Jason Geiser, Bert Phetterplace, and Sticks Sigler. (Courtesy of the Smithsburg Historical Society.)

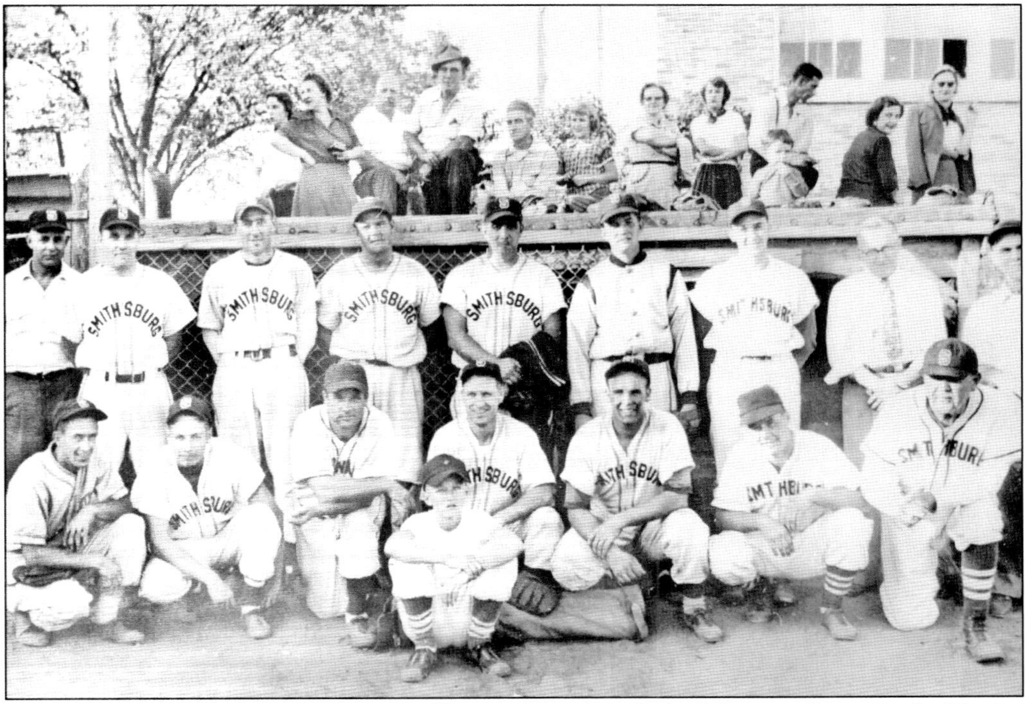

The 1950s Smithsburg baseball team is (first row) unidentified, ? Thomas, Omar Rock, Charles "Boots" Meagher, ? Ramer, Butch Miller, and Clyde Shaver; (second row) Arnold Myers, Bob Haugh, Skeets Chamberlain, Tom Brown, Bill Smith, two unidentified, Reno Harp, and Roy Warrenfeltz. The batboy is Steve Smith. (Courtesy of the Smithsburg Historical Society.)

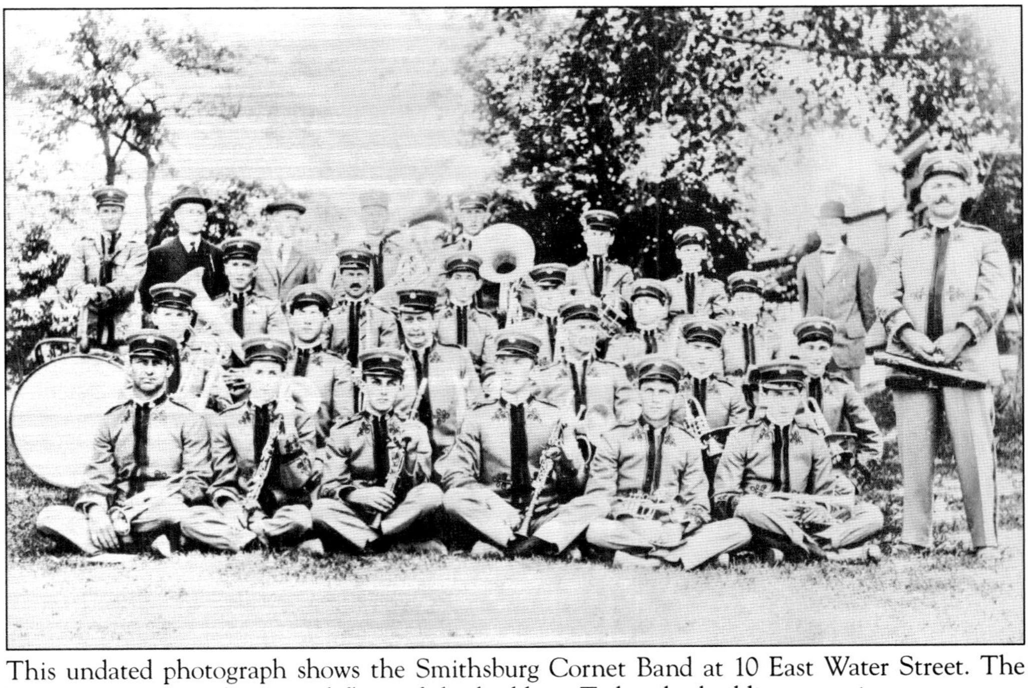

This undated photograph shows the Smithsburg Cornet Band at 10 East Water Street. The band practiced on the second floor of the building. Today the building contains apartments. (Courtesy of the Smithsburg Historical Society.)

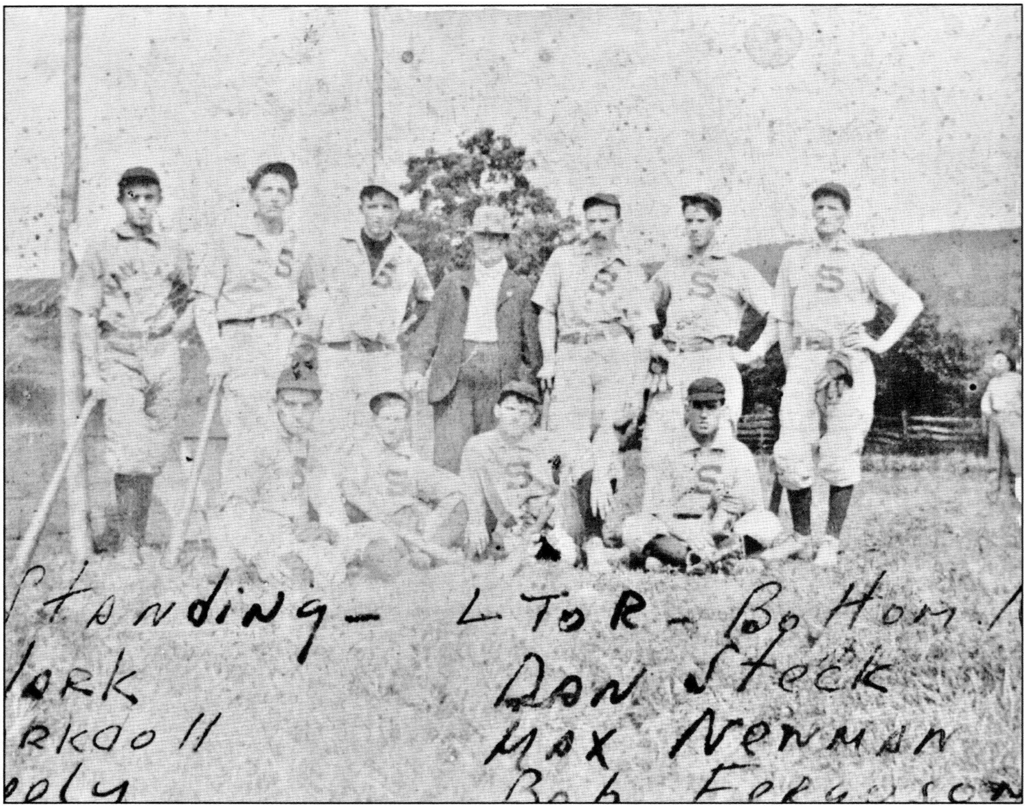

The Smithsburg School baseball team is pictured at an unknown date. (Courtesy of the Smithsburg Historical Society.)

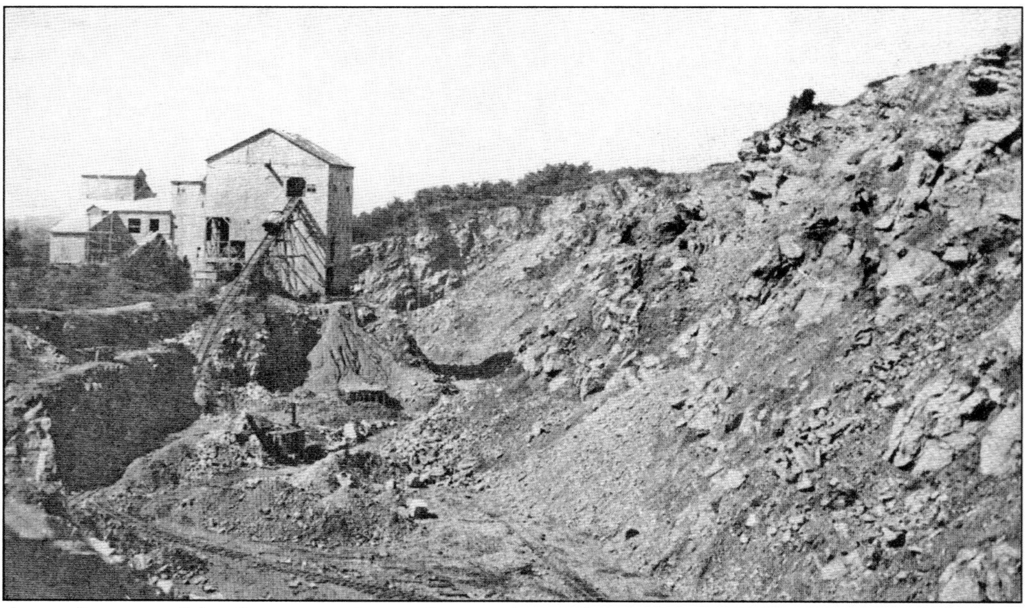

An early view of the Cavetown Stone Quarry, located on West Water Street in Smithsburg, is shown here. (Courtesy of the Smithsburg Historical Society.)

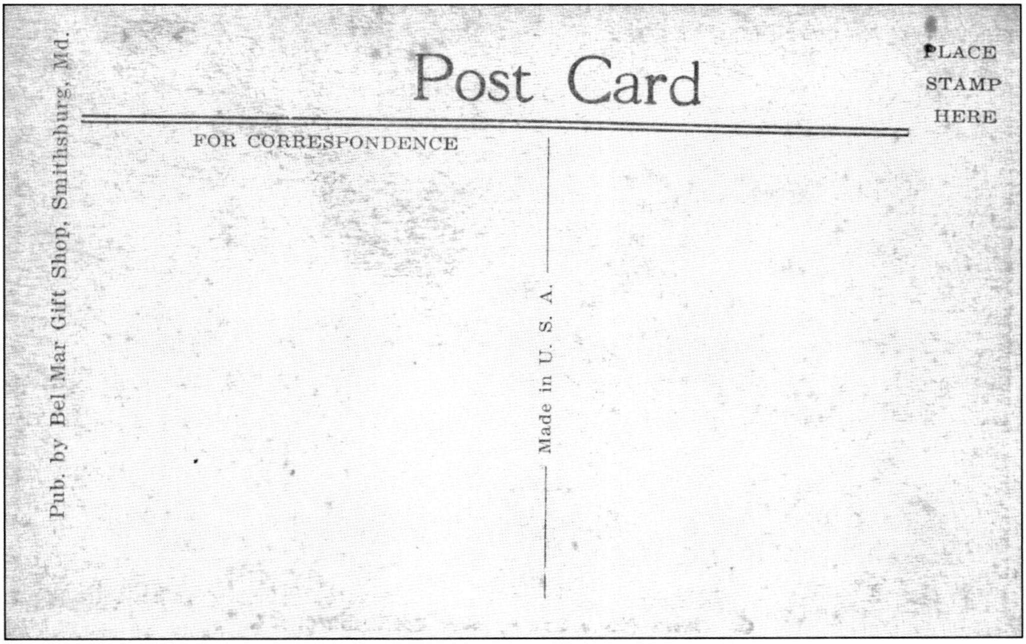

This postcard is from the Bel Mar Gift Shop in Smithsburg, Maryland. The shop no longer exists, but pieces of nostalgia, such as this postcard, have survived. (Courtesy of the Smithsburg Historical Society.)

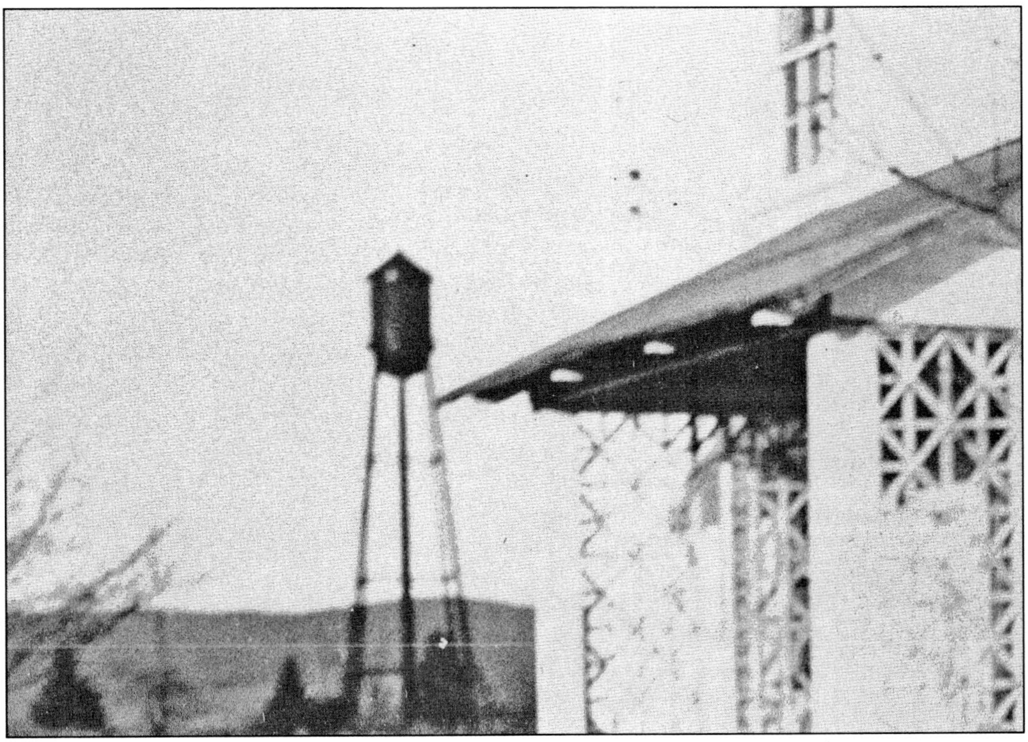

The Smithsburg water tower was constructed in 1931 and dismantled in 1957. It was located north of West Water Street just beyond the cemetery. (Courtesy of the Smithsburg Historical Society.)

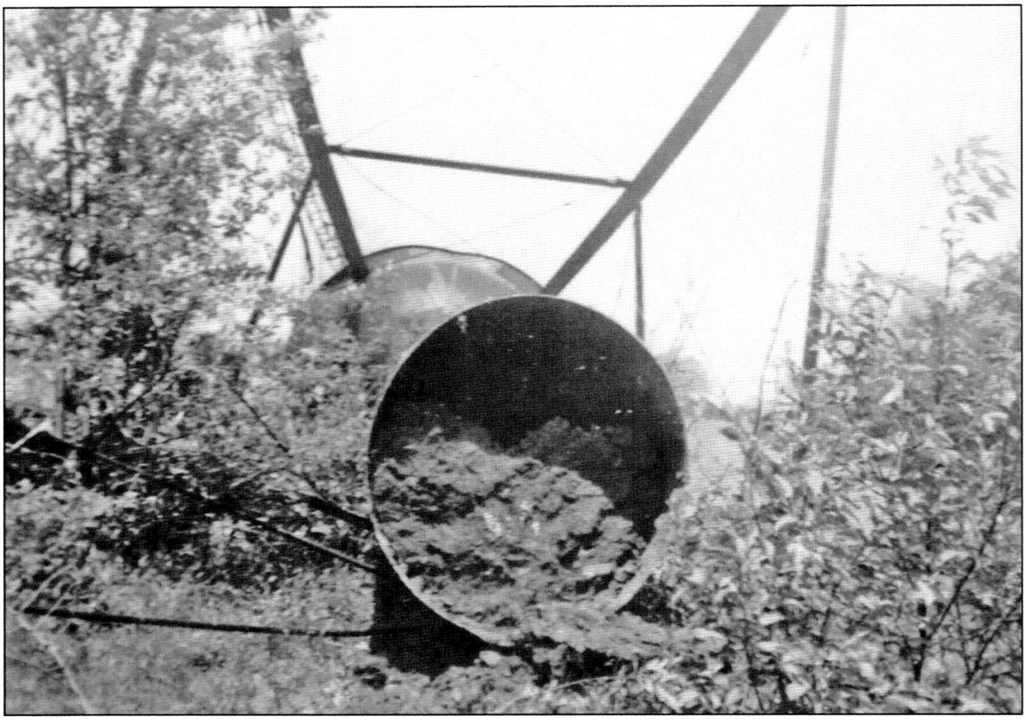

This photograph shows the demolition of the Smithsburg Water Tower in 1957. (Courtesy of the Smithsburg Historical Society.)

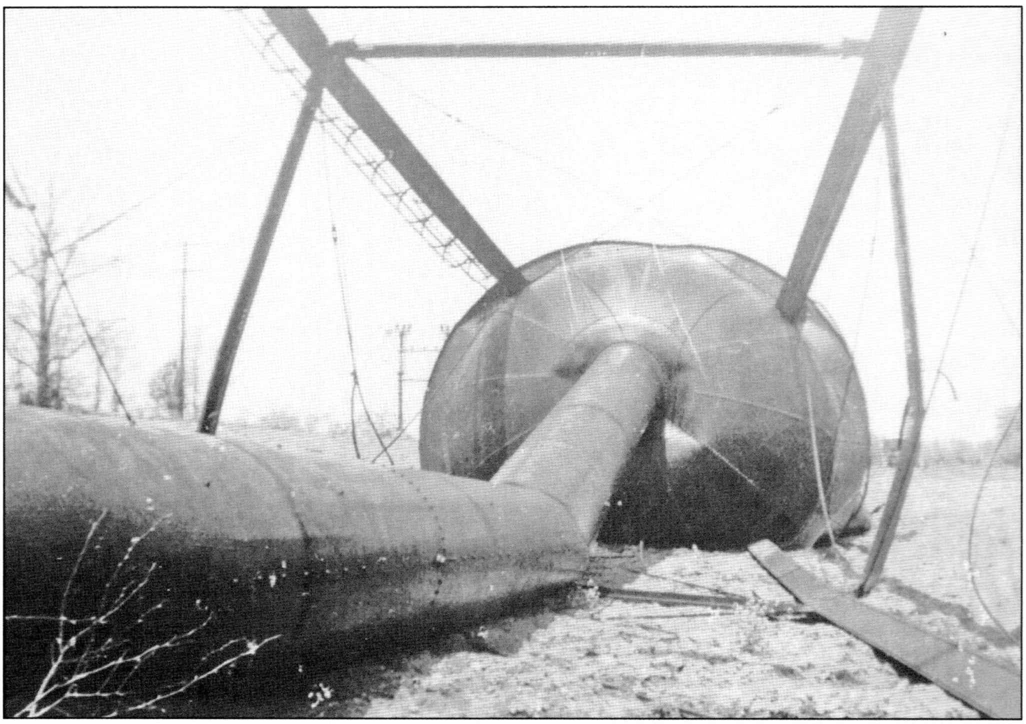

Here is another view of the Smithsburg Water Tower demolition in 1957. (Courtesy of the Smithsburg Historical Society.)

Pres. Lyndon B. Johnson, his wife, Lady Bird Johnson, and their daughter, Lynda Bird Johnson, visited St. Ann's Episcopal Church in Smithsburg on Easter Sunday, March 26, 1967. The image at right is of President Johnson. The below images are of Lady Bird Johnson, left, and Lynda Bird Johnson, right. These photographs plus a lengthy article ran in the *Morning Herald* newspaper of Hagerstown, Maryland. Over the course of his term, President Johnson visited the Smithsburg area many times. Camp David, the presidential retreat, is located in close proximity to Smithsburg. (Courtesy of Sari Slick Kilheffer.)

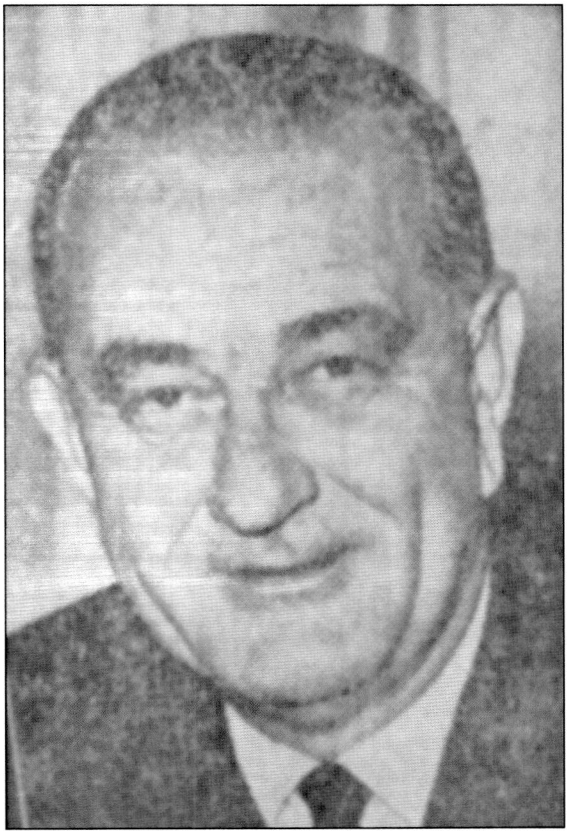

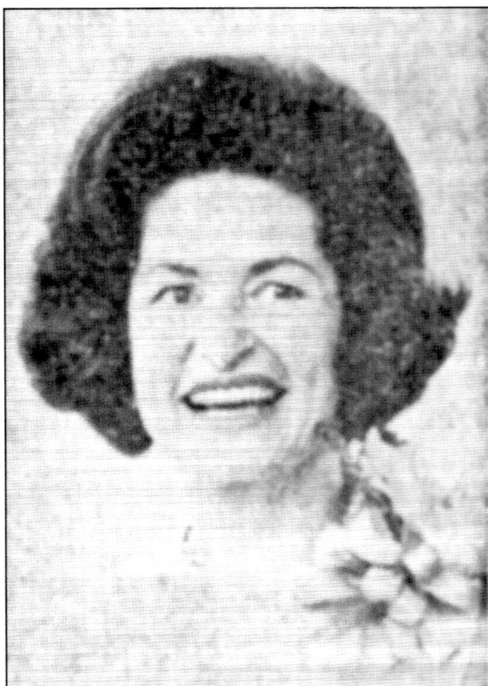

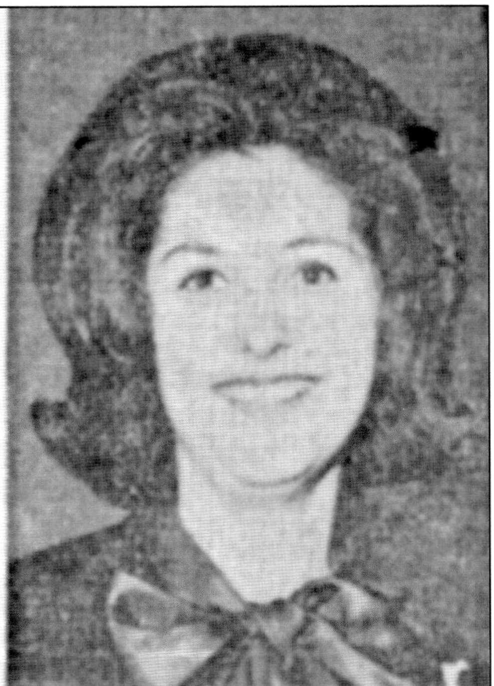

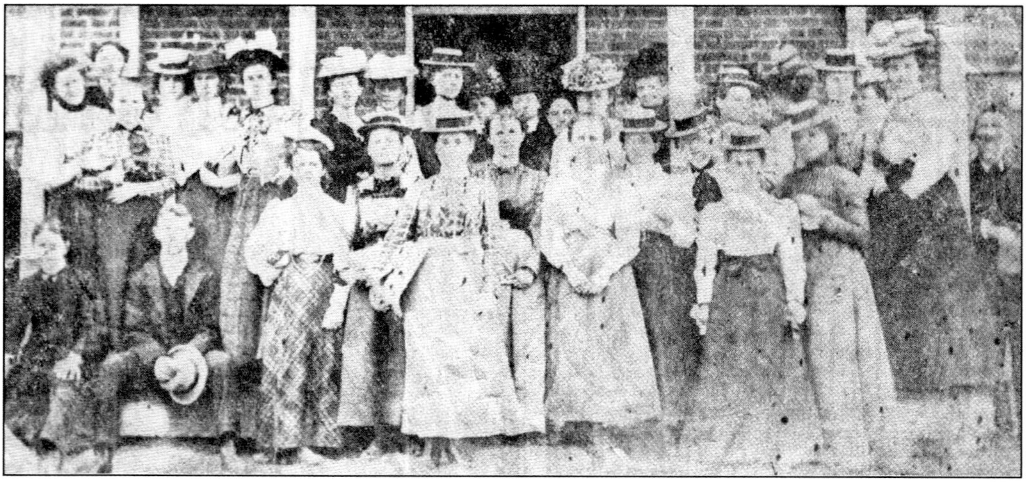

The *Morning Herald* newspaper reported in 1898 on "oral examination day," when the two upper classes of Smithsburg School were tested. (Courtesy of the Smithsburg Historical Society.)

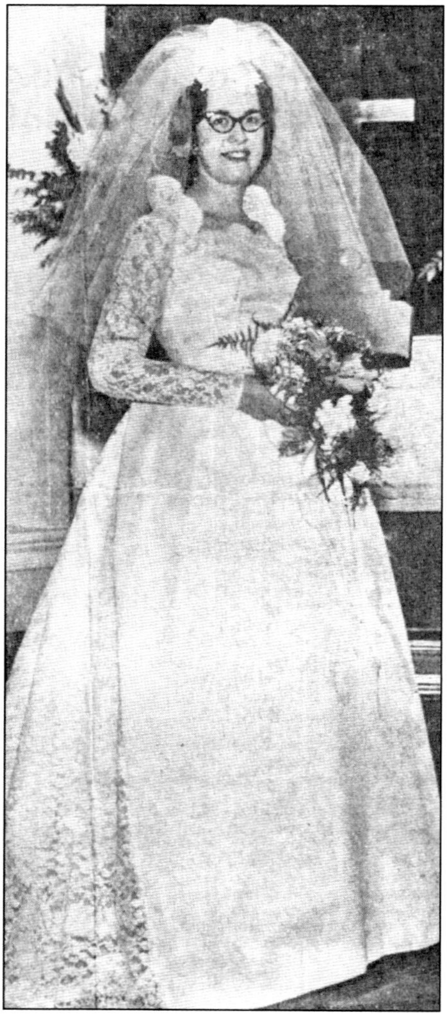

In 1964, the wedding announcement of this Smithsburg bride appeared in one of Hagerstown's newspapers. (There are three papers in Hagerstown—the *Morning Herald*, the *Daily Mail*, and the *Herald Mail*.) Married in Trinity Lutheran Church on Easter Sunday, the bride, Beatrice Lee Myers Hessong, wore a "period adaptation of white silk organdy" and a "Queen Anne collar of chantilly lace." (Courtesy of the Smithsburg Historical Society.)

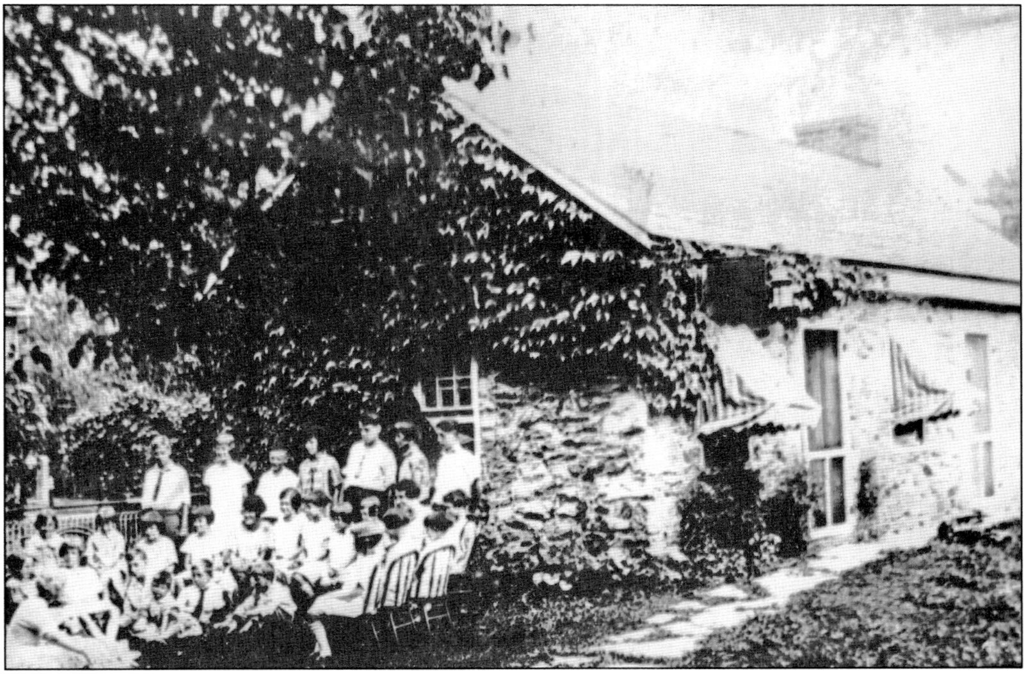

This 1930s photograph shows Reading Hour at the former Smithsburg Library at 20 East Water Street. This building is one of the originals in Smithsburg and has served as a jail, a library, and a residence, as well as the site of the Smithsburg Historical Society. (Courtesy of the Smithsburg Historical Society.)

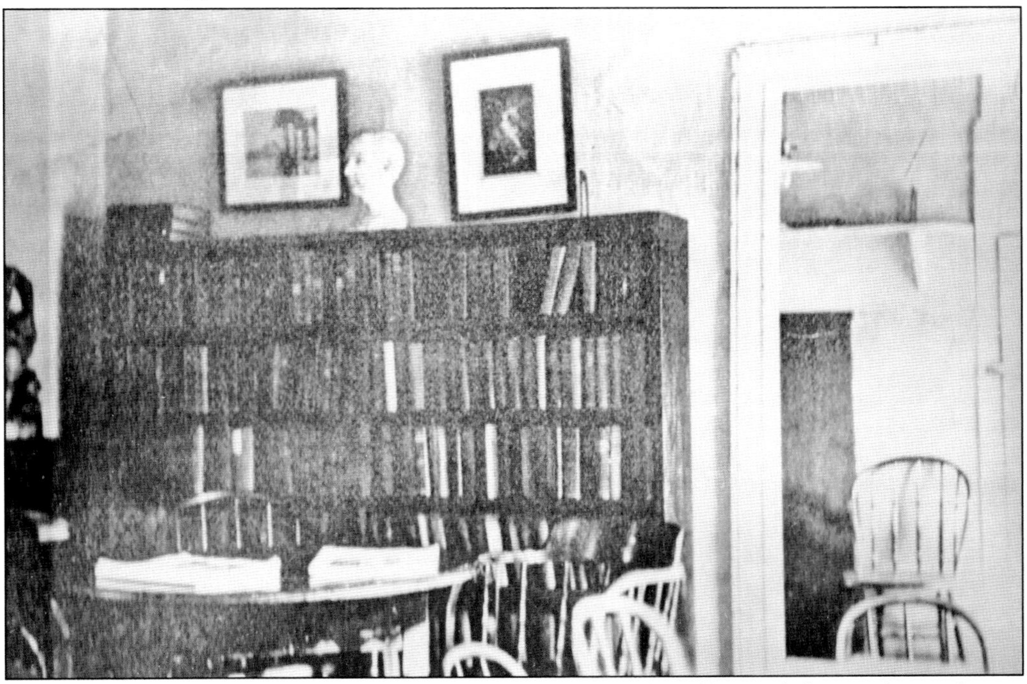

This photograph, taken in 1921, reveals the interior of the old Smithsburg Library. It was originally built as a private residence but has served as much more. (Courtesy of the Smithsburg Historical Society.)

TABLE OF RATES

Adopted by the

WASHINGTON COUNTY MEDICAL SOCIETY.

1866.

FEE TABLE.

Visits in town, exclusive of Medicine, each	$1.00
Visits in town, at night, (from 10 P. M. to Sunrise,)	2.00
Detention all night, not less than	5.00
Examination of patients, with directions looking to their future condition of health,	$3.00 to 10.00
First consultation,	5.00
Each subsequent consultation not less than	2.00
Professional opinion in writing, not less than	5.00
Office prescription, not less than	50
Visits out of town, for the first mile,	1.50
Each additional mile,	50
Night visits, for the first mile,	2.00
Each additional mile,	1.00
Special call and extracting Placenta,	5.00 to 10.00
Attending case in labor, one subsequent visit additional,	8.00 to 10.00
Vaginal Examination by Speculum,	5.00
" " Digital,	2.00
Venesection and extracting teeth, each, not less than	50
Single Vaccination at office, or in town	1.00
In the country, mileage added.	
Case of Gonorrhœa or Syphilis, fee in advance,	10.00 to 30.00
Amputation of large limbs, through continuity of bone,	25.00 to 75.00
Amputation of large joints,	50.00 to 100.00
" " fingers and toes,	5.00 to 20.00
" " tarsal and metarsal bones,	25.00
Excision of diseased joints,	50.00 to 100.00
Operation for Exostosis or Necrosis,	20.00 to 40.00
Trepanning,	20.00 to 50.00
Reduction of dislocations,	10.00 to 30.00
" " fingers and toes,	5.00
Adjusting fracture of long bones,	10.00 to 30.00
Lithotomy,	50.00 to 200.00
Tracheotomy,	20.00 to 40.00
Reduction of Hernia by Taxis,	5.00 to 20.00
Operation for Strangulated Hernia,	25.00 to 100.00
Important Operations on the Eye,	25.00 to 100.00
Minor " " "	5.00 to 20.00
Dressing recent Wounds, opening Abcess, introducing Seton or Issue,	1.00 to 5.00
Each subsequent Dressing,	50 to 2.00
Extirpation of Polypus,	5.00 to 30.00
Extirpation of Tumors,	5.00 to 50.00
Removing Tonsils or Uvula, each	5.00 to 10.00
Operation for Fistula in Ano or Perineo,	10.00 to 50.00
Passing Catheter or Boujie,	1.00 to 5.00
Paracentisis Abdom, Thoracis, or Vesicae,	5.00 to 20.00
Applying Cups or Leeches,	1.00 to 5.00
Operation for Hydrocele,	10.00 to 30.00
" " Aneurism,	5.00 to 100.00
Applying Ligatures to large arteries in Wounds	10.00 to 50.00
Operation for Hair Lip,	10.00 to 30.00
Examination and application of Truss,	2.00 to 5.00

MEDICINES.

Calomel Bolus,	25
Six Febrifuge Powders,	75
Six Tonic or other do.,	75
Pills per dozen,	50
Tinctures Vinous or Alcoholic, per oz.,	20 to 50
Aqueous Solutions per bottle,	25 to 75
Blisters,	50 to 1.00
Use of Syringe,	50
Administering Enema not less than	1.00
Verbal Prescription	50 to 1.00
Gonorrhœa Mixture, per oz.,	50
Quinine, per grain,	5

The subscribers, having been duly constituted members of the Medical Society of Washington County, do hereby pledge their honors to conform themselves thereto, and to all such other rules and regulations as may hereafter be adopted, so long as they shall severally continue to be members of said Society. In testimony whereof they have affixed their respective signatures.

District No. 1.
AUGUSTIN A. BIGGS,
BENJ. D. DEKALB.

District No. 2.
J. JOHNSON,
S. WEISEL,
H. ZELLER,
J. A. CROFT.

Hagerstown.
J. B. McKEE,
N. B. SCOTT,
M. J. McKINNON,
T. W. SIMMONS,
JNO. E. MILLER,
FRED. DORSEY,
JOSHUA JONES

District No. 4.
H. F. PERRY,
FRED. C. DOYLE,
W. W. SHAPELY.

District No. 5.
JAMES B. DELAPLANE,
JAMES BREATHED,
EDW. BORCK.

District No. 6.
H. B. WILSON,
OTHO J. SMITH,
J. F. SMITH.

District No. 7
E. BISHOP,
E. TRACY BISHOP,
W. A. RIDDLEMOSER.

District No. 8.
JAMES H. CLAGET.

District No. 9.
SAM'L. M. GOOD,
OTHO M. MUNCASTER.

District No. 10.
WM. BOOTH,
R. H. E. BOTELER.

District No. 12,
THOS. MADDOX.

Smithsburg was noted for George Pearson and other fine teachers producing doctors, lawyers, and other professionals. Here is a listing of rates that the doctor would charge for medical attention. Amputation of large joints could cost up to $100. (Courtesy of the Smithsburg Historical Society.)

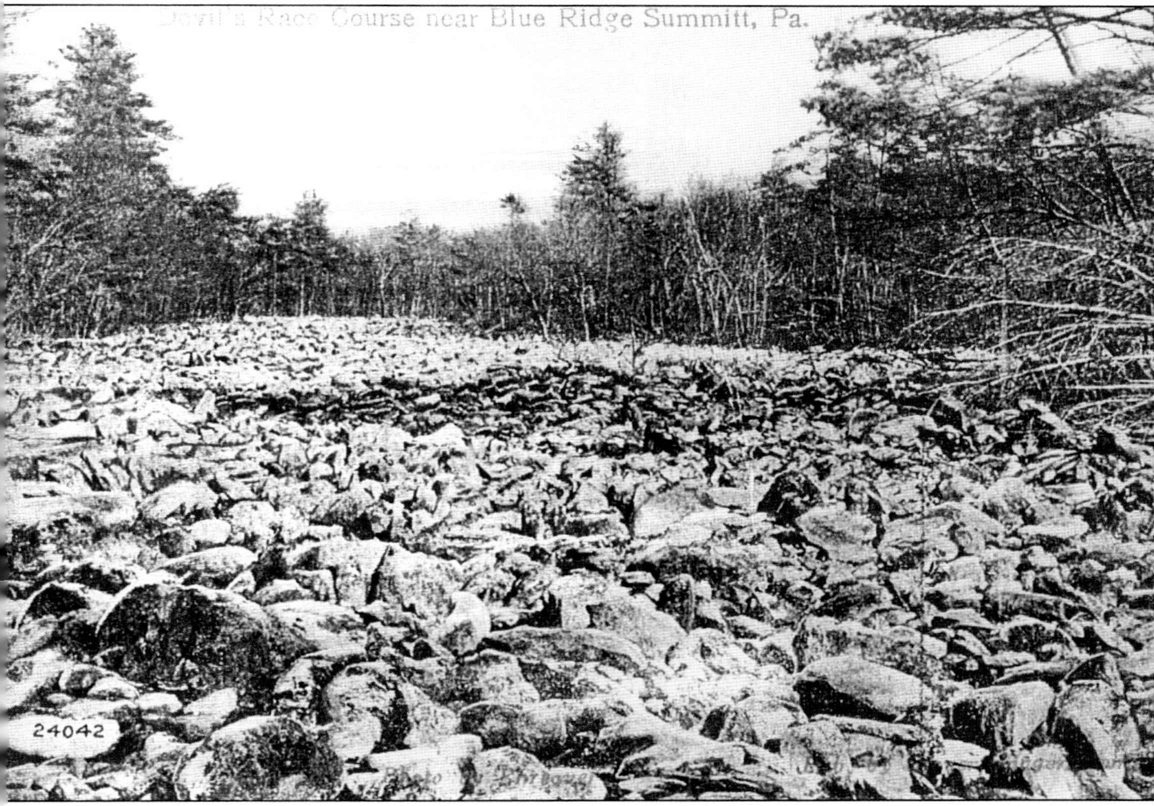

The Devil's Racecourse is a natural rock formation near Smithsburg. According to local legend, if one stands on the rocks, water can be heard running underneath. The Devil's Racecourse can be accessed at Fort Ritchie Road or on the Appalachian Trail. This postcard is postmarked April 18, 1921. (Courtesy of the Smithsburg Historical Society.)

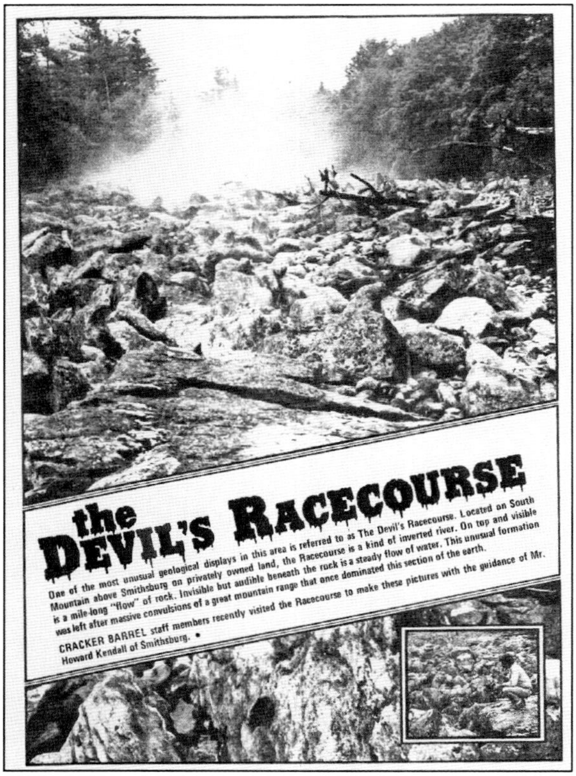

the DEVIL'S RACECOURSE

One of the most unusual geological displays in this area is referred to as The Devil's Racecourse. Located on South Mountain above Smithsburg on privately owned land, the Racecourse is a kind of inverted river. On top and visible is a mile-long "flow" of rock. Invisible but audible beneath the rock is a steady flow of water. This unusual formation was left after massive convulsions of a great mountain range that once dominated this section of the earth.

CRACKER BARREL staff members recently visited the Racecourse to make these pictures with the guidance of Mr. Howard Kendall of Smithsburg. •

The *Cracker Barrel* magazine provided an advertisement in their July 1976 edition. Howard Kendall and various *Cracker Barrel* staff members traveled to Devil's Racecourse to take photographs. (Courtesy of the Smithsburg Historical Society and *Maryland Cracker Barrel*.)

C. C. Fishack and Sons Wagon Repair Shop was located in Smithsburg, Maryland. The town map shows that the repair shop, situated at 10 East Water Street, was in business in the early 1900s. The building still stands and is presently is a residence. Quinn Fogle donated the photograph. (Courtesy of the Smithsburg Historical Society.)

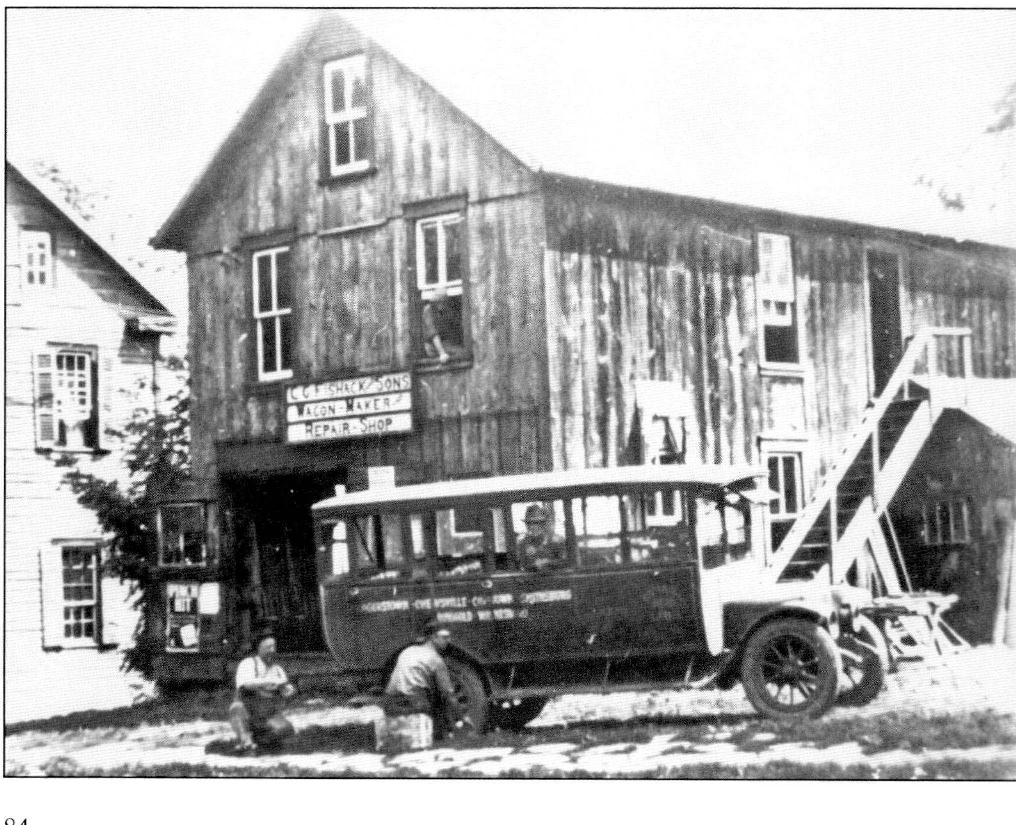

Four

TRAINS
ALL ABOARD

With the advent of transportation, specifically locomotives, trade became a possibility for Smithsburg. Orchards were able to pack and ship "Mountain Peaches" and "Smithsburg Pride" to more towns, cities, and states. Word of mouth was spreading, and the introduction of the Western Maryland Railroad Passenger Station tremendously benefited the town of Smithsburg and its residents. From the first train that steamed through town in 1872 until the last in June 1957, the railroad had been an influential and profitable addition to Smithsburg.

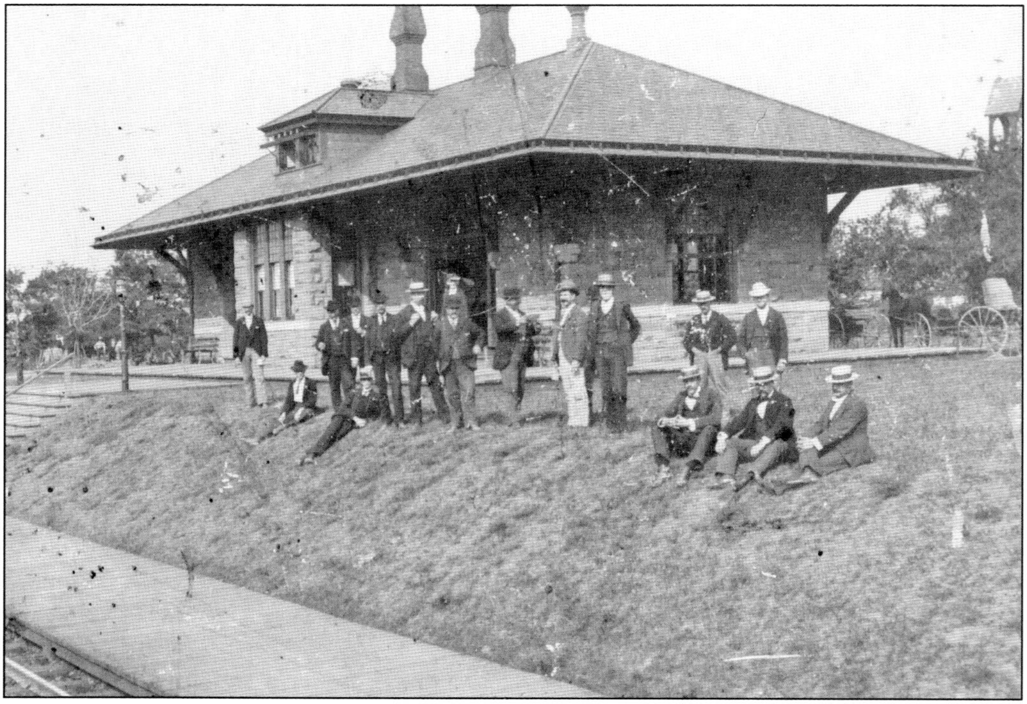

Located at 63 Railroad Lane, the Smithsburg railroad station is shown in 1895 near St. Ann's Episcopal Church. The cross atop the church can be seen in the background, as can horses and their wagons. (Courtesy of the Smithsburg Historical Society.)

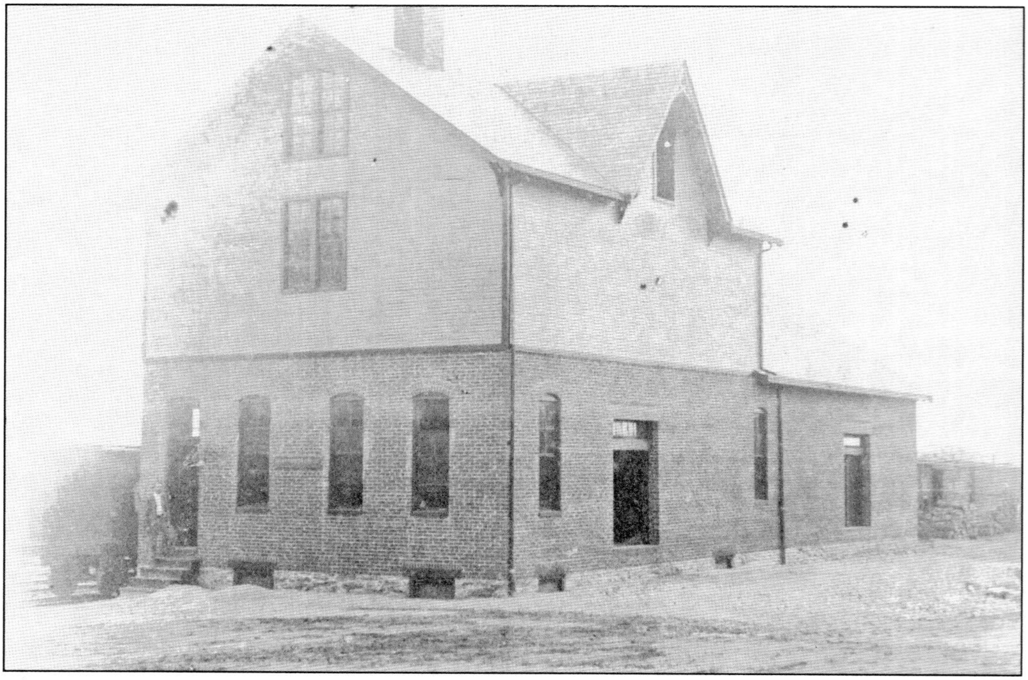

The Western Maryland Railroad Freight Station is seen around 1910. The freight station was the second structure located here. A fire destroyed the original station in 1900. (Courtesy of the Smithsburg Historical Society.)

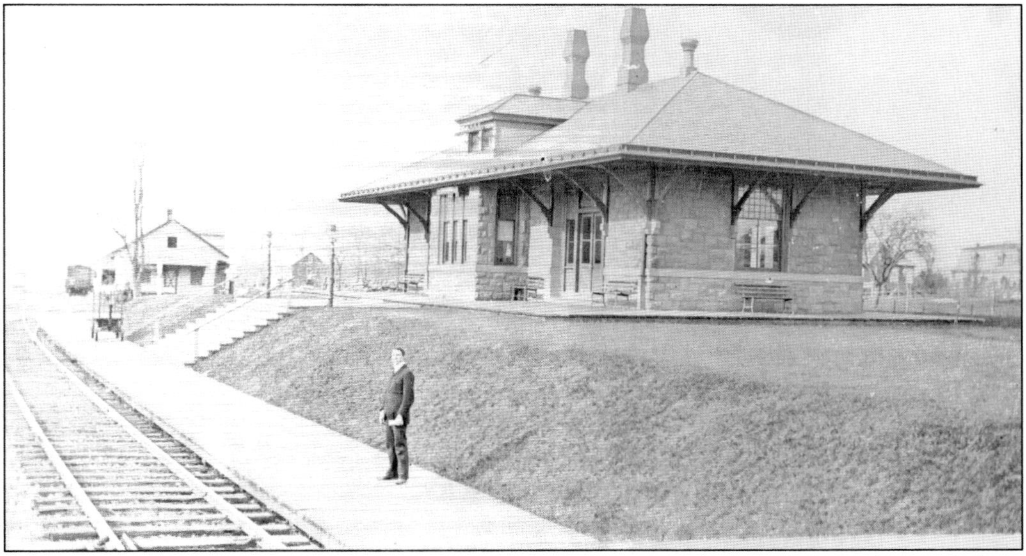

On June 6, 1872, the first train from Baltimore to Hagerstown steamed through Smithsburg Railroad Station. At the end of the 19th century, 32 trains daily stopped at the station. (Courtesy of the Smithsburg Historical Society.)

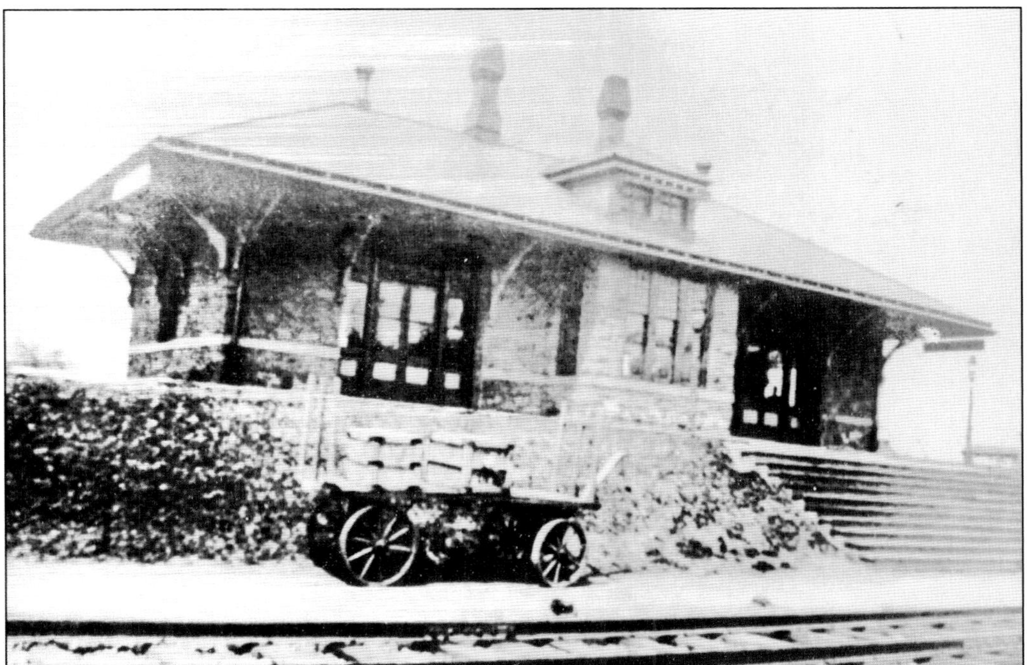

The Smithsburg railroad station is seen from across the tracks. Passenger service was discontinued in 1957, and the station was deeded to Farmers and Merchants Bank in 1964. The following year, the bank opened for business. (Courtesy of the Smithsburg Historical Society.)

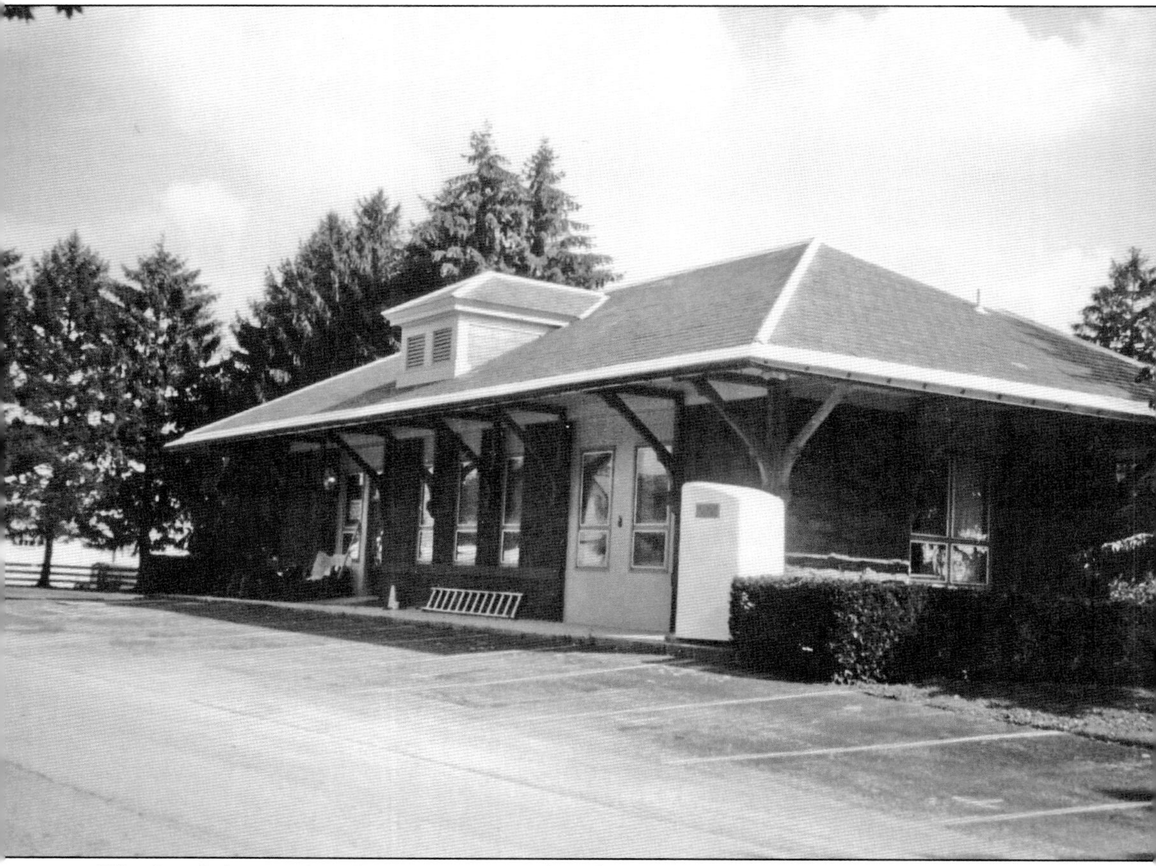

The Smithsburg railroad station is pictured in the 1980s. After the bank left in 1989, the building was purchased by a private investor and housed a laundry and hair salon. The building has also been home to an imported jewelry distributor. (Courtesy of the Smithsburg Historical Society.)

Five

ORCHARDS
PEACHY KEEN

Smithsburg's roots are literally in the ground. Realizing that peaches could grow hearty and robust in the rough mountain terrain, many area farmers cultivated a place in the world of agriculture by producing some of the best produce in the mid-Atlantic states. Apples, peaches, plums, cherries, pears, and more became the staples of the local diet. Known as "Smithsburg Pride," local orchards grew, packed, and shipped the fruits of their labor to neighboring towns, cities, and states. Most of the orchards are still operating at full production today. The pride of Smithsburg, the orchards are still a thriving business.

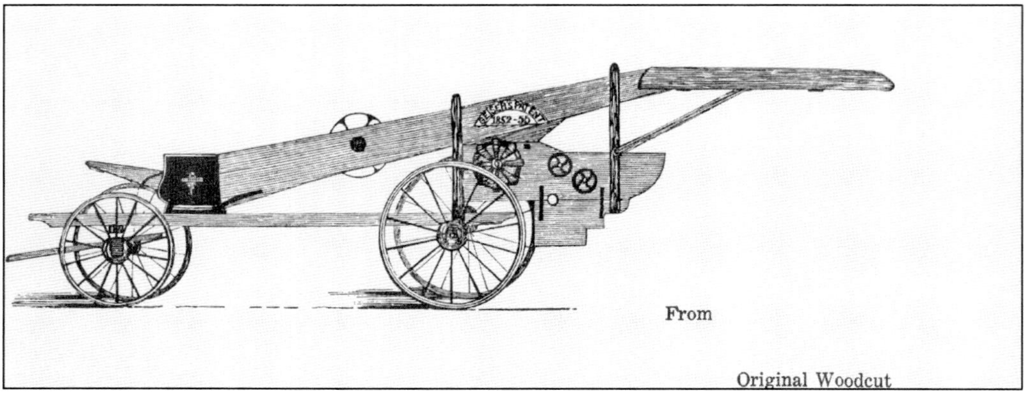

This is the original woodcut design of Peter Geiser's grain separator, patented in 1852. Geiser worked the farm he and his brother owned and tried out his inventions there. Before 1854, Geiser built and sold three more machines. The invention of this machine, and many more from Geiser, revolutionized the agricultural industry. (Courtesy of the Smithsburg Historical Society.)

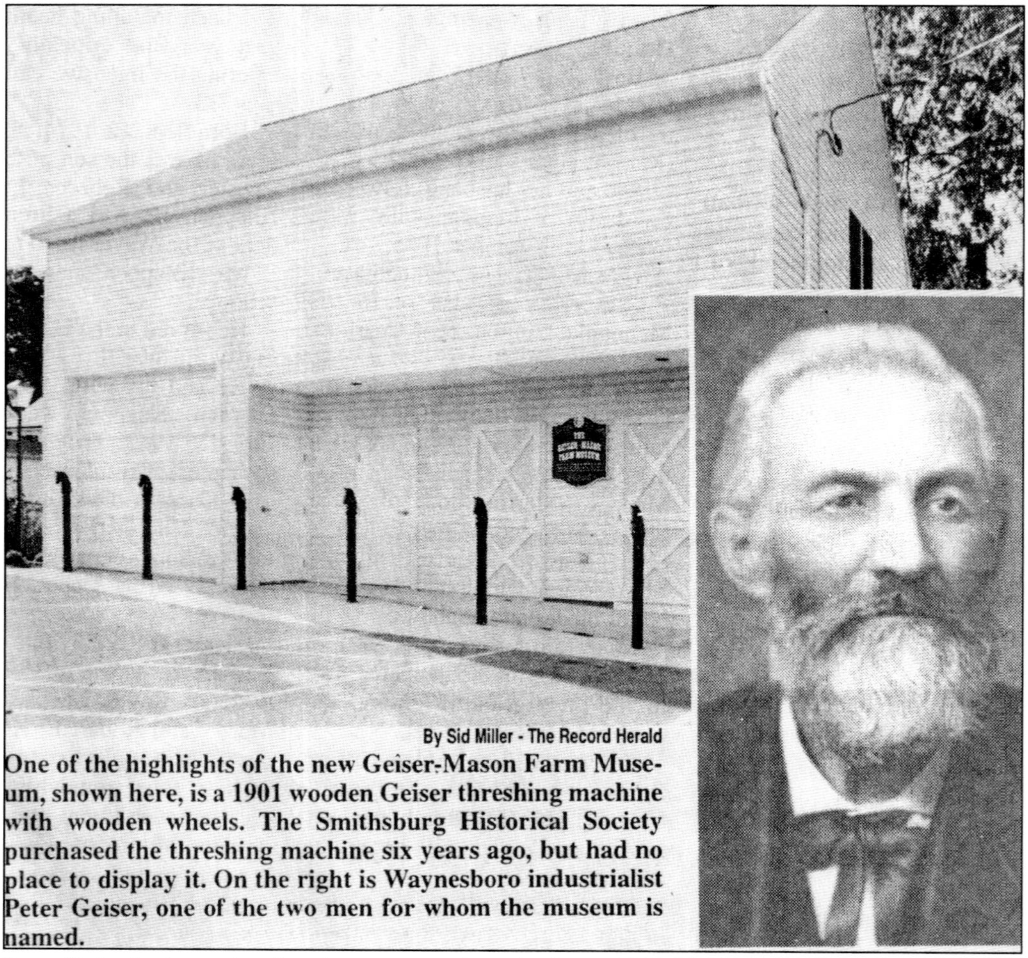

Peter Geiser's picture is taken from an article in the *Record Herald* of Waynesboro, Pennsylvania. The article explains about the new Geiser threshing machine, now housed in the Geiser-Mason Farm Museum in Smithsburg, Maryland. (Courtesy of the Smithsburg Historical Society.)

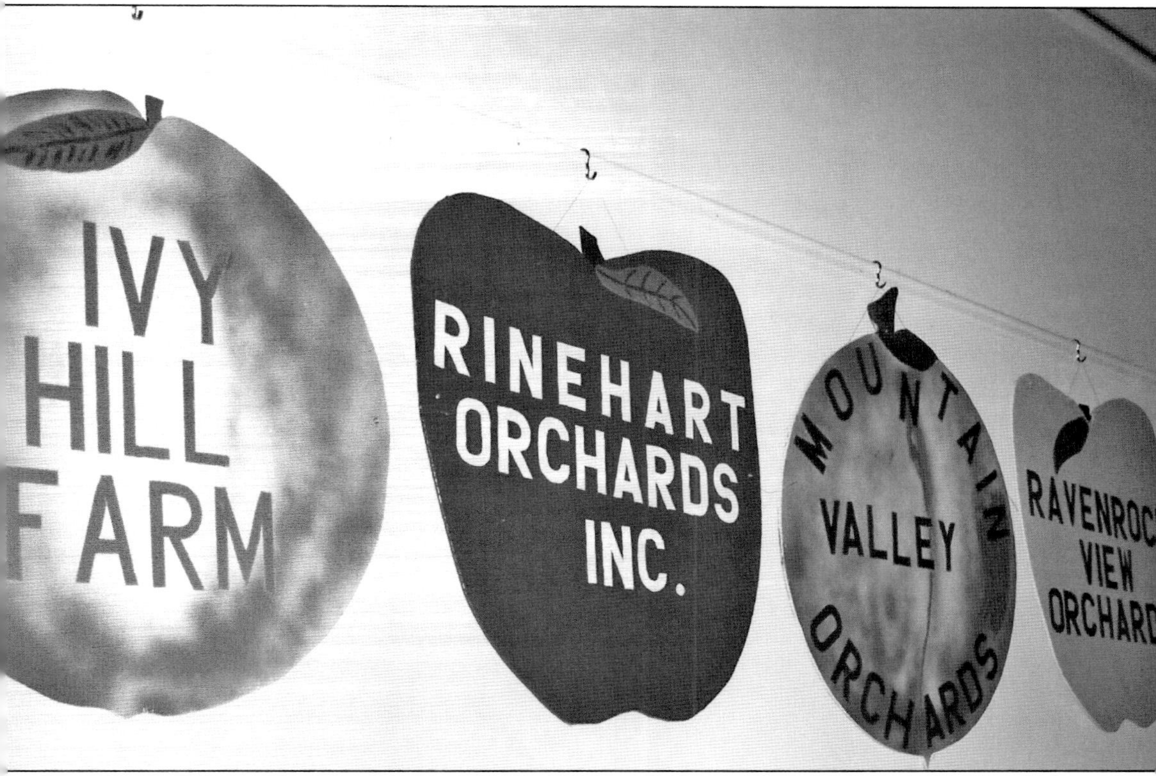

Here are various signs for some of the local orchards, including Ivy Hill Farm, Rinehart Orchards, Mountain Valley Orchards, and Ravenrock View Orchards. These signs, and more, are housed at the Geiser-Mason Farm Museum in Smithsburg, Maryland. (Courtesy of the Smithsburg Historical Society.)

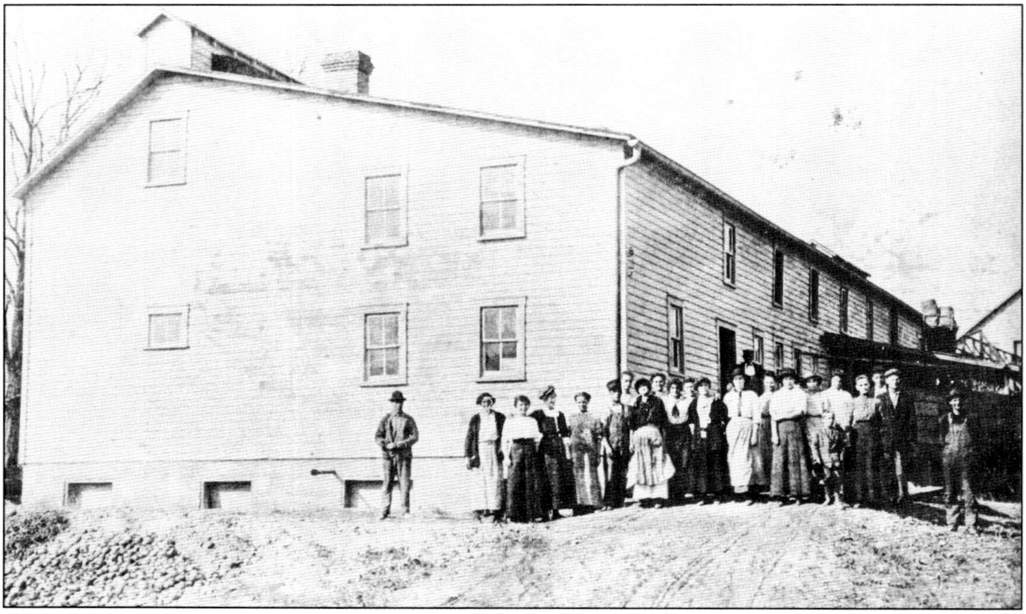

This photograph shows the Smithsburg Fruit Cooperative and Evaporating Company. The unidentified people in this photograph are fruit pickers ready to start their day. (Courtesy of the Smithsburg Historical Society.)

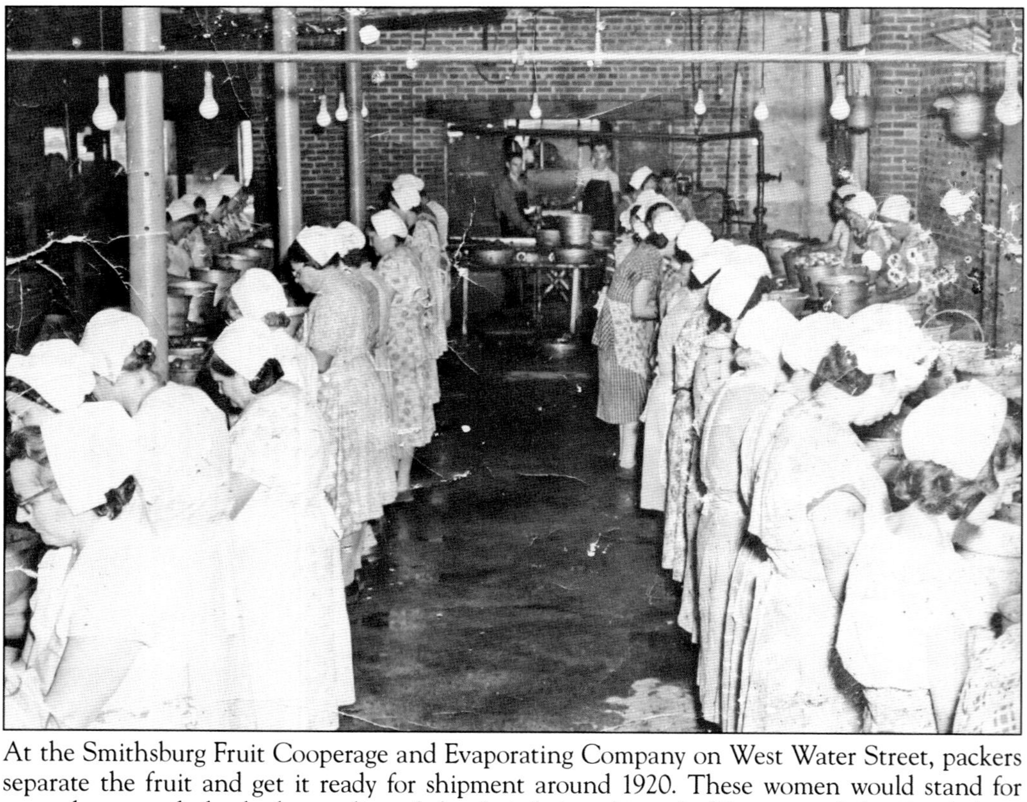

At the Smithsburg Fruit Cooperage and Evaporating Company on West Water Street, packers separate the fruit and get it ready for shipment around 1920. These women would stand for many hours and check the quality of the fruit being shipped. (Courtesy of the Smithsburg Historical Society.)

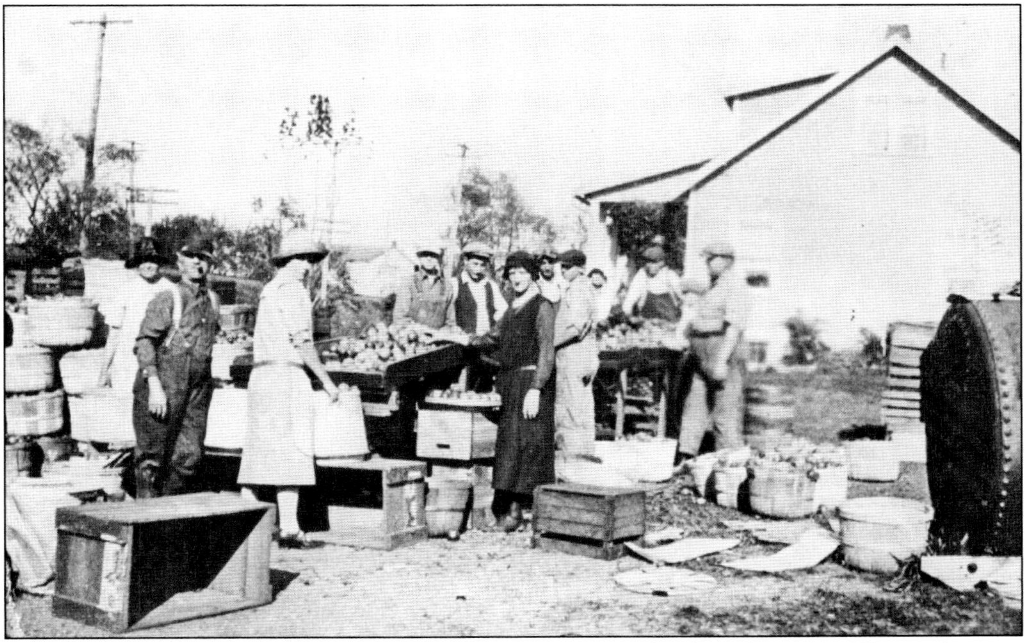

Maryland Packing Company was located in Cavetown, Maryland, in the 1920s. The workers are separating the crop and weighing the apples for packing and shipping to various destinations. From left to right are Ethel Oswald, Henry Baker, Luella Shaver, Wilmer Oswald, Ben Smith, Gertie Smith, Raymond Hershberger, unidentified, Hattie Walters, two unidentified, and J. Clyde Shaver. (Courtesy of the Smithsburg Historical Society.)

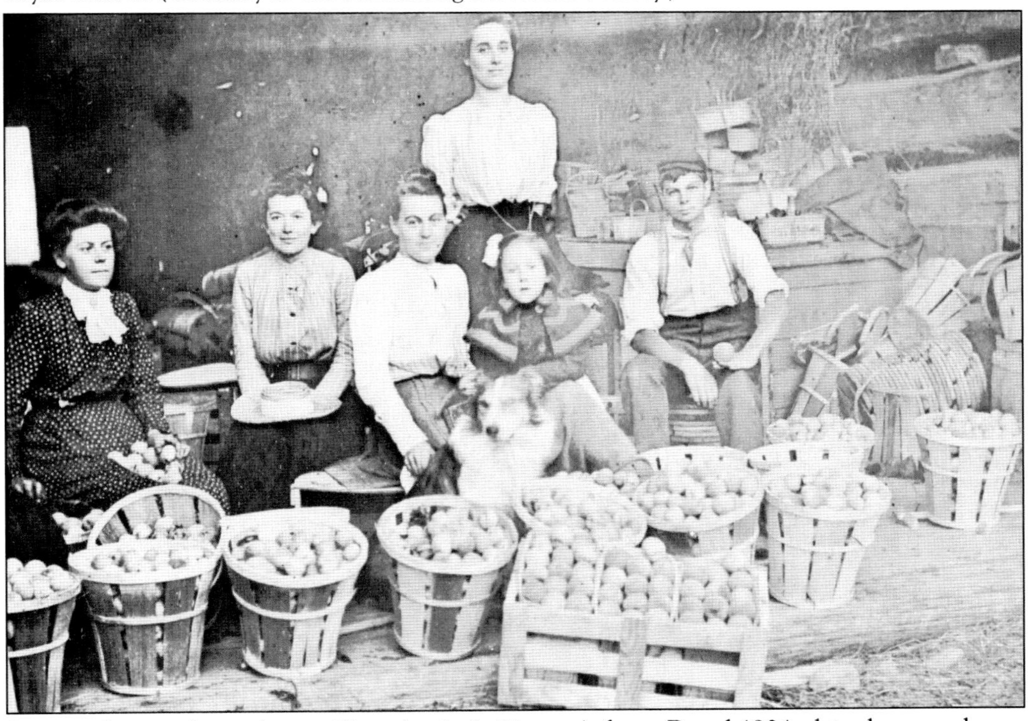

Fruit packers pack peaches at Cloverly, A. L. Towson's farm. Dated 1904, this photograph was taken by George W. Reid of Hagerstown. (Courtesy of the Smithsburg Historical Society.)

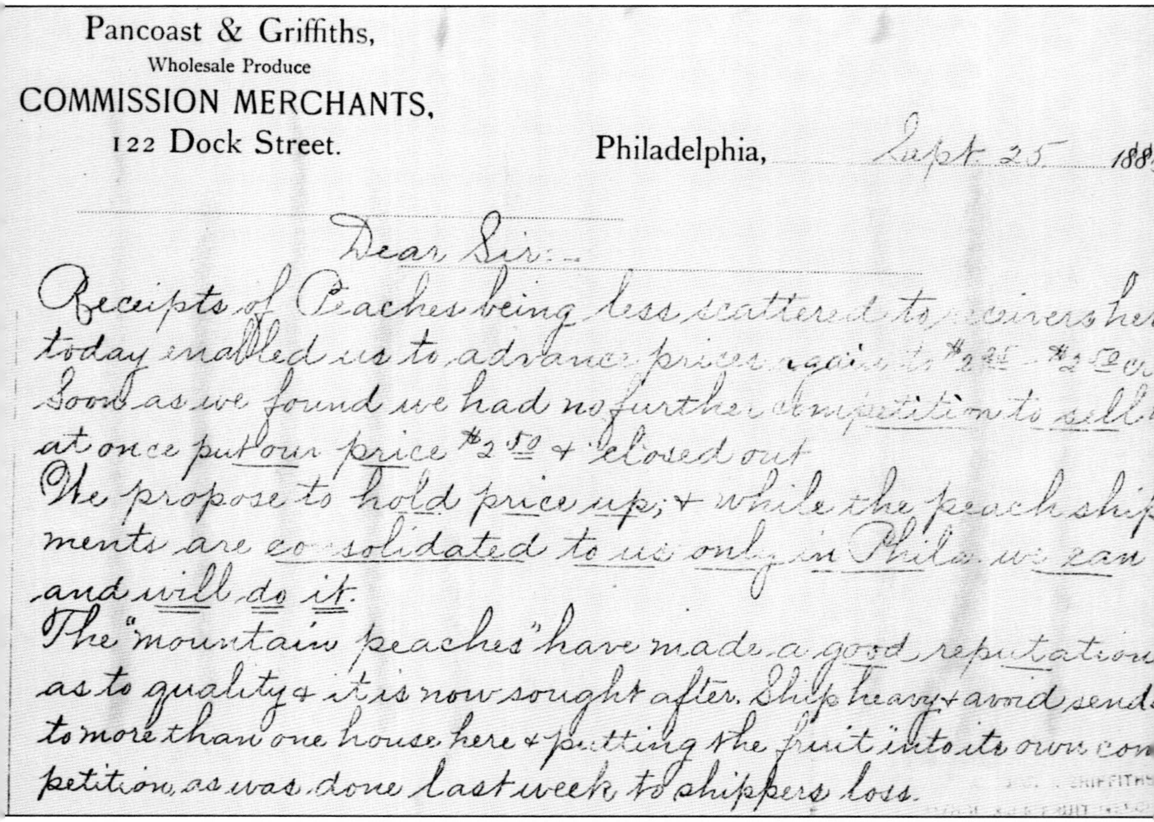

Pancoast & Griffiths,
Wholesale Produce
COMMISSION MERCHANTS,
122 Dock Street. Philadelphia, Sept. 25 188

Dear Sir:-
Receipts of Peaches being less scattered to receivers here today enabled us to advance prices again to $2.25 - $2.50 or. Soon as we found we had no further competition to sell at once put our price $2.50 + closed out
We propose to hold price up; + while the peach shipments are consolidated to us only in Phila. we can and will do it.
The "mountain peaches" have made a good reputation as to quality + it is now sought after. Ship heavy + avoid sending to more than one house here + putting the fruit into its own competition, as was done last week to shippers loss.

This invoice from Pancoast and Griffiths in Philadelphia is dated September 25, 1888. The subject is Smithsburg's famous mountain peaches. "The 'mountain peaches' have made a good reputation as to quality and it is now sought after." (Courtesy of the Smithsburg Historical Society.)

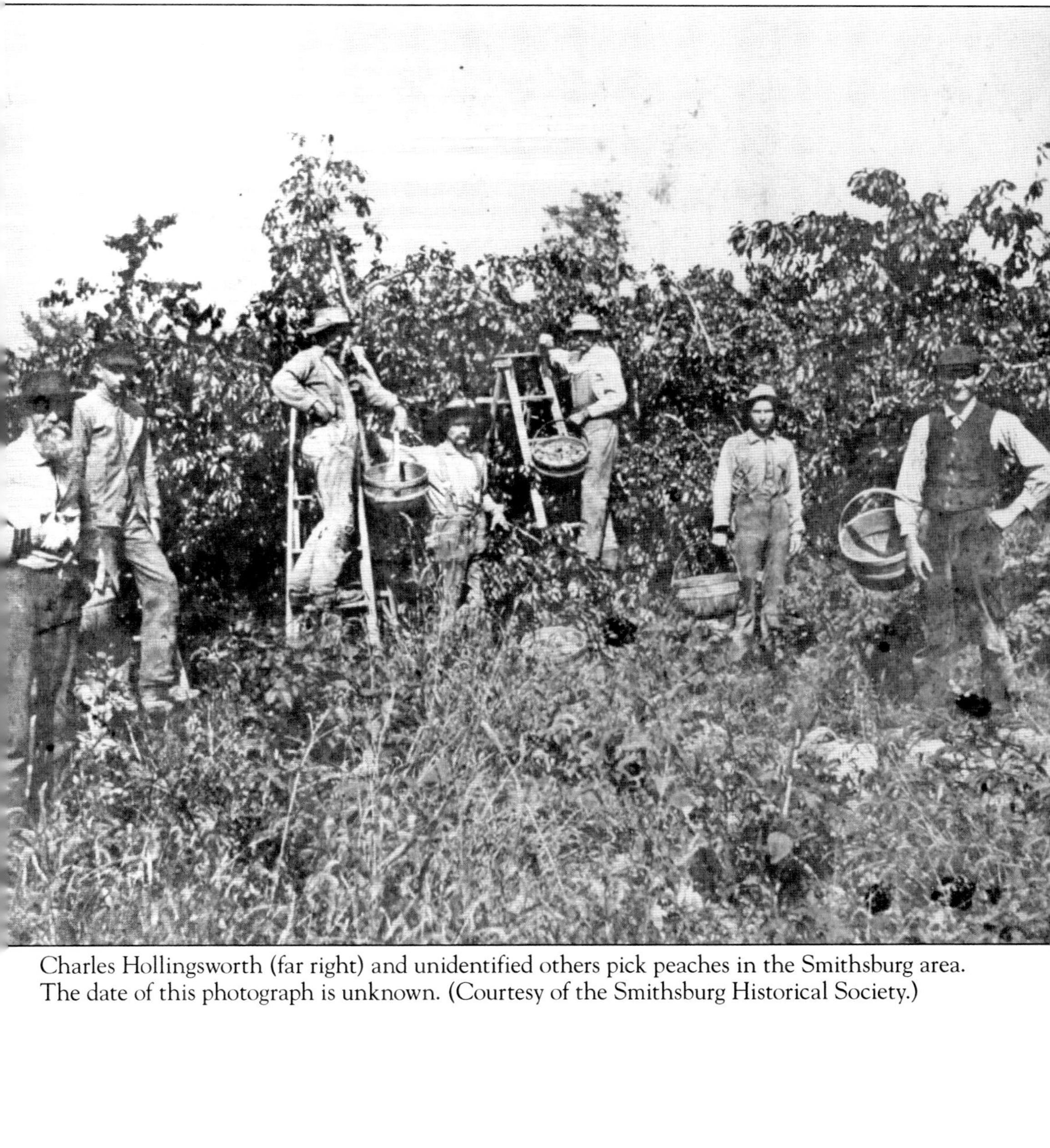

Charles Hollingsworth (far right) and unidentified others pick peaches in the Smithsburg area. The date of this photograph is unknown. (Courtesy of the Smithsburg Historical Society.)

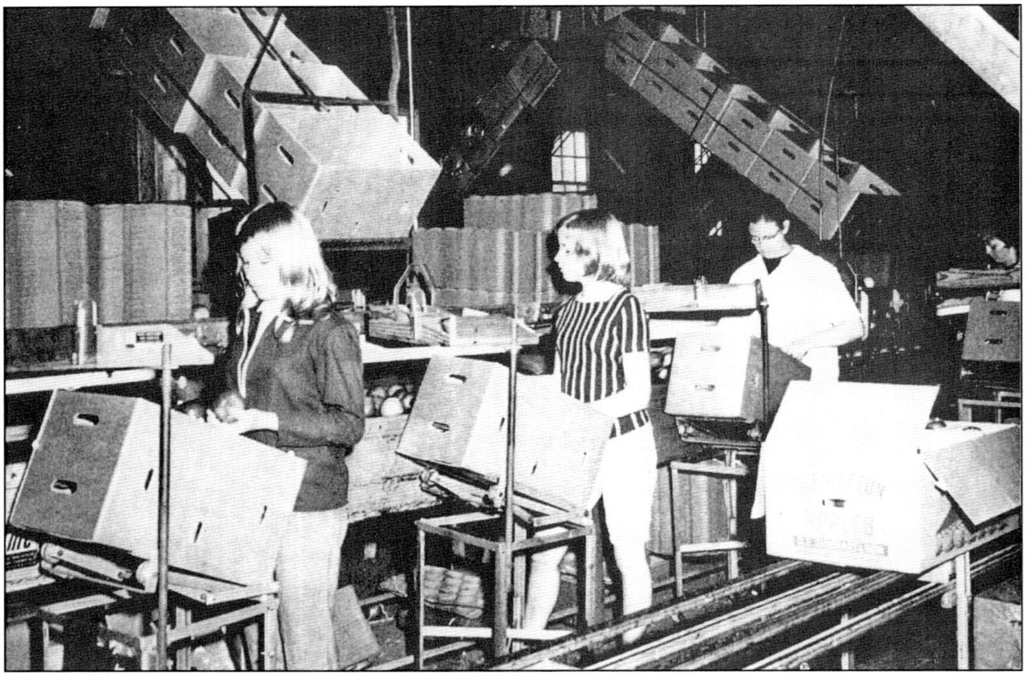

This 1969 photograph shows Rinehart's Glen Afton Farm workers packing fruit to be shipped to various cities. (Courtesy of the Smithsburg Historical Society.)

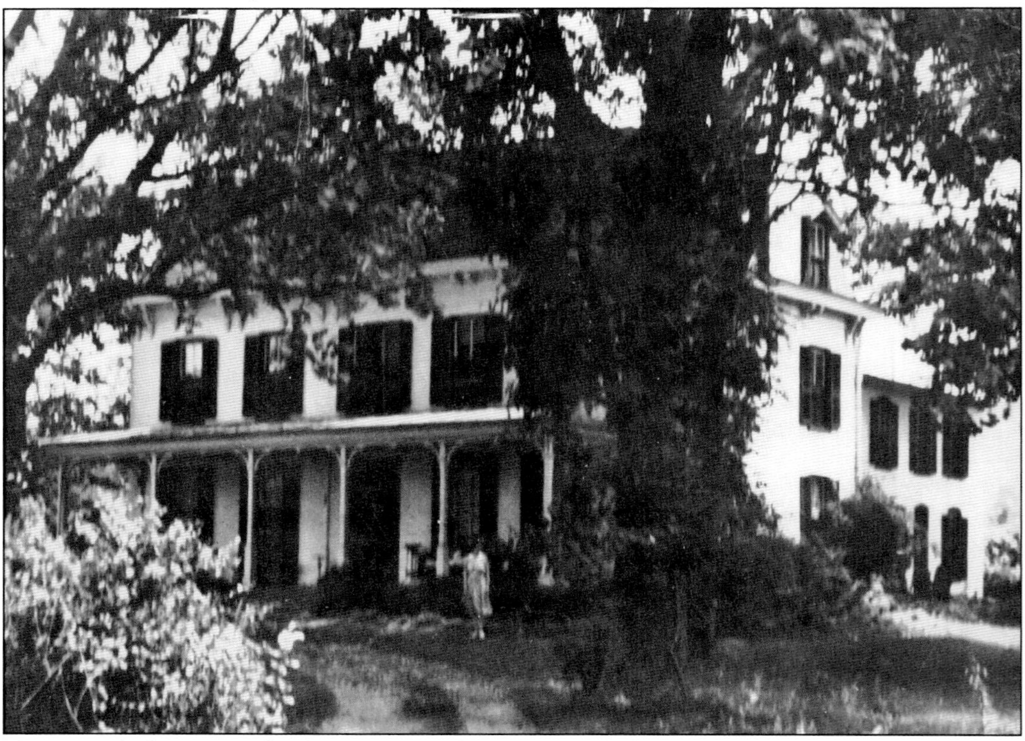

Homewood, the name of Robert Towson's home in Smithsburg, Maryland, is pictured here. An unidentified young lady stands near the front porch of the home, which is nearly concealed by the trees. (Courtesy of the Smithsburg Historical Society.)

A. L. Towson's obituary ran in the *Daily Mail*, Hagerstown's newspaper, on July 3, 1958. The pioneer fruit grower and retired grain and feed businessman died at age 91. One little-known fact about Towson is that he holds the record for longest service as an Episcopalian choir member. He had been a member of St. Ann's Episcopal Church for 80 years. (Courtesy of the Smithsburg Historical Society.)

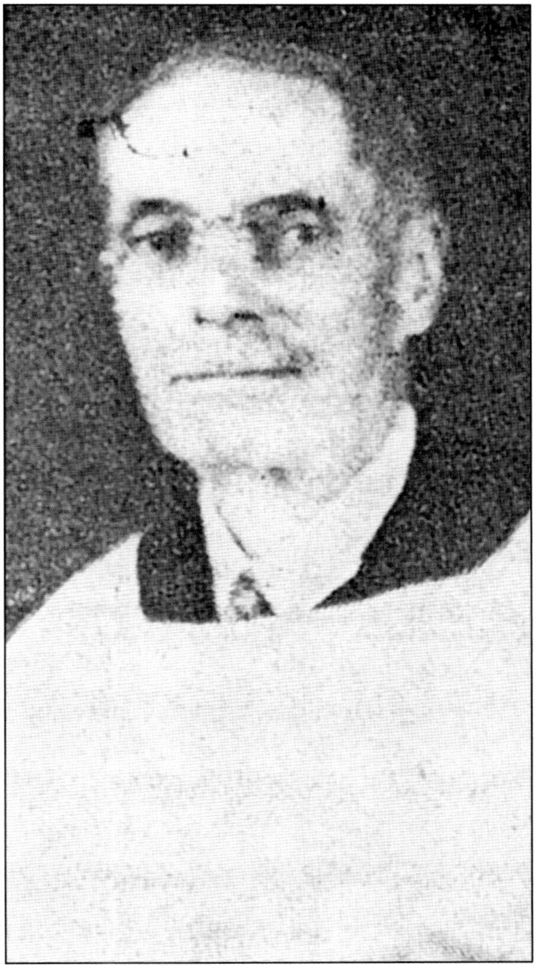

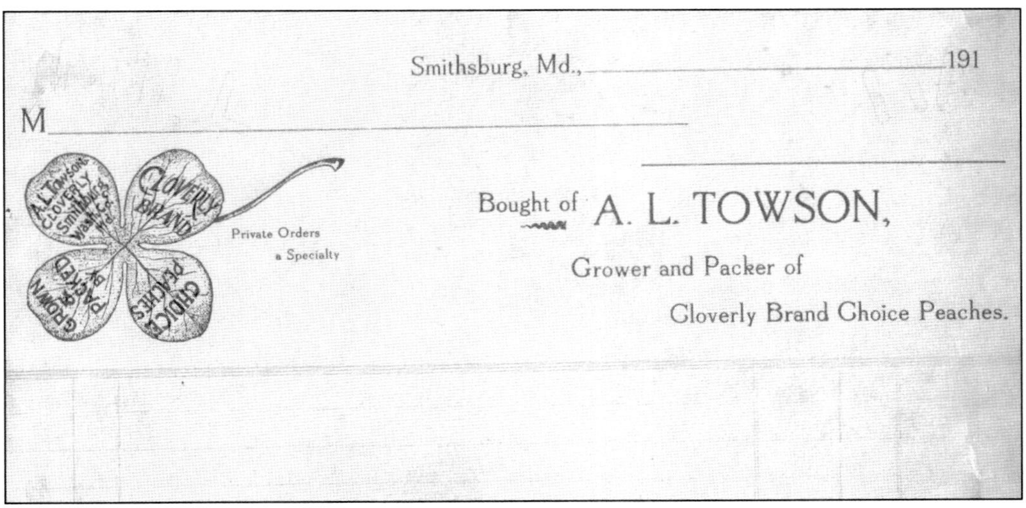

Smithsburg, Md., ______________ 191

M______________

A. L. Towson
Cloverly
Smithsburg
Wash. Co.
Md.

Cloverly Brand

Grown Packed

Choice Peaches

Private Orders
a Specialty

Bought of A. L. TOWSON,

Grower and Packer of

Cloverly Brand Choice Peaches.

This unused receipt is from A. L. Towson's Cloverly farm in Smithsburg, Maryland. The receipt shows the option of private orders as well as specialty orders available from Cloverly. (Courtesy of the Smithsburg Historical Society.)

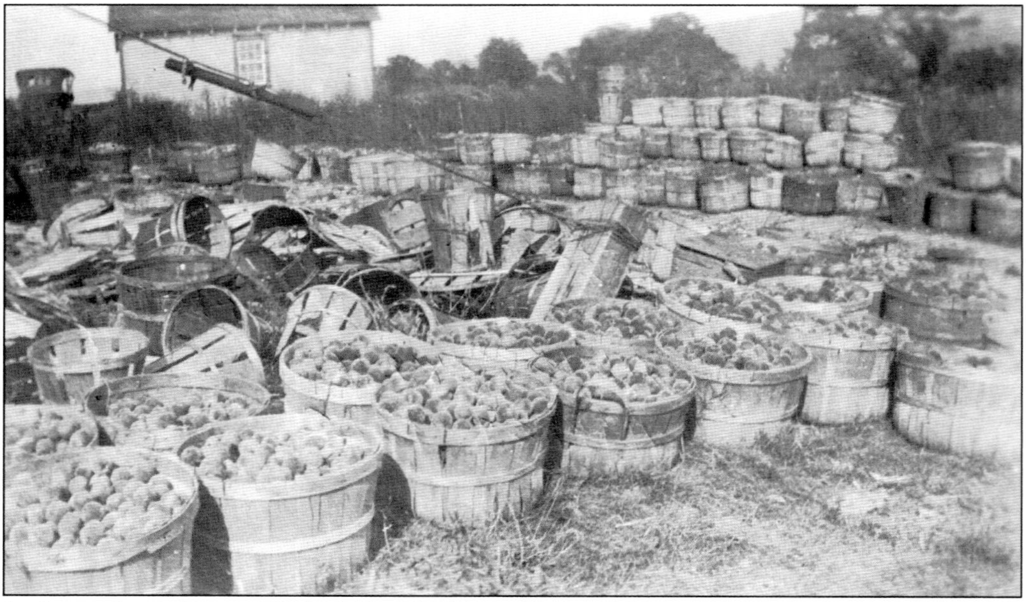

In this undated photograph, bushels of freshly picked peaches wait for distribution to neighboring towns or even states. The rows of bushels of produce stacked up in the background indicate that they are ready to be shipped. (Courtesy of the Smithsburg Historical Society.)

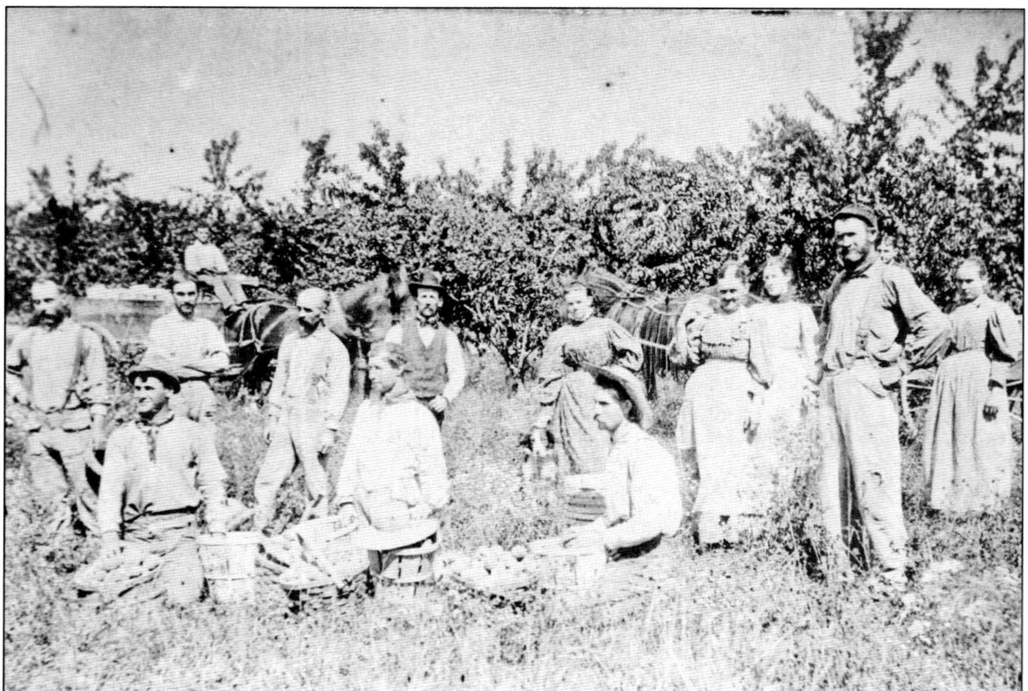

Maintaining and running a successful orchard takes many laborers. From picking the crop to packing it, many skilled hands are needed. This photograph, taken in the early 1900s, shows Joseph Sleasman's orchard and gives only one example of how many people an orchard would need to work on a particular day. (Courtesy of the Smithsburg Historical Society.)

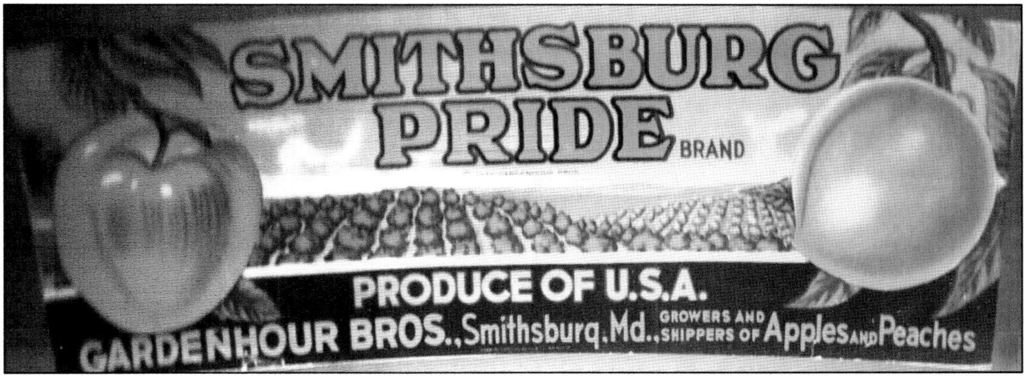

A sign from Gardenhour Orchards touts the Pride of Smithsburg. Locally grown fruits, especially peaches and apples, are a way of life in Smithsburg, Maryland. (Courtesy of the Smithsburg Historical Society.)

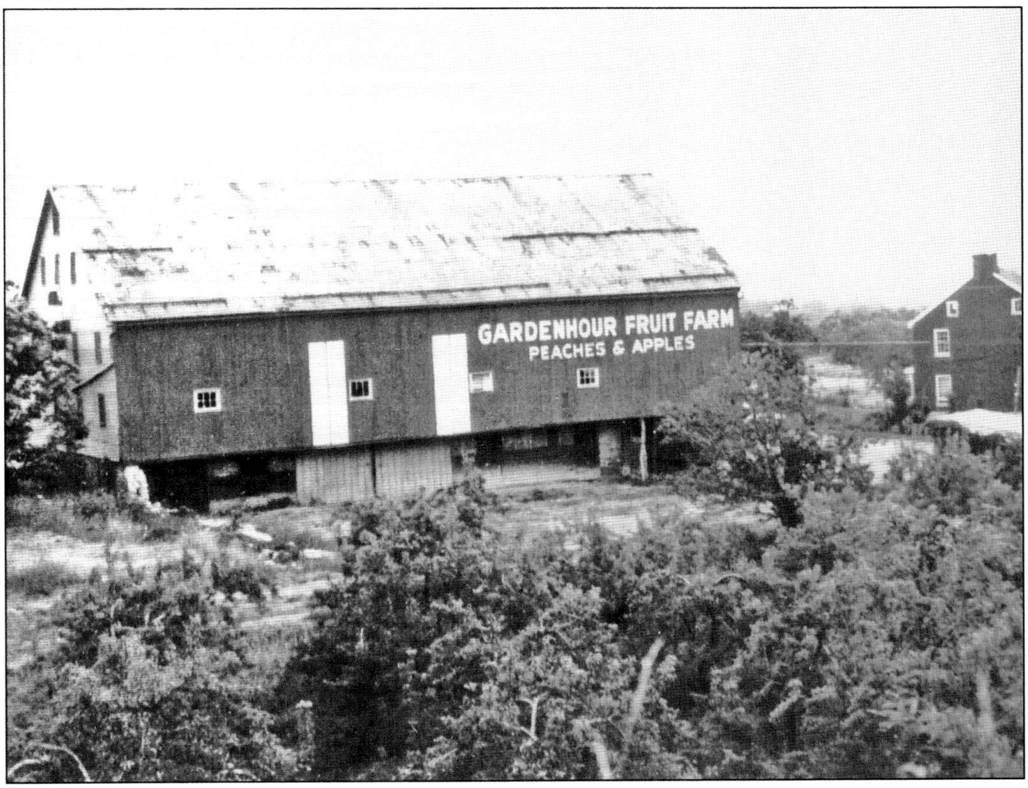

Gardenhour Orchards is a prominent orchard in the Smithsburg area specializing in peaches and apples. The large barn advertises the produce. (Courtesy of the Smithsburg Historical Society.)

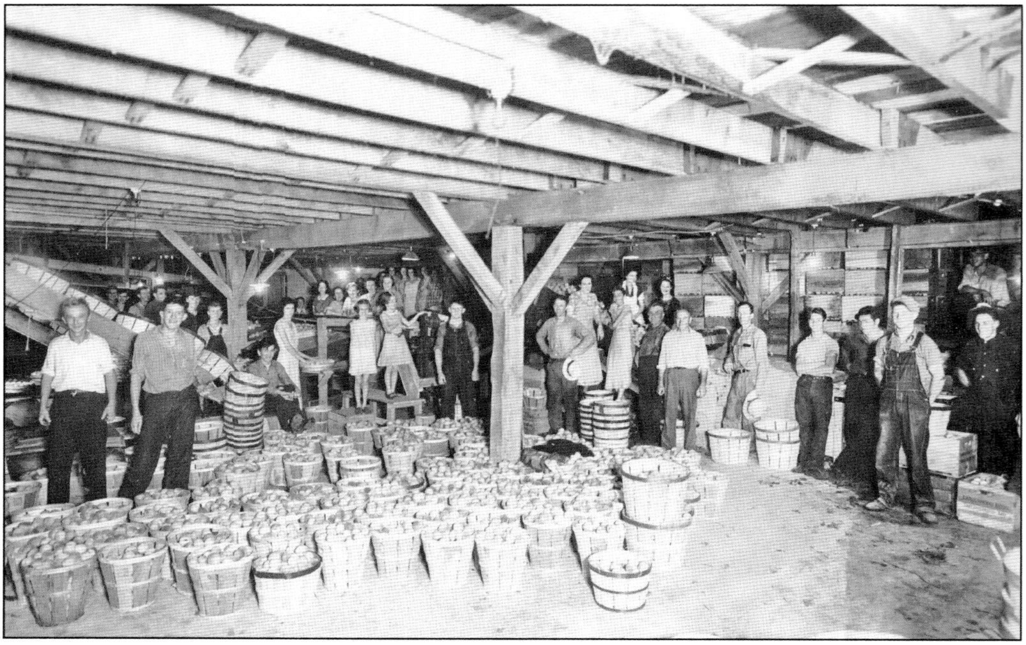

Various workers at Gardenhour Orchards are pictured around 1935. From left to right are Victor Cline, Sol Hershberger, George Martin, Page Brown, Mary Catherine Gardenhour, Louelle Gardenhour, Tom Hessong, Willie Gardenhour, Alice Hershberger, three unidentified, Keller Beard, Amos Shockey, Raymond Gardenhour, and five unidentified. The rest of the people in the image are unidentified. (Courtesy of the Smithsburg Historical Society.)

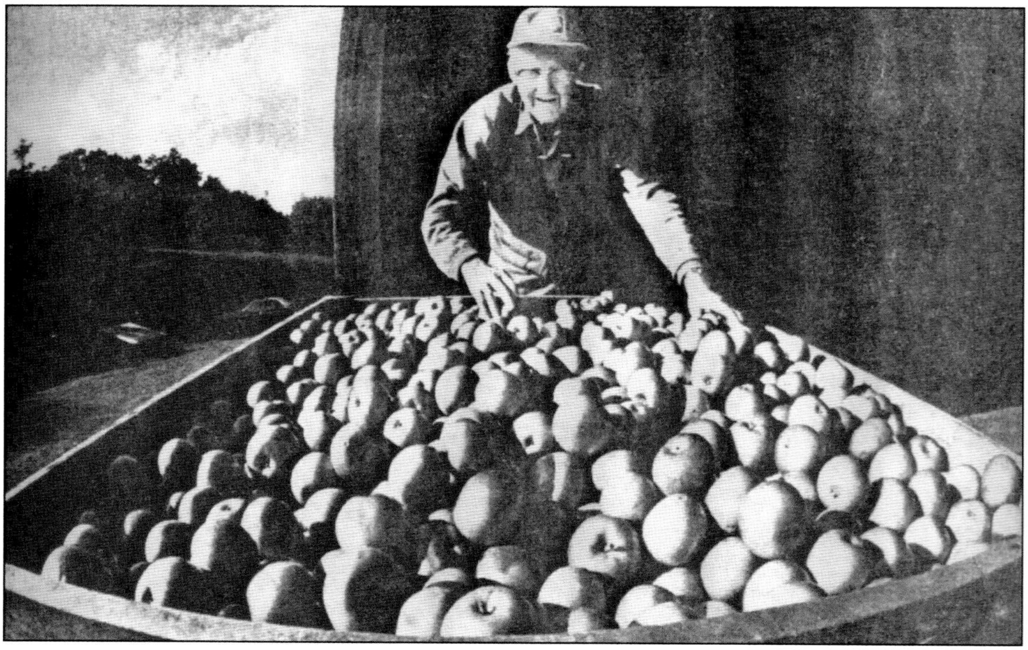

An important moment in agriculture took place in 1880, when various farmers realized that the rough mountainsides had good soil for peaches and other fruits. Pictured here is G. William "Bill" Gardenhour of Gardenhour Orchards. He is checking the crop of freshly picked apples. (Courtesy of the Smithsburg Historical Society.)

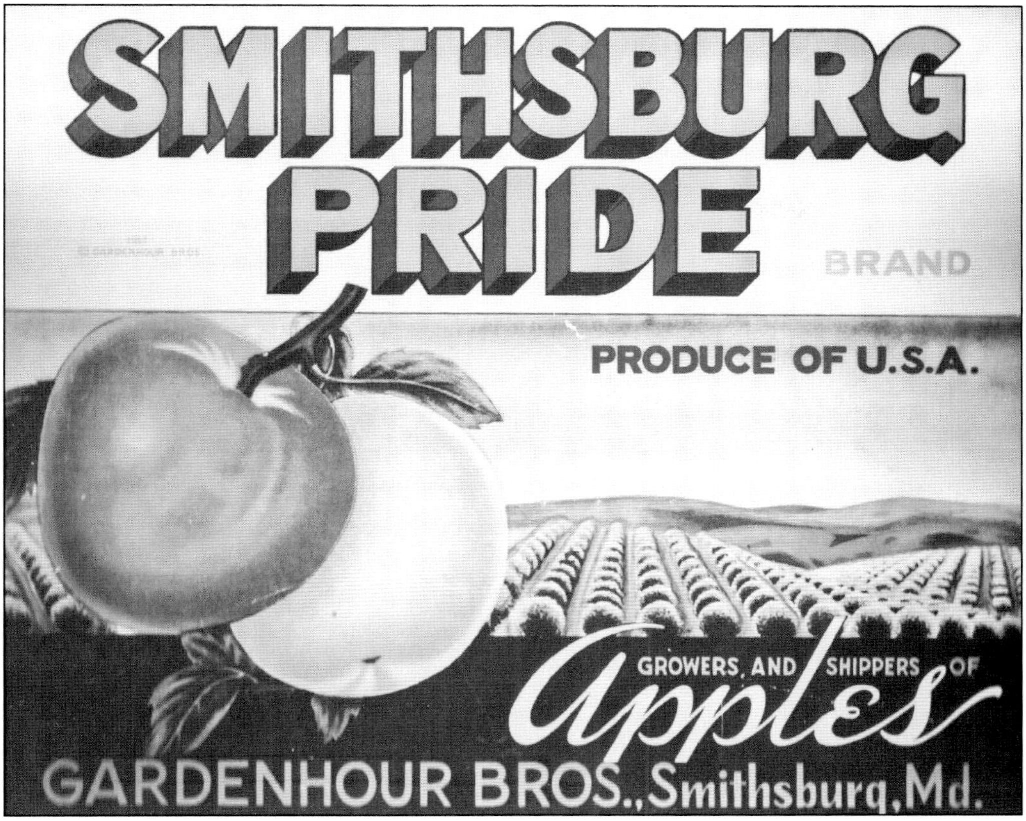

Another sign from Gardenhour Orchards from 1957 touts Smithsburg Pride. The orchards and farms of Smithsburg are the pride of the town. In the first part of the 20th century, the high demand for produce and the infestation of codling moths and other insects led to the use of spray materials to control any possible damage to the fruit. (Courtesy of the Smithsburg Historical Society.)

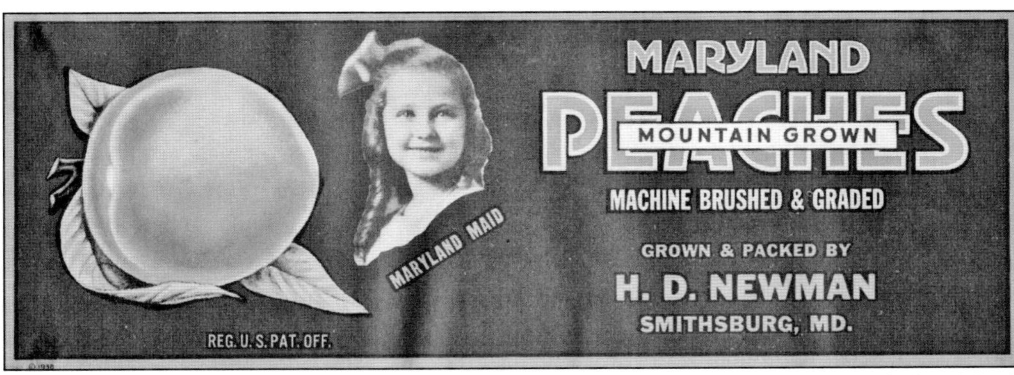

A sign from Newman's Orchards advertises the "mountain grown" peaches. Bushels of fresh peaches and other fruits are available for those who do not live in the area and have direct access to the mountain-grown crop. (Courtesy of the Smithsburg Historical Society.)

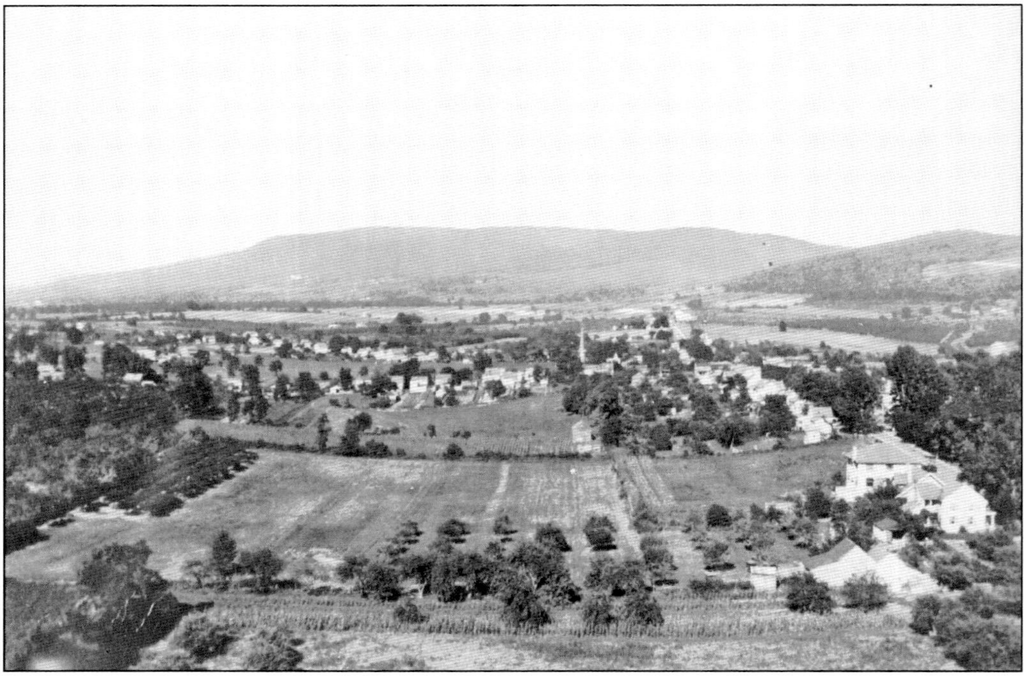

Smithsburg, with Newman's Orchards in the foreground, is viewed from the top of the water tower. The right side of the picture shows houses lining West Water Street. To the right of center, one can see the church steeple. (Courtesy of the Smithsburg Historical Society.)

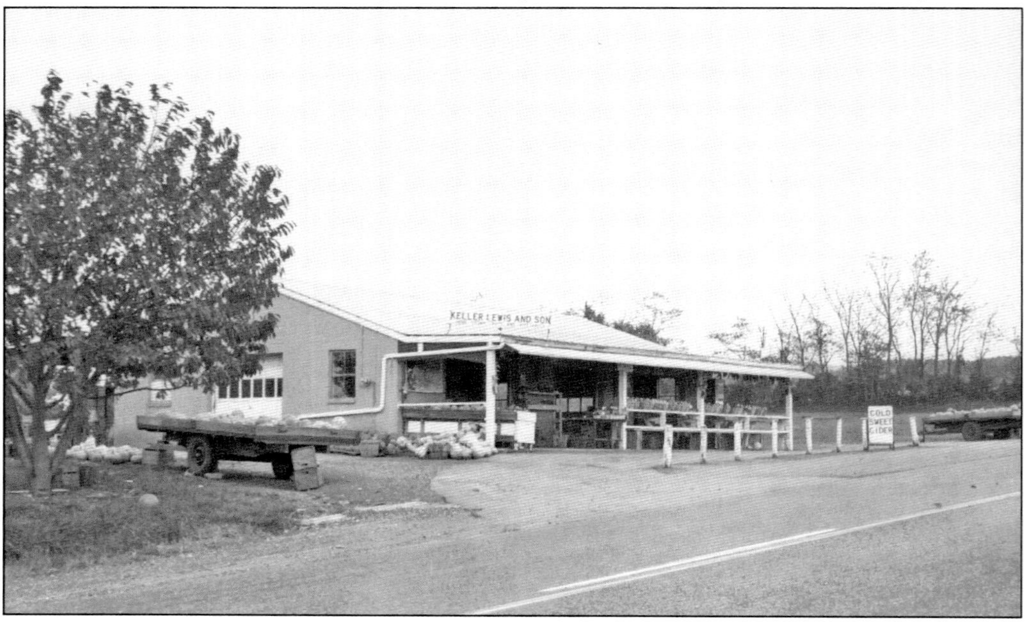

Keller Lewis and Sons Fruit Stand is located on State Route 64 in Smithsburg, Maryland. This fruit stand has been a mainstay in the fruit business for decades. Begun by Jacob Hoffman more than 100 years ago, and passed down to his daughter Minnie, who later married Keller Lewis, more than 17 different varieties grow on their orchard property. They provide customers with their choice in fresh produce, and their location is ideal to anyone traveling in or out of town. (Courtesy of the Smithsburg Historical Society.)

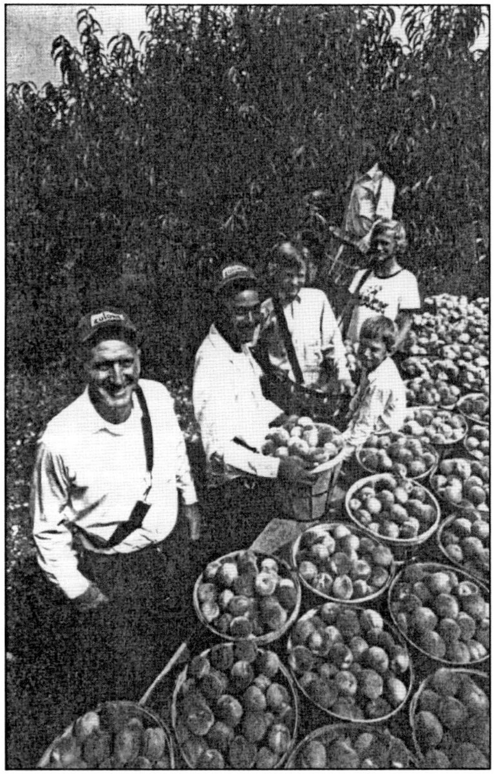

The Lewis tradition continues today. Keller and Minnie's son Nevin and family have been responsible for the largest expansion of the business, from 12 acres to as much as 350 acres at one time. Still thriving today, the Lewis fruit stand provides Smithsburg natives and tourists with locally grown produce, jams, jellies, and more. The family motto is "Fresh quality produce, from our family, to yours." (Courtesy of the Smithsburg Historical Society.)

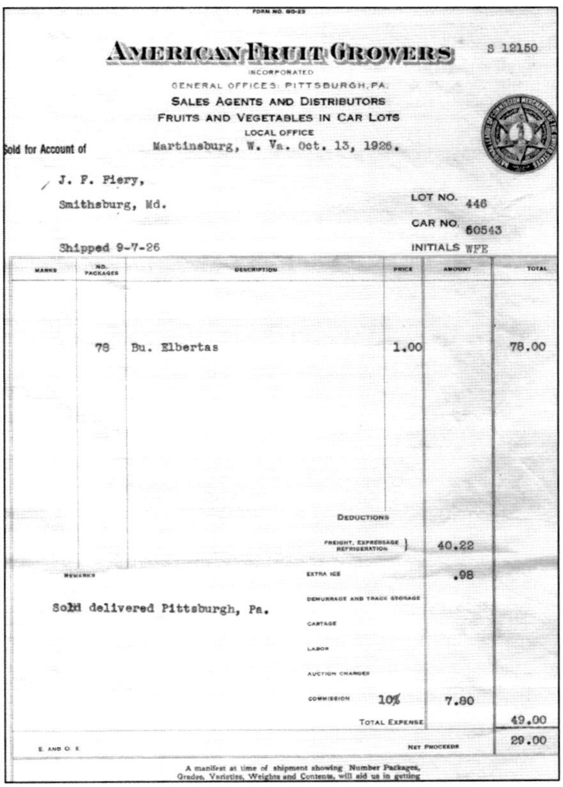

FORM NO. 60-23

AMERICAN FRUIT GROWERS
INCORPORATED
GENERAL OFFICES: PITTSBURGH, PA.
SALES AGENTS AND DISTRIBUTORS
FRUITS AND VEGETABLES IN CAR LOTS
LOCAL OFFICE

S 12150

Sold for Account of — Martinsburg, W. Va. Oct. 13, 1926.

J. F. Piery,
Smithsburg, Md.

LOT NO. 446
CAR NO. 60543
Shipped 9-7-26 — INITIALS WFE

MARKS	NO. PACKAGES	DESCRIPTION	PRICE	AMOUNT	TOTAL
	78	Bu. Elbertas	1.00		78.00
		DEDUCTIONS			
		FREIGHT, EXPRESSAGE REFRIGERATION		40.22	
		EXTRA ICE		.98	
		DEMURRAGE AND TRACK STORAGE			
		CARTAGE			
		LABOR			
		AUCTION CHARGES			
		COMMISSION	10%	7.80	
		TOTAL EXPENSE			49.00
		NET PROCEEDS			29.00

REMARKS
Sold delivered Pittsburgh, Pa.

E. AND O. E.

A manifest at time of shipment showing Number Packages, Grades, Varieties, Weights and Contents, will aid us in getting

This invoice shows how Smithsburg orchards are instrumental in delivering fresh fruit to various parts of the country. This particular invoice is for Pittsburgh, Pennsylvania. The purchaser bought 78 bushels of Elbertas for $1 each. (Courtesy of the Smithsburg Historical Society.)

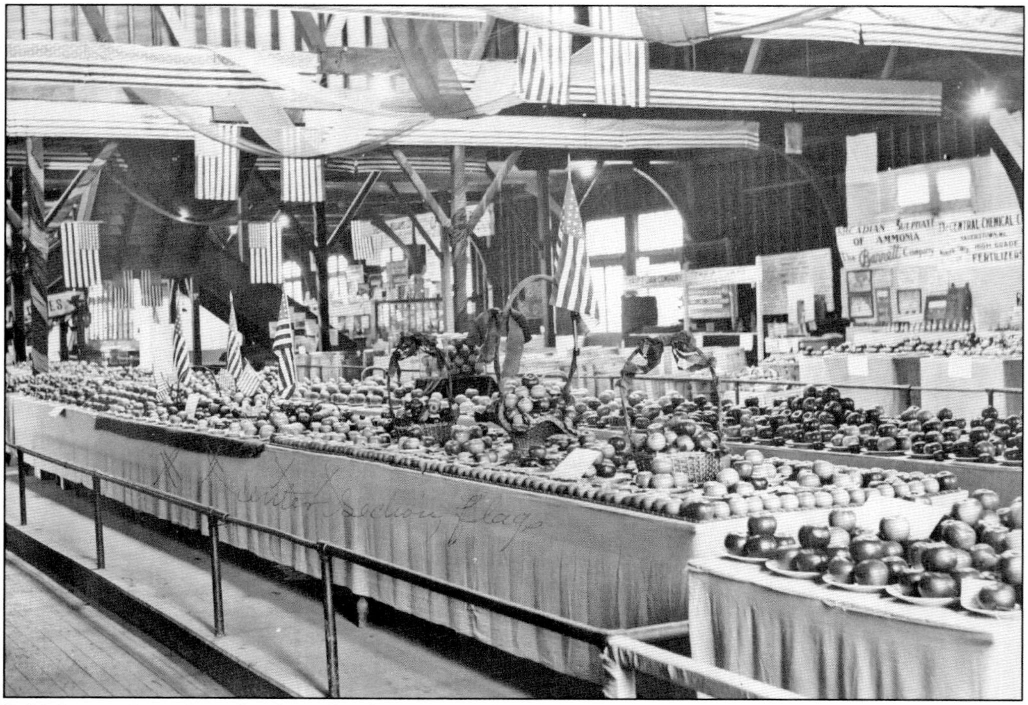

Bikle's won first place for their display. Every table holds the many types of apples grown on Bikle's Fruit Farm. Many American flags hang throughout the enormous display, symbolizing American pride and the town pride for produce. (Courtesy of the Smithsburg Historical Society.)

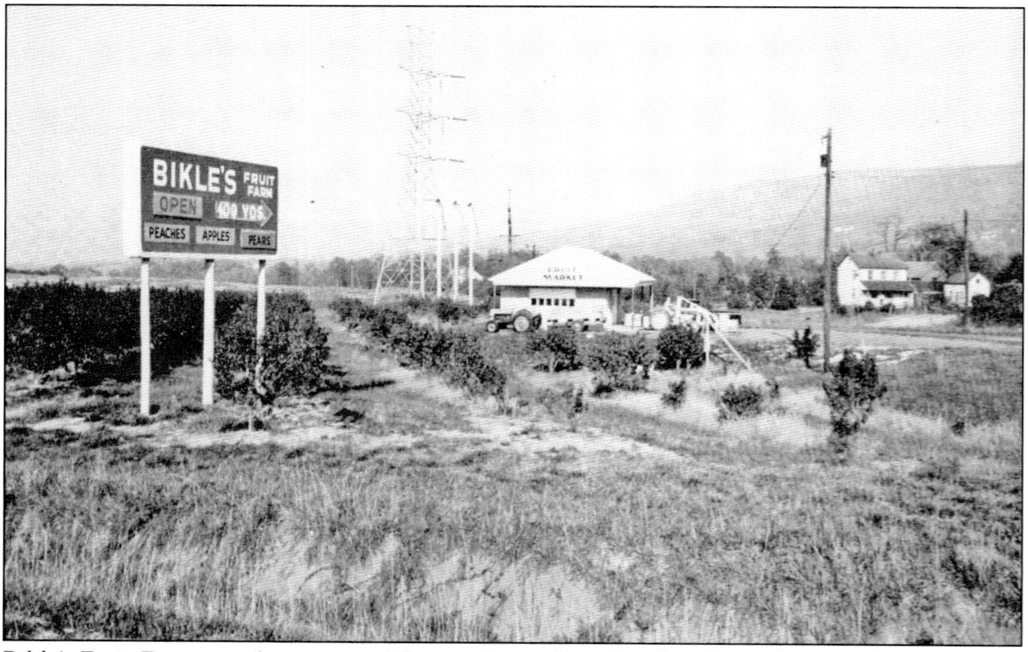

Bikle's Fruit Farm, on the corner of former Greensburg Road and Route 64, was one of many prominent fruit farms in Smithsburg that sold mountain peaches, apples, and pears, among other fruits. Greensburg Road was later renamed Bikle Road. (Courtesy of the Smithsburg Historical Society.)

On the front porch of Sari Kilheffer's house sits an old orchard crate, filled with flowers, from Ben Clopper's orchard. The site of Clopper's orchard was originally a dairy farm purchased by Ben Clopper in 1948. He turned it into a prosperous orchard in 1960. (Courtesy of Shay Mace.)

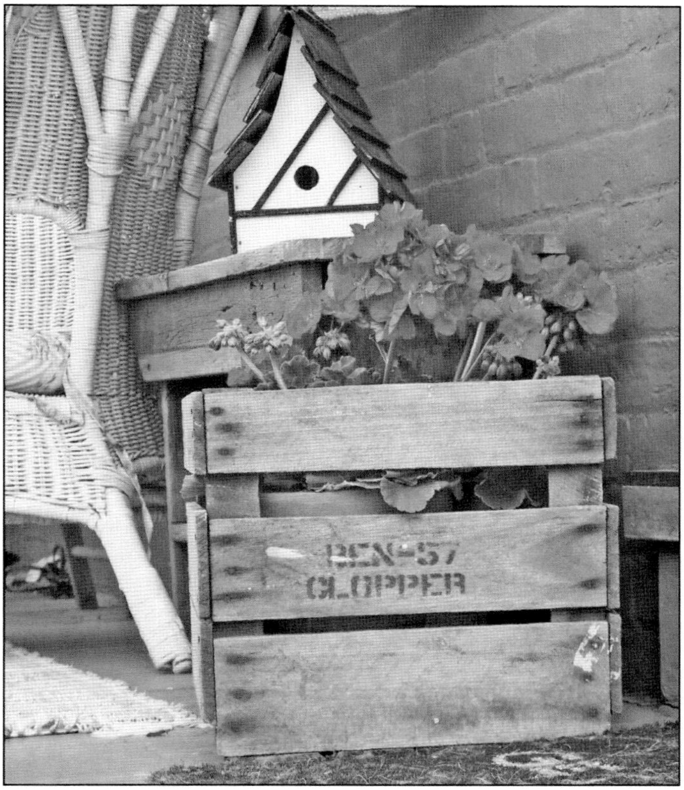

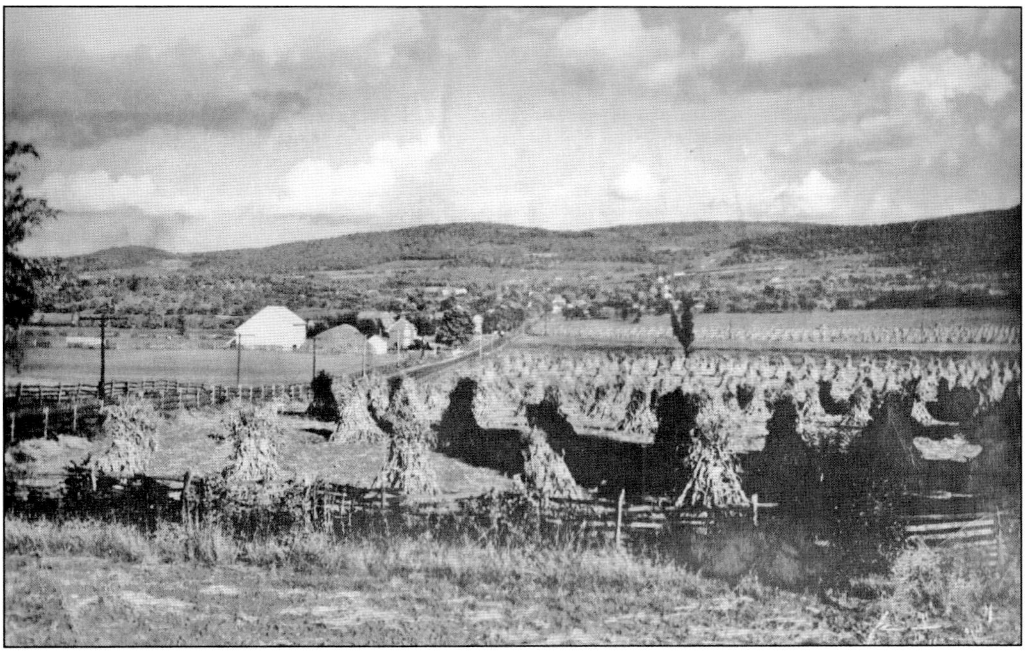

This farm in Smithsburg used corn shocks. Once mechanical harvesters appeared, this method of drying corn was quickly replaced. Corn shocks are commonly seen in fall displays that usually include pumpkins and bales of straw. The location of this picture is south of Jefferson Boulevard leading into Smithsburg. (Courtesy of the Smithsburg Historical Society.)

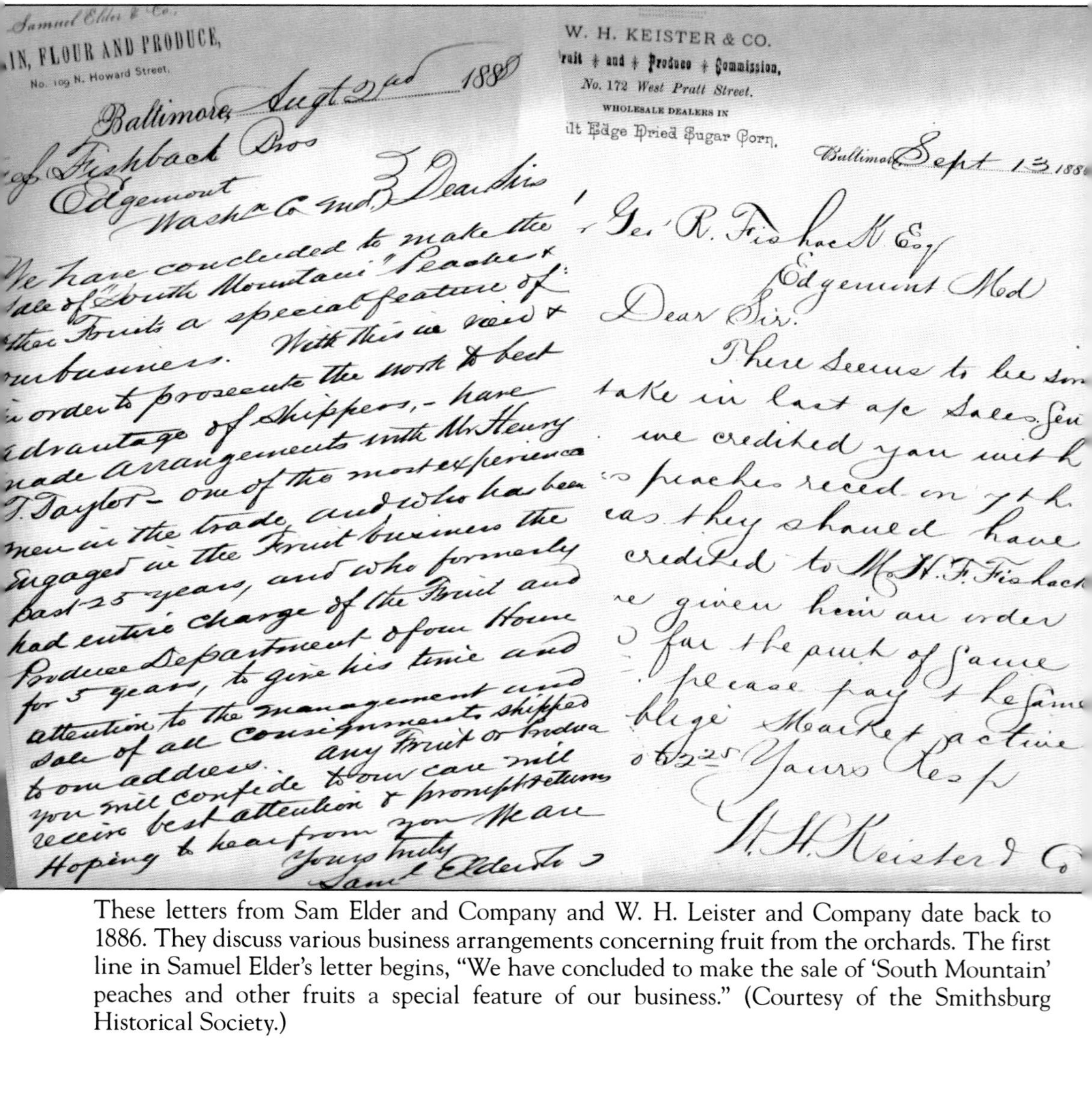

Samuel Elder & Co.
...IN, FLOUR AND PRODUCE,
No. 109 N. Howard Street.

Baltimore, Augt 2nd 1886

Fishback Bros
Edgemont
Wash Co Md
Dear Sirs

We have concluded to make the sale of "South Mountain" Peaches & other Fruits a special feature of our business. With this in view & in order to prosecute the work to best advantage of Shippers, - have made arrangements with Mr Henry T. Taylor - one of the most experienced men in the trade, and who has been engaged in the Fruit business the past 25 years, and who formerly had entire charge of the Fruit and Produce Department of our House for 5 years, to give his time and attention to the management and sale of all consignments shipped to our address. Any Fruit or Produce you will confide to our care will receive best attention & prompt returns. Hoping to hear from you We are

Yours truly
Saml Elder & Co

W. H. KEISTER & CO.
Fruit and Produce Commission,
No. 172 West Pratt Street.
WHOLESALE DEALERS IN
Gilt Edge Dried Sugar Corn.

Baltimore Sept 13 1886

Geo R. Fishback Esq
Edgemont Md
Dear Sir.

There seems to be some take in last a/c Sales. we credited you with peaches reced on 7th as they should have credited to M H. F. Fishback given him an order for the amt of same please pay the same blige Market active @ 2.25 Yours Resp

W. H. Keister & Co

These letters from Sam Elder and Company and W. H. Leister and Company date back to 1886. They discuss various business arrangements concerning fruit from the orchards. The first line in Samuel Elder's letter begins, "We have concluded to make the sale of 'South Mountain' peaches and other fruits a special feature of our business." (Courtesy of the Smithsburg Historical Society.)

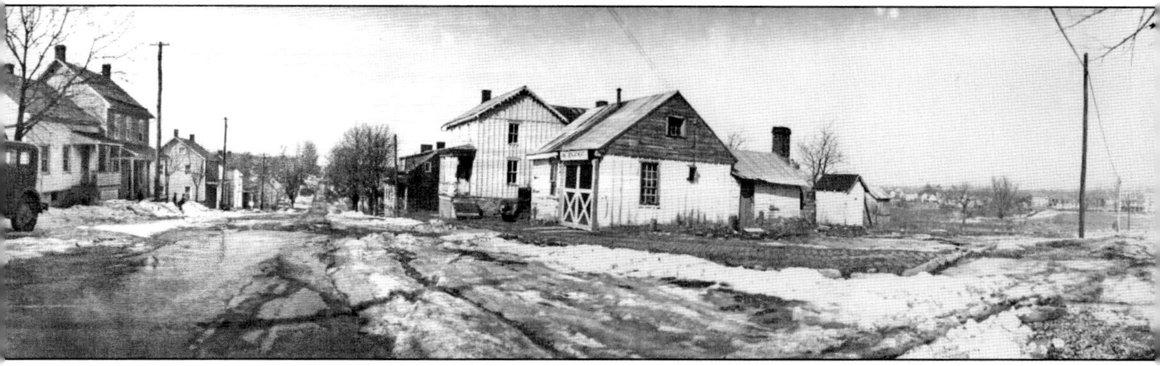

Snow still lies in piles on both sides of Main Street in winter during the early 1900s. The small building on the right is the first Smithsburg Fire Department. In 1814, when the town plat was published, this lot (no. 52) stood vacant. In 1875, Dr. J. A. Riddlemoser owned a one-and-a-half-story log dwelling on this site. In 1933, this property was known as the Eleanora Shank property. The log house was converted to use as a firehouse. (Courtesy of the Smithsburg Historical Society.)

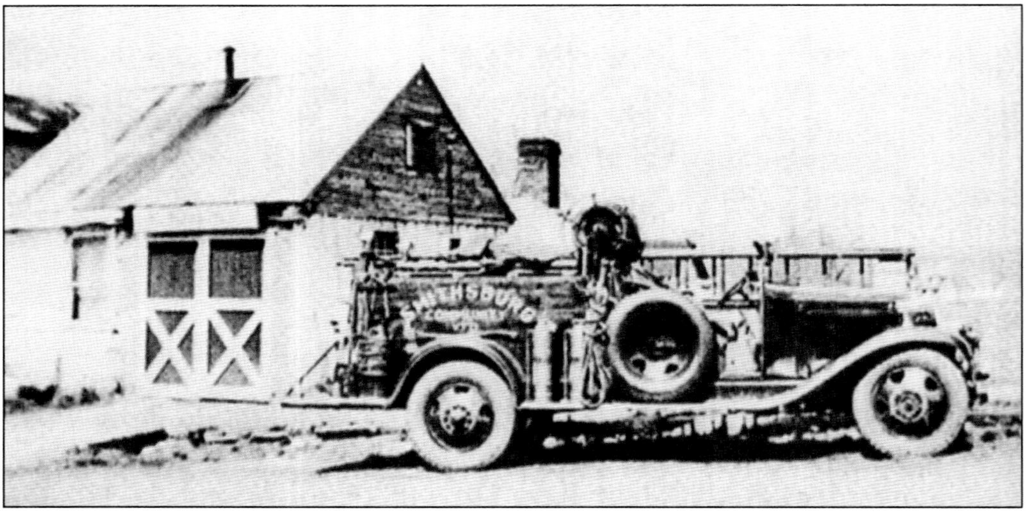

The first Smithsburg Volunteer Fire Company fire truck is pictured next to the first fire hall. Located at 22 North Main Street, the fire company building is set on the original lot 52. According to the town plat of 1814, no owner was listed. (Courtesy of the Smithsburg Historical Society.)

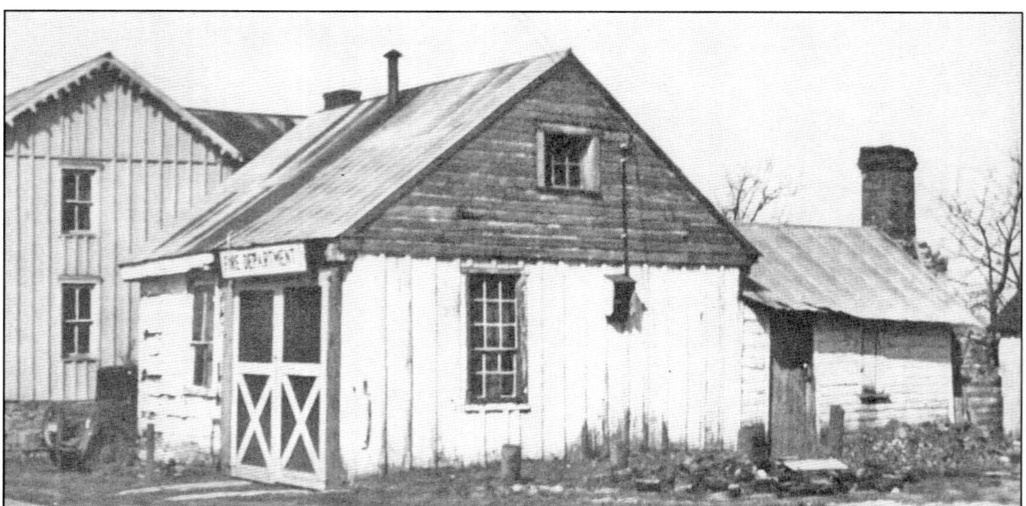

In this closer look at the fire hall, note the sign hanging over the doorway that says "Fire Department." In December 1933, the recently formed fire company agreed to purchase the property. The log house was replaced in 1938 by a one-story, three-bay brick building.

Six

Careers and Volunteers

Hold Your Fire

It takes a special person to fill the boots of a volunteer—more specifically, filling the boots of a volunteer firefighter. The Smithsburg Community Volunteer Fire Company members exhibit courage, dedication, discipline, and a desire to help their neighbors. The town honors their spirit of commitment and values that the company members have passed down from one generation to the next. As with the fire company, many volunteer positions turn into viable career moves. The ladies of the Telephone Exchange, located at 11 East Water Street, made their careers in communication, helping Smithsburg residents connect with one another.

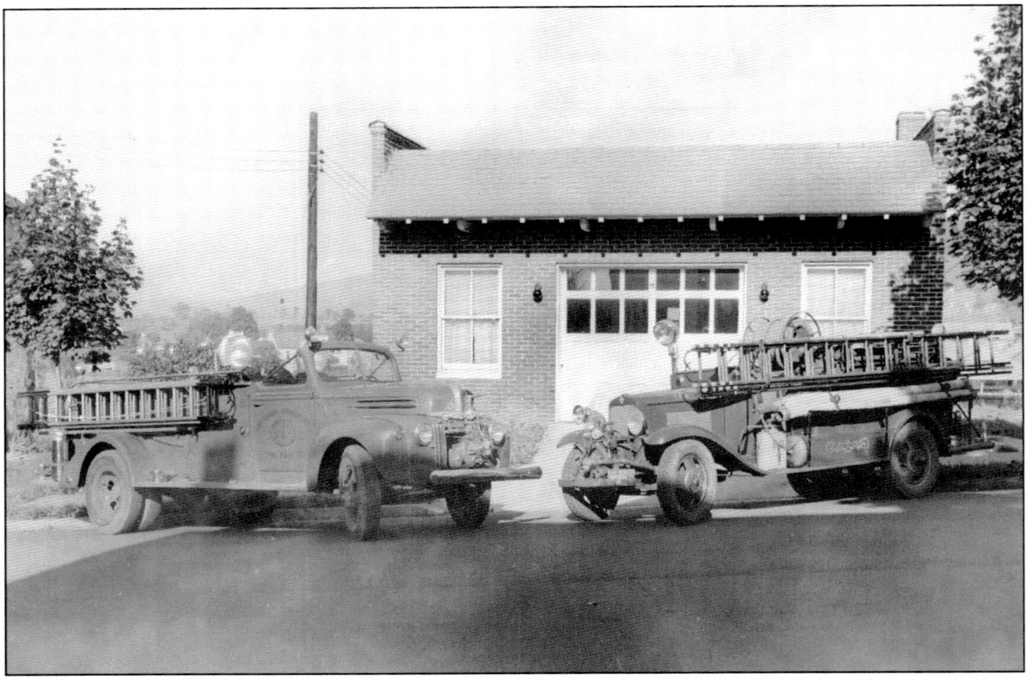

The two fire trucks are a 1946 Ford on the left and a 1932 Chevrolet on the right. The Smithsburg Community Volunteer Fire Company's firehouse was constructed in 1938. (Courtesy of the Smithsburg Historical Society.)

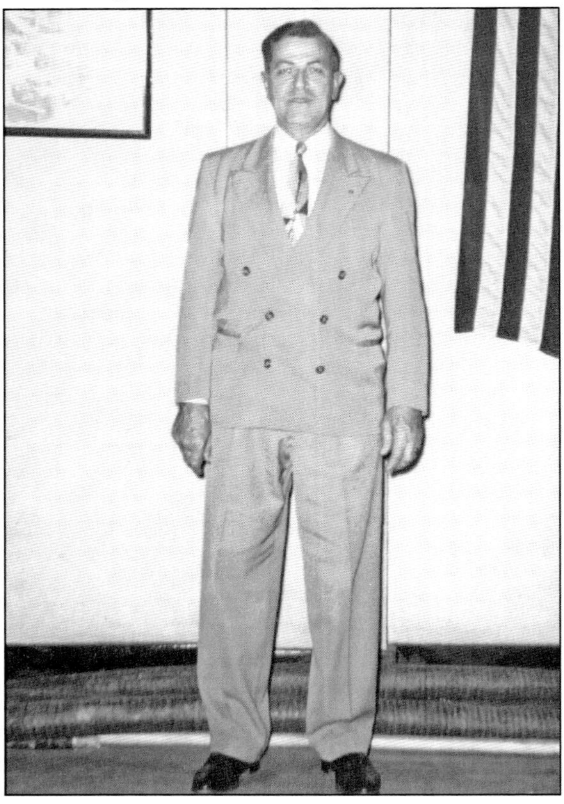

Richard Kline, pictured in 1956, was a driver for the Smithsburg Volunteer Fire Company. He also served as fire chief from 1980 to 1986. Julia Wiles donated the photograph. (Courtesy of the Smithsburg Historical Society.)

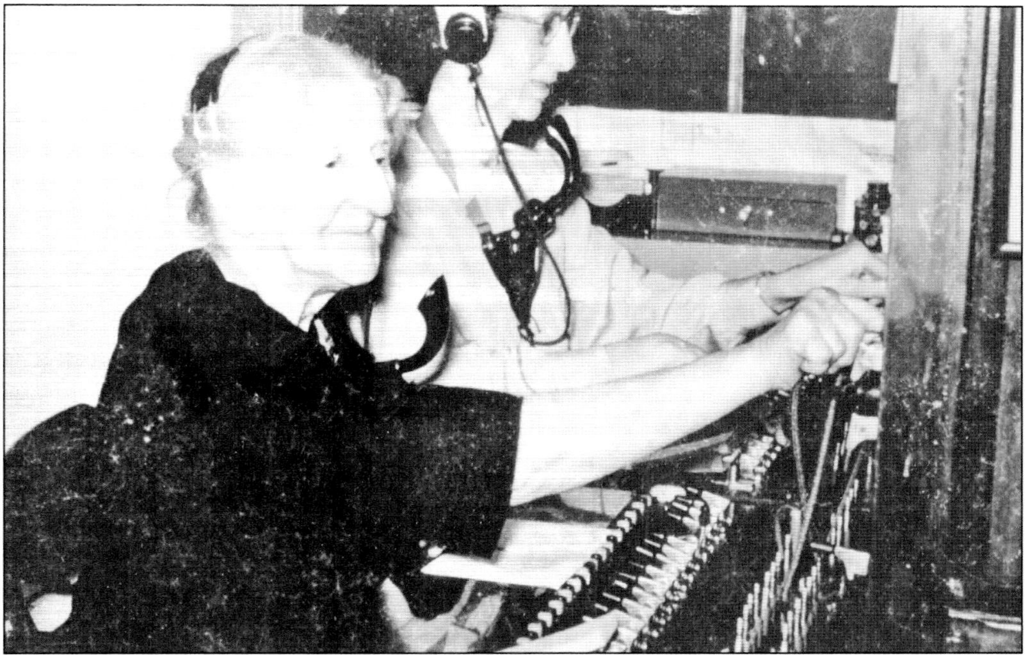

The ladies of the Smithsburg Telephone Exchange seemed to enjoy their job as telephone operators. Notice the hands-free speakers attached to the headpieces. Annie Schlosser is in the forefront of this photograph. The Telephone Exchange was run out of Annie Schlosser's residence on East Water Street. (Courtesy of the Smithsburg Historical Society.)

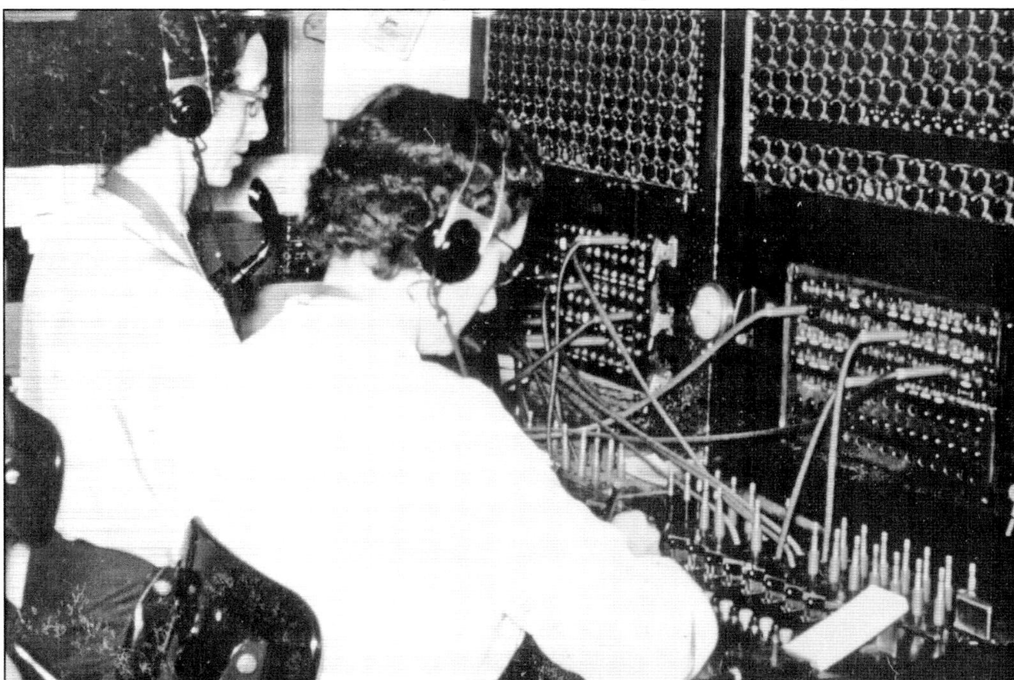

Located at 11 East Water Street, the Smithsburg Telephone Exchange operated at this residence from 1916 until 1952, when the new dial-up system became available. (Courtesy of the Smithsburg Historical Society.)

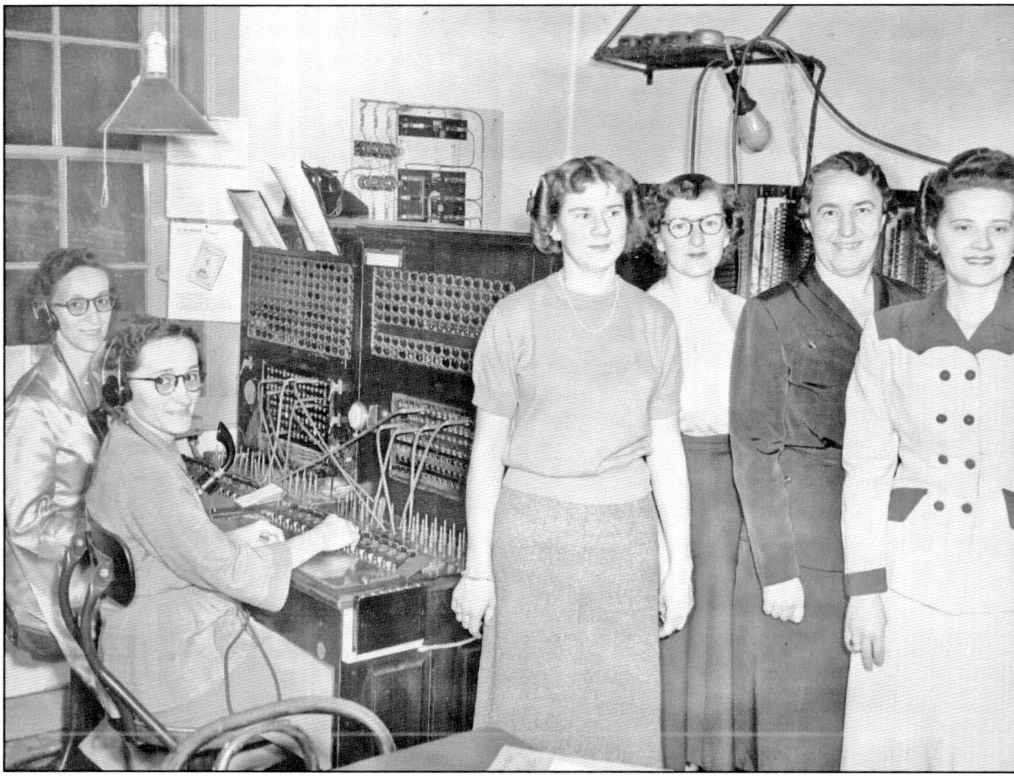

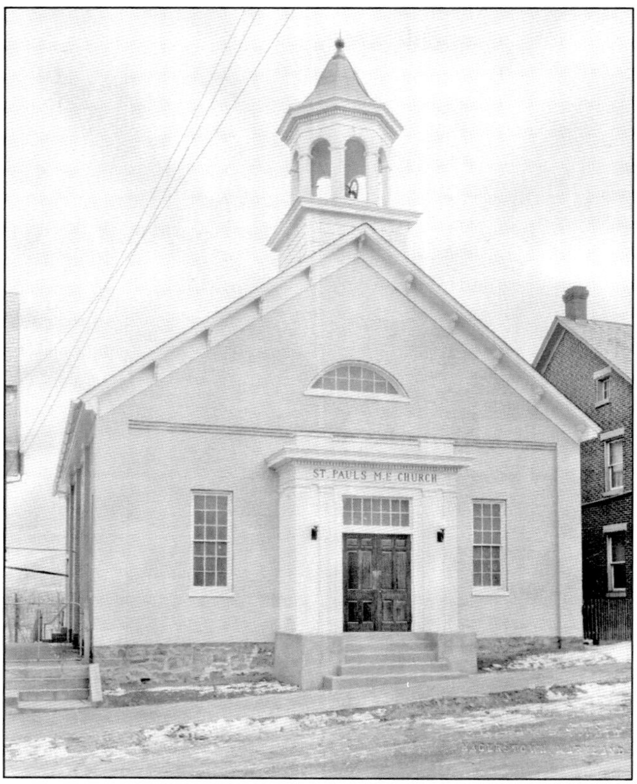

The Smithsburg Telephone Exchange operators are, from left to right, Evelyn Hershberger, Margaret Hershberger Ross, Gloria Kendle, Margaret Ferguson, Mary Catherine Grove, and Anna E. Diehl. This photograph was donated by William Diehl Sr. of Williamsport, Maryland. (Courtesy of the Smithsburg Historical Society.)

St. Paul's United Methodist Church is a one-and-a-half-story, three-bay brick church. The main focus of the building is the Colonial Revival steeple, which provides a visual landmark for Main Street. (Courtesy of the Smithsburg Historical Society.)

Seven

Churches
Say a Little Prayer

The town of Smithsburg is one of core values and faith, so it is not surprising that there are quite a number of churches within the town, Episcopalian, Methodist, and Lutheran, among other denominations. The townspeople gather strength and guidance from their chosen faith. Over the years, community and visitors alike have shared their devotion with one another. Former president Lyndon B. Johnson and his wife, Lady Bird Johnson, have visited Smithsburg many times, often stopping to attend St. Ann's Episcopal Church. The churches in Smithsburg date back as far as the founding of the town. Christopher Smith, the town founder, is buried in an unmarked grave in the cemetery adjacent to the Trinity Lutheran Church at 20 North Main Street.

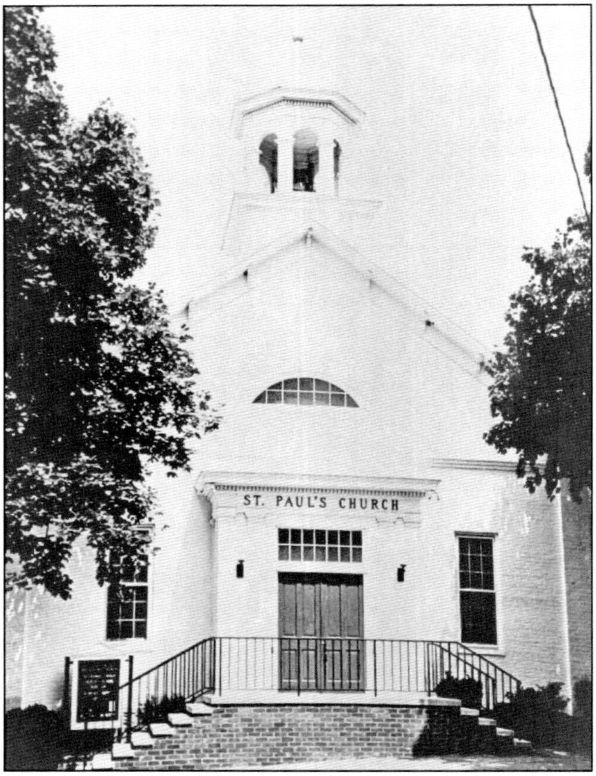

St. Paul's United Methodist Church stands at 53 South Main Street. After being extensively damaged by an 1868 storm, the building was repaired and rebuilt. Major remodeling was done to the church in 1929. (Courtesy of the Smithsburg Historical Society.)

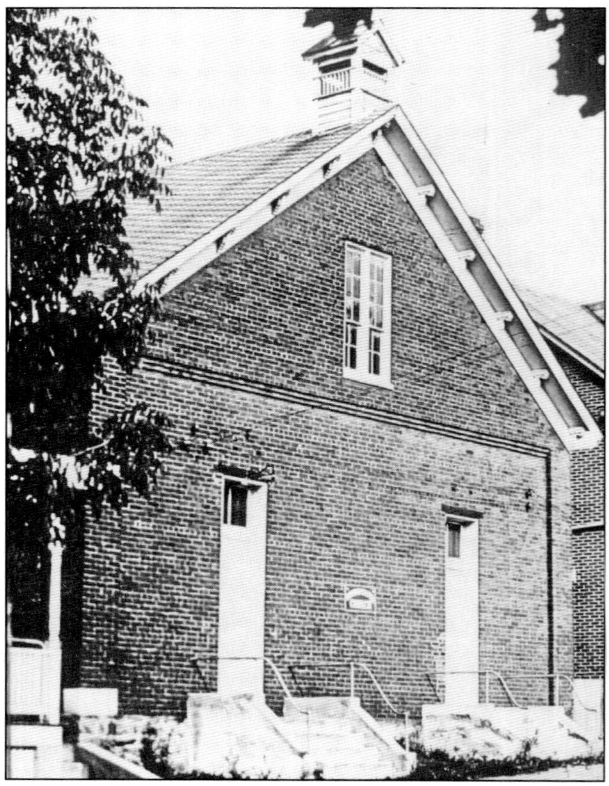

St. Paul's United Methodist Church is seen in the 1850s. (Courtesy of the Smithsburg Historical Society.)

Christ's Reformed Church is now called the Cavetown United Church of Christ. The church barely missed being built directly in the town of Smithsburg. (Courtesy of the Smithsburg Historical Society.)

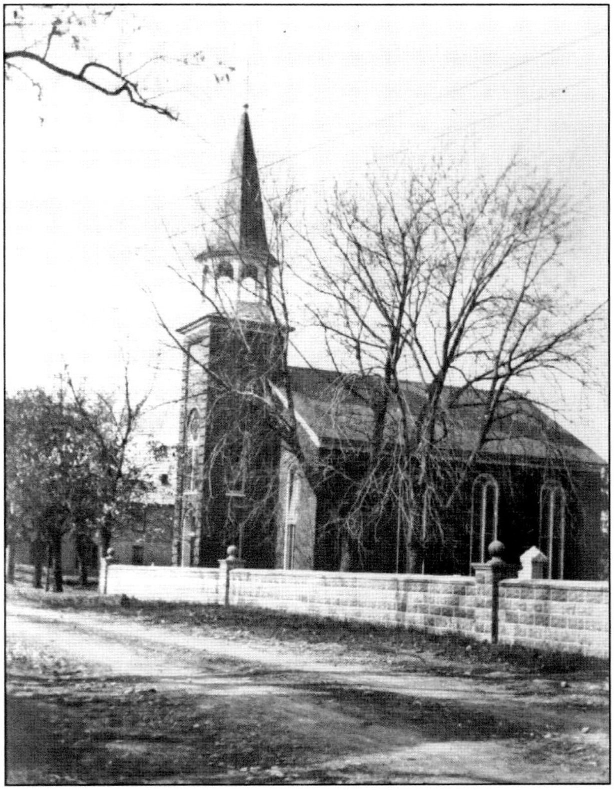

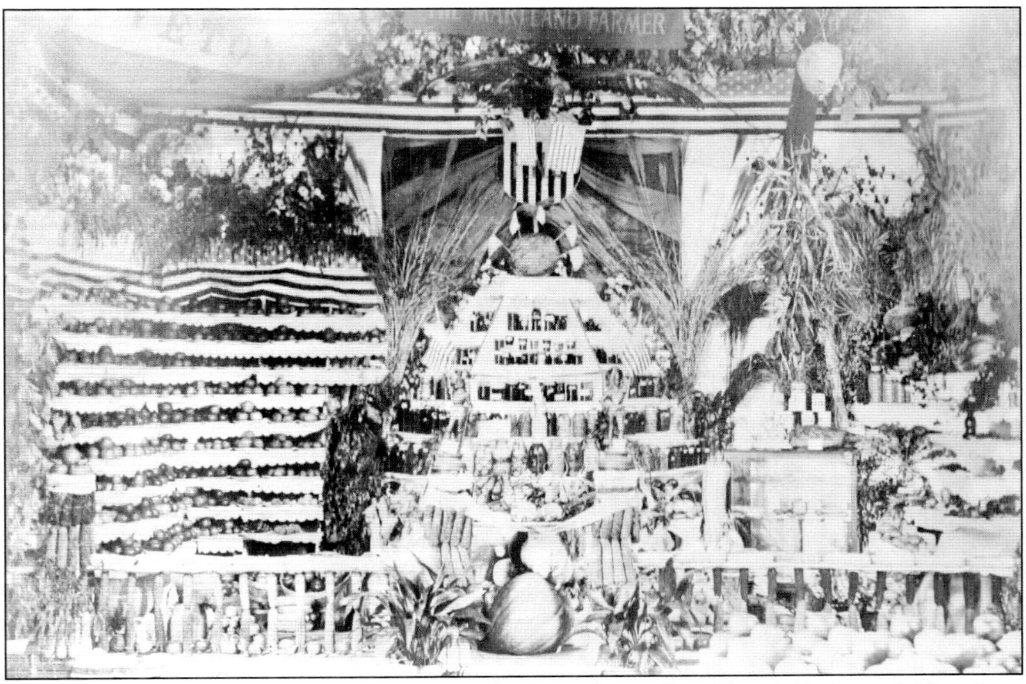

The Cavetown community's Harvest Home display is located at Christ's Reformed Church in Cavetown, Maryland. Canned preserves, pumpkins, apples, fruits, and vegetables of the harvest are exhibited as Maryland farmers are celebrated. (Courtesy of the Smithsburg Historical Society.)

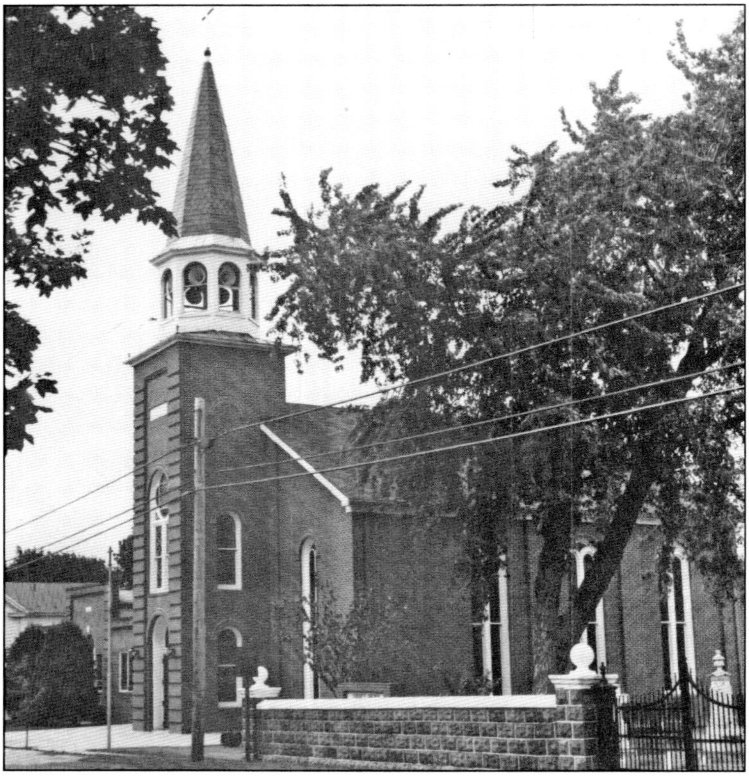

Seen here is a more recent photograph of Christ's Reformed Church. Christ's Reformed Church in Cavetown almost became a Smithsburg church. This church was organized in 1827 and missed being built directly in Smithsburg by one vote of the committee that established the congregation. (Courtesy of the Smithsburg Historical Society.)

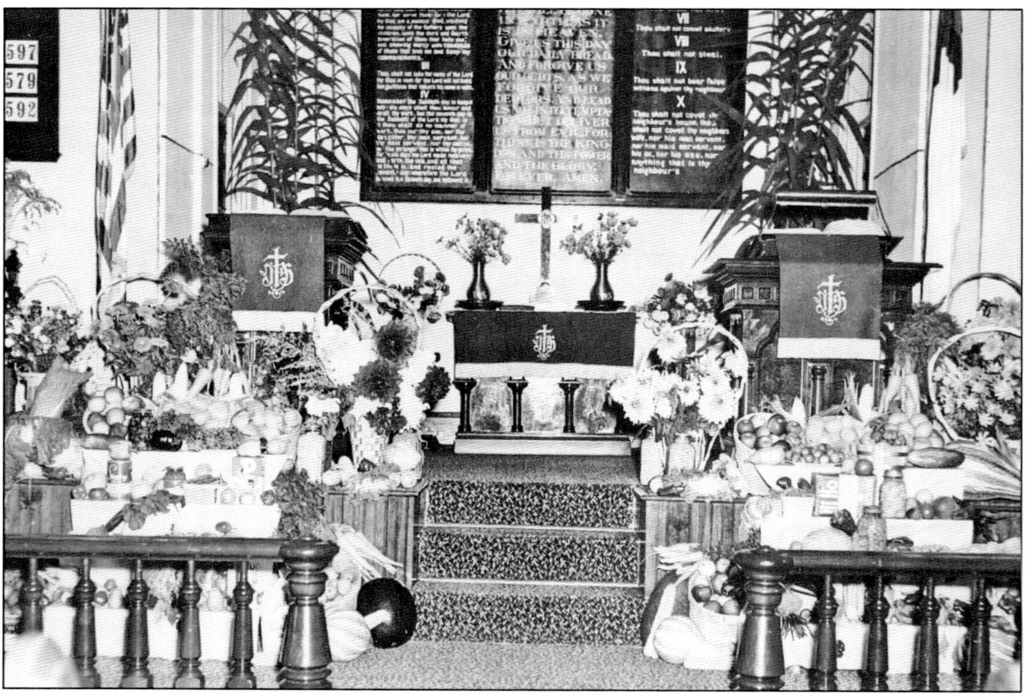

The Harvest Altar at Christ's Reformed Church is an annual tradition in which the altar is laden with fruits of the current year's harvest. Apples, corn, vegetables, and flowers adorn the altar as the congregation gives thanks. (Courtesy of the Smithsburg Historical Society.)

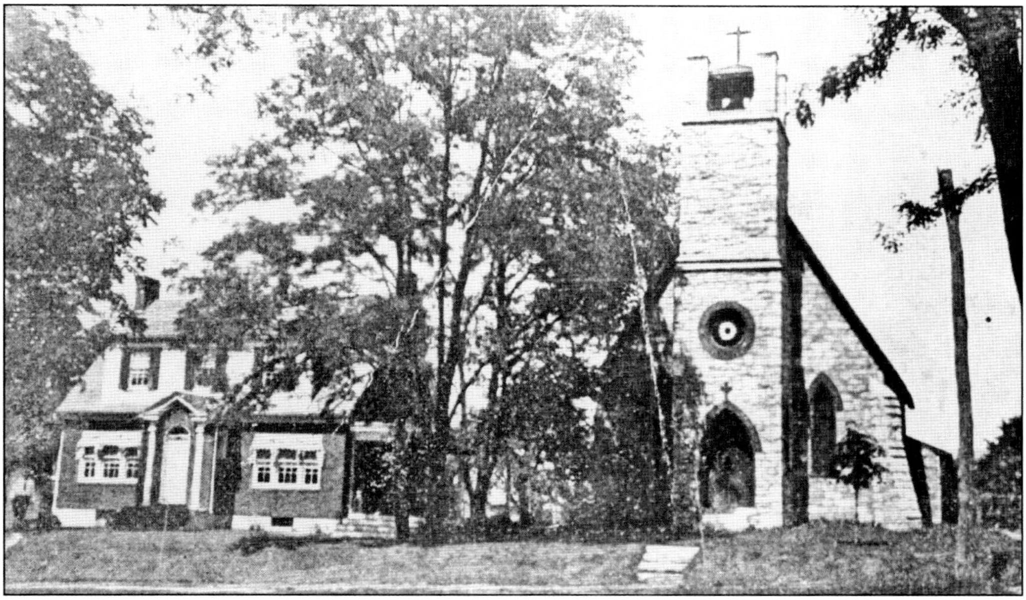

This *c.* 1926 photograph shows St. Ann's Episcopal Church and the new rectory directly beside it. Situated close to Camp David, the presidential retreat, Smithsburg often played host to Pres. Lyndon B. Johnson and family. (Courtesy of the Smithsburg Historical Society.)

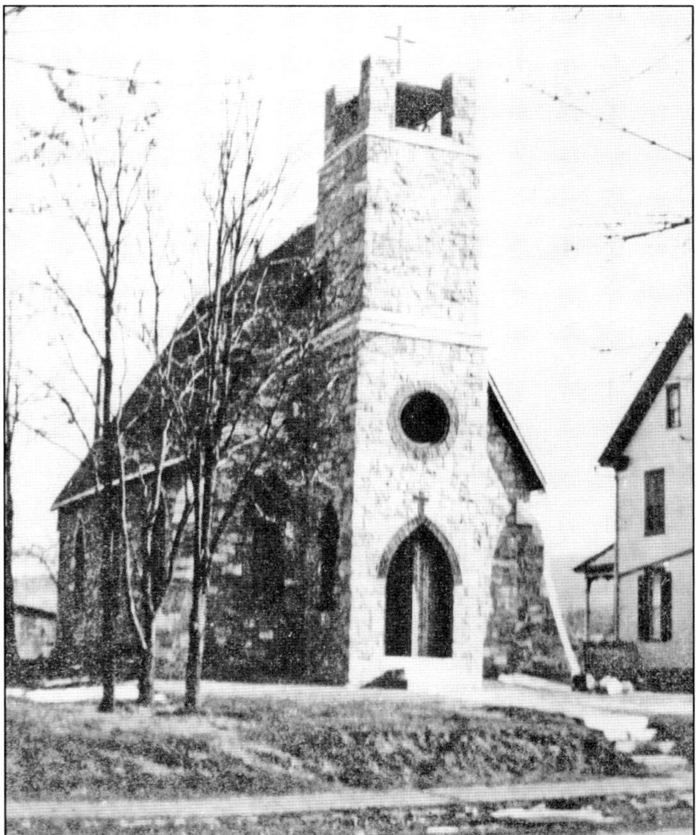

The building of St. Ann's Episcopal Church in Smithsburg began in May 1873 on a lot donated by Emily Bishop. The bell tower was added in 1916. On two occasions, the congregation of St. Ann's welcomed Pres. and Mrs. Lyndon B. Johnson in worship. The first visit, during his presidential term, was May 16, 1965. The second was on Easter Sunday, March 31, 1969, after his presidential service. St. Ann's has saved the pew where the Johnsons sat. (Courtesy of the Smithsburg Historical Society.)

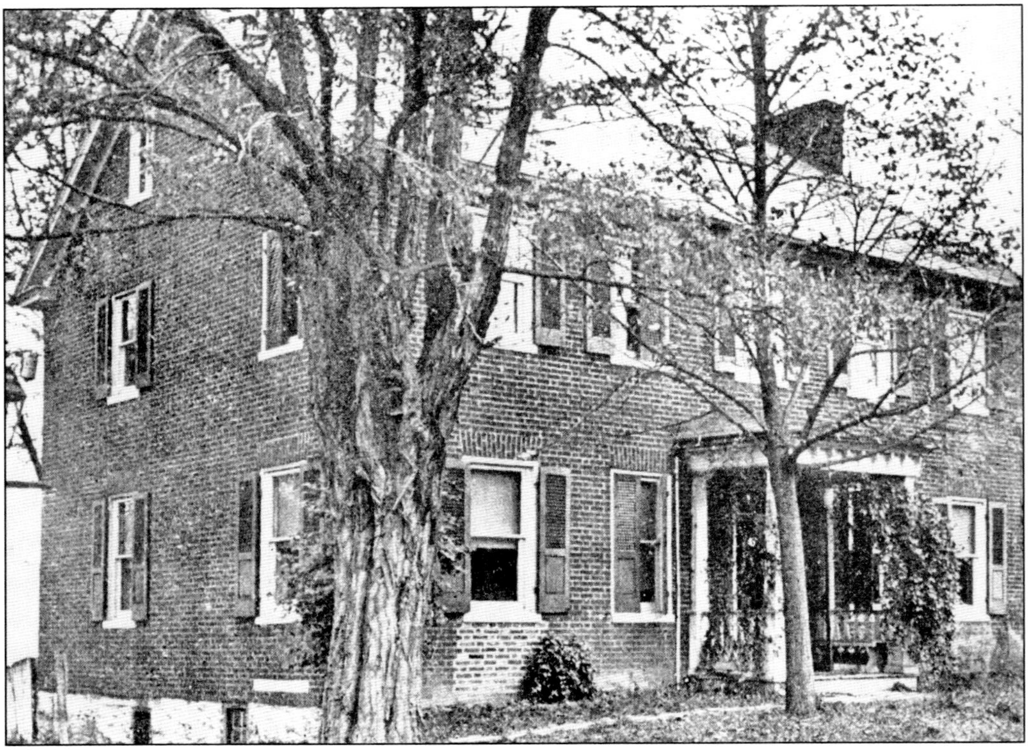

The Lutheran parsonage was used from 1863 to 1963. The parsonage still stands today on the corner of East Water Street and Bradbury Avenue. (Courtesy of the Smithsburg Historical Society.)

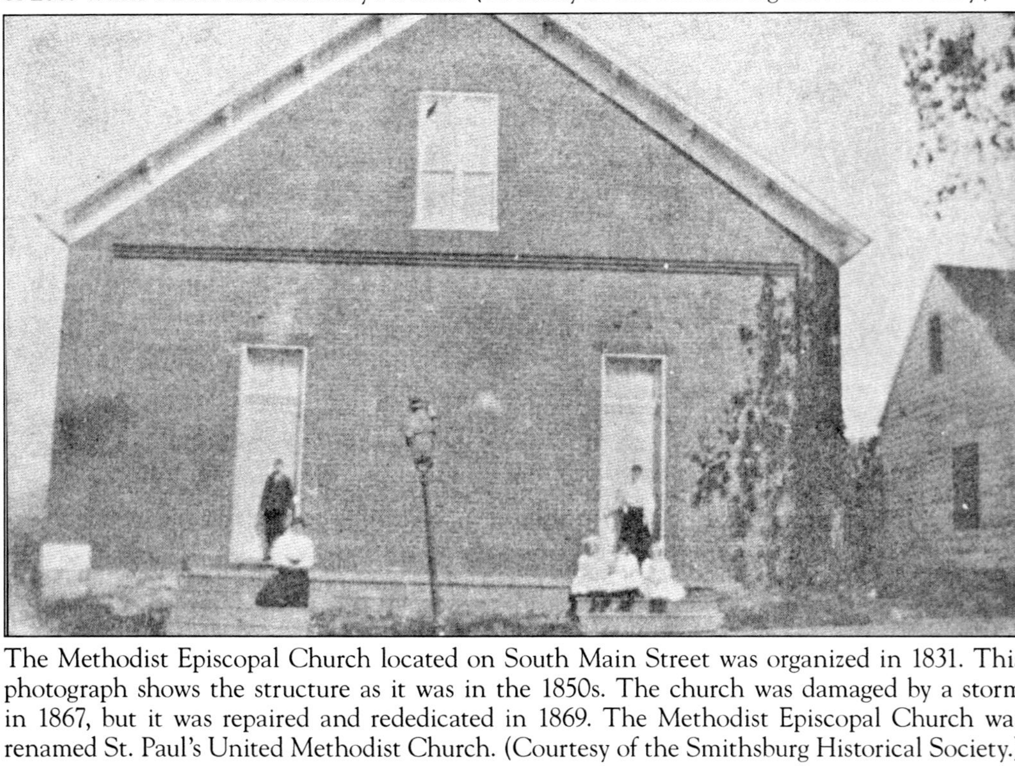

The Methodist Episcopal Church located on South Main Street was organized in 1831. This photograph shows the structure as it was in the 1850s. The church was damaged by a storm in 1867, but it was repaired and rededicated in 1869. The Methodist Episcopal Church was renamed St. Paul's United Methodist Church. (Courtesy of the Smithsburg Historical Society.)

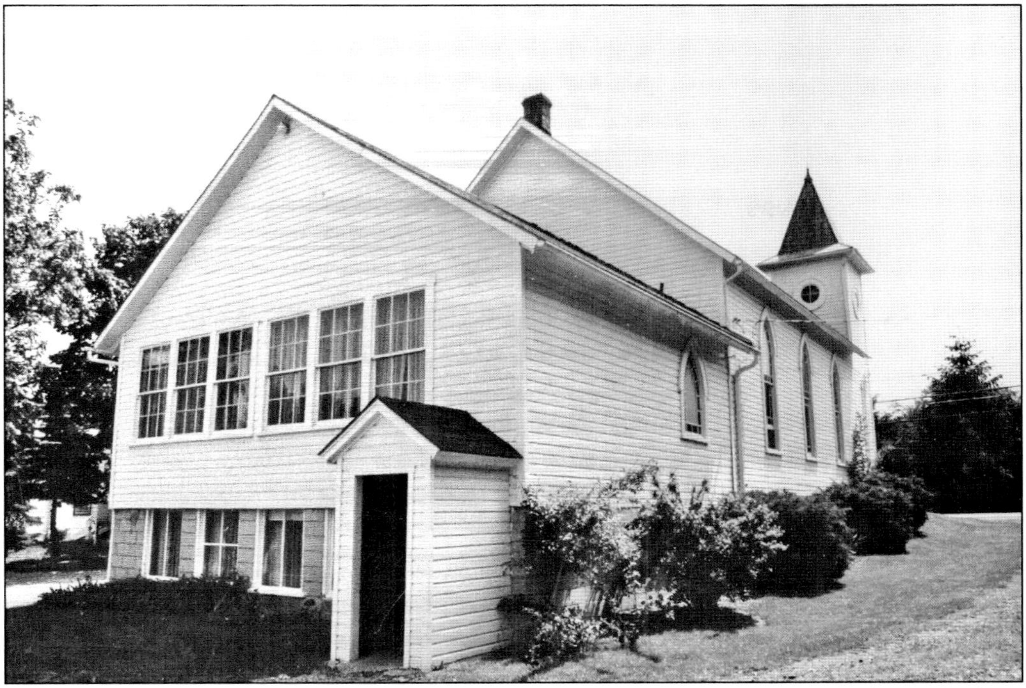

The Seventh-day Adventist church is located on Bradbury Avenue. The church was built in 1915 and still stands. For quite a while, two ladies of German descent occupied the church as a home. Today it still serves as a residence. (Courtesy of the Smithsburg Historical Society.)

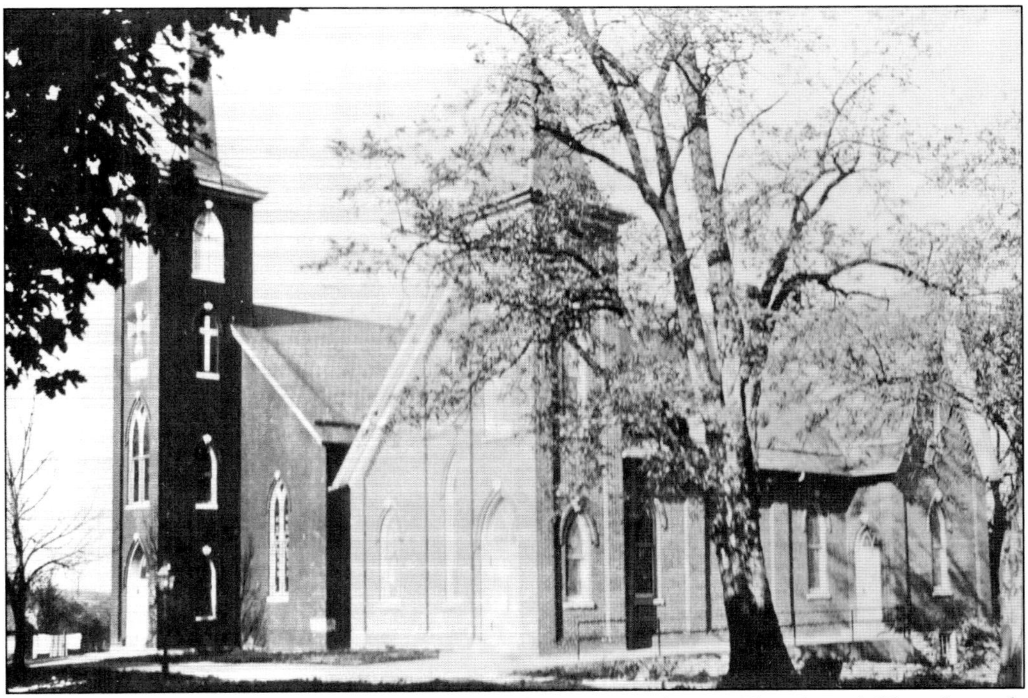

Located directly beside the Smithsburg Fire Hall, Trinity Lutheran Church and Chapel stands on lot 50 of the original plot of the town. The church windows bear stained-glass designs. (Courtesy of the Smithsburg Historical Society.)

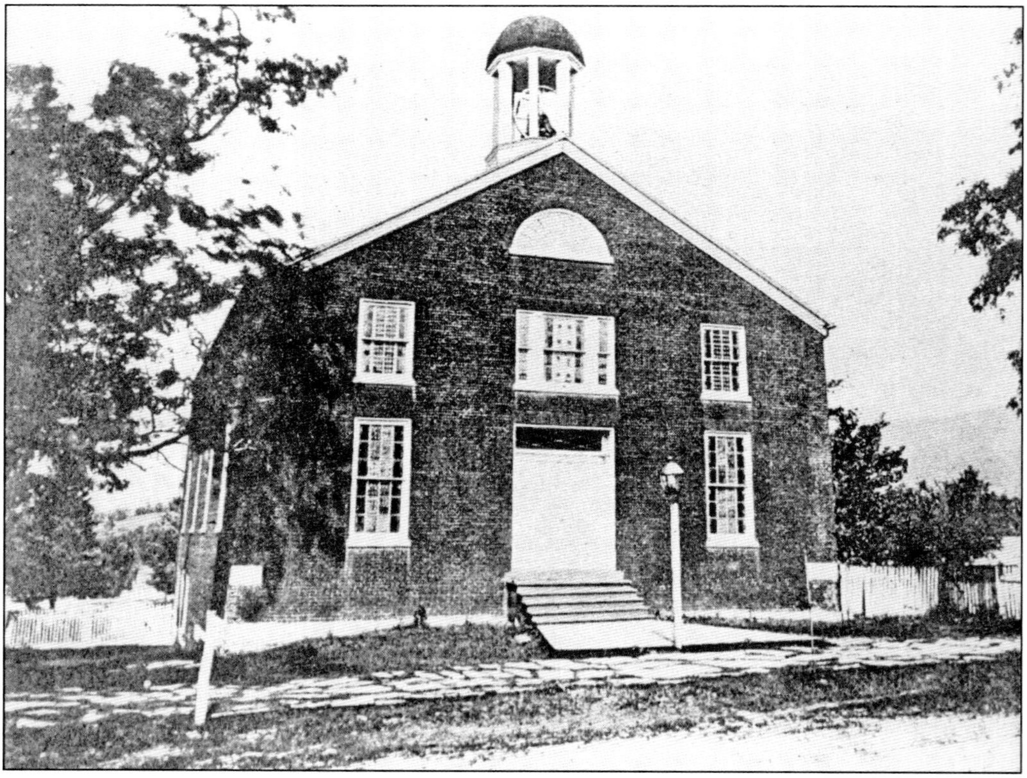

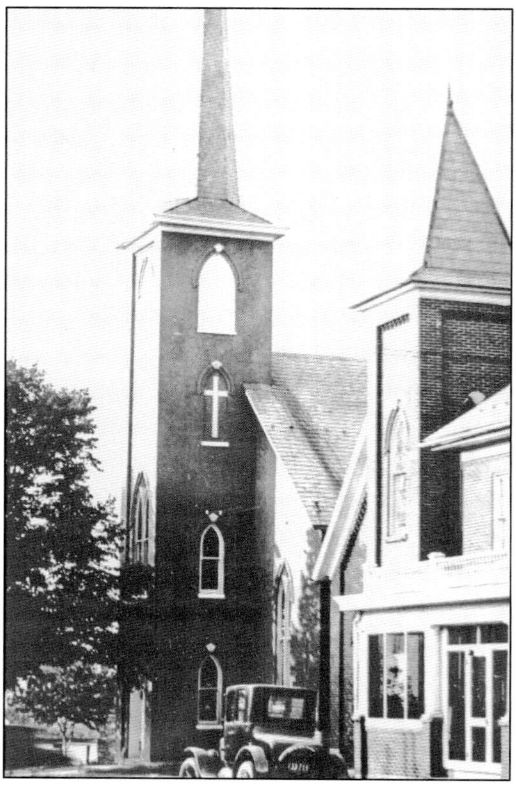

This photograph shows the brick Trinity Lutheran Church. The church was the first to be organized and built in Smithsburg. The original church was built in 1822 of common stone and cast over with lime mortar. The stone building was taken down and replaced by brick in 1850. (Courtesy of the Smithsburg Historical Society.)

A different view of Trinity Lutheran Church, located at 20 Main Street, is shown here. The same brick structure stands today but has undergone many renovations, including the addition of a bell tower. The Gothic chapel was built in 1909. (Courtesy of the Smithsburg Historical Society.)

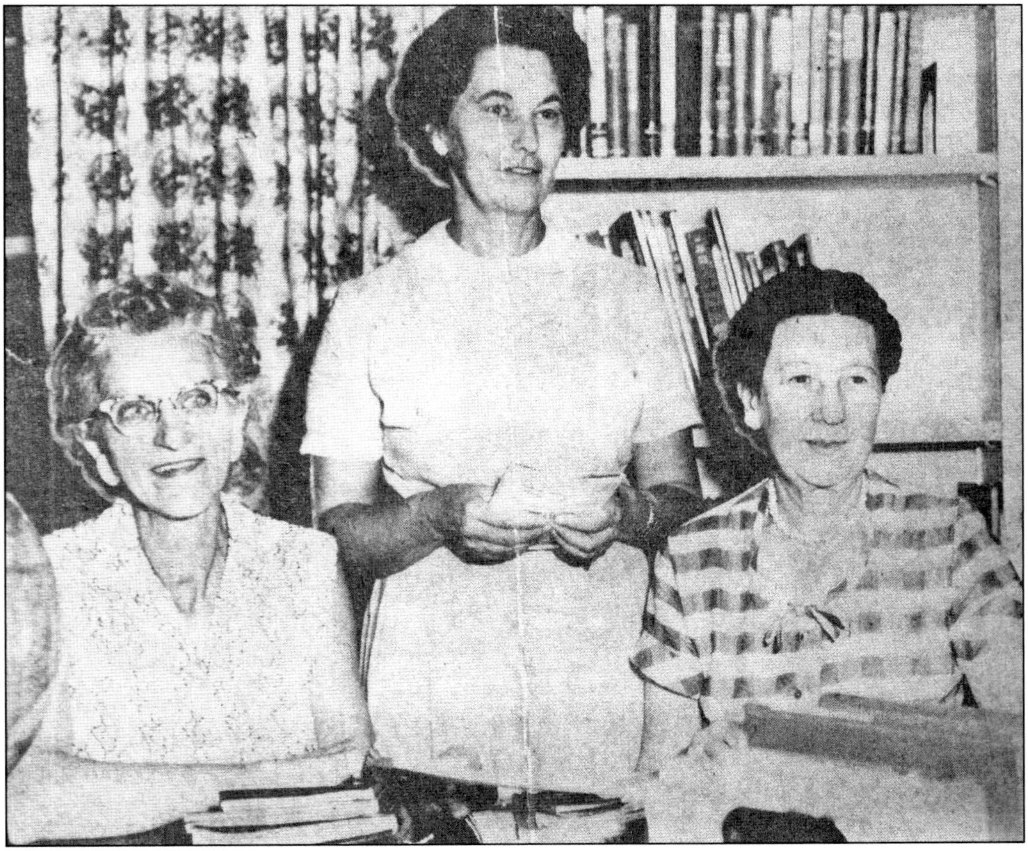

The Smithsburg Library is pictured when it was located on 20 East Water Street in Smithsburg. The drapery in the background (green and white) still hangs in the same window at the Smithsburg Historical Society, which occupies this building. From left to right are Mrs. Edward Bachtell Sr., librarian Mrs. Max Newman, and Mrs. Richard K. Newcomer. (Courtesy of the Smithsburg Historical Society.)

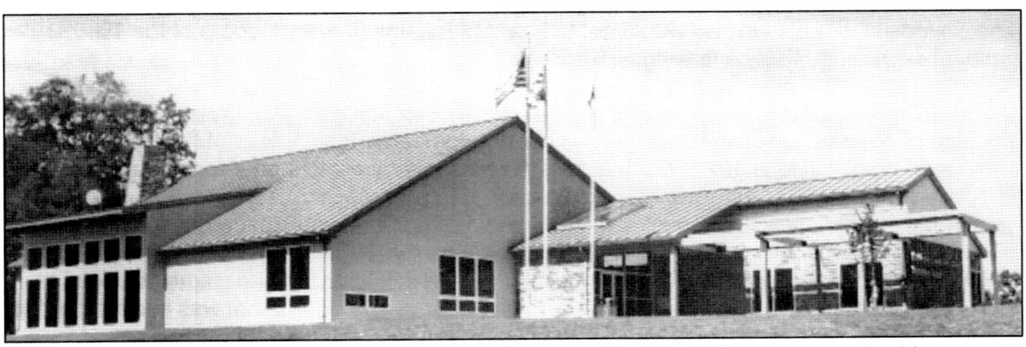

The new Smithsburg Library is located at Veteran's Park. Originally set in the building on 20 East Main Street, the library and its patrons have grown considerably over the years. The new library opened in August 2006. (Courtesy of the Smithsburg Historical Society.)

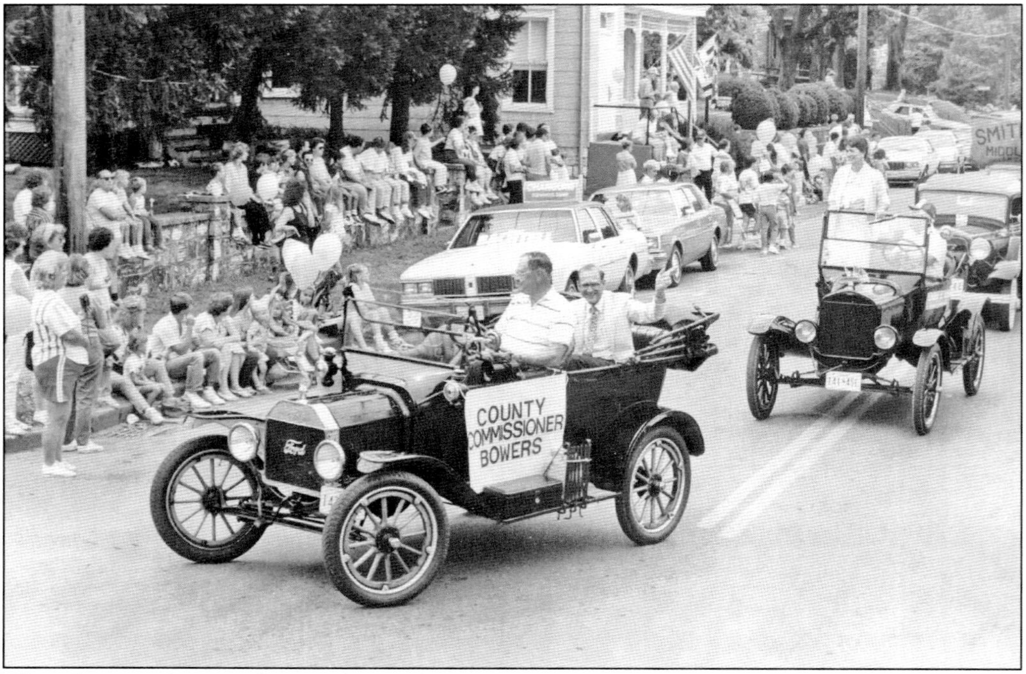

This photograph was taken at the 175th anniversary of the founding of Smithsburg. Town hall can be seen in the background. The crowd has gathered on West Water Street awaiting the parade. Behind the third car in this parade is a partial banner from Smithsburg Middle School. (Courtesy of the Smithsburg Historical Society.)

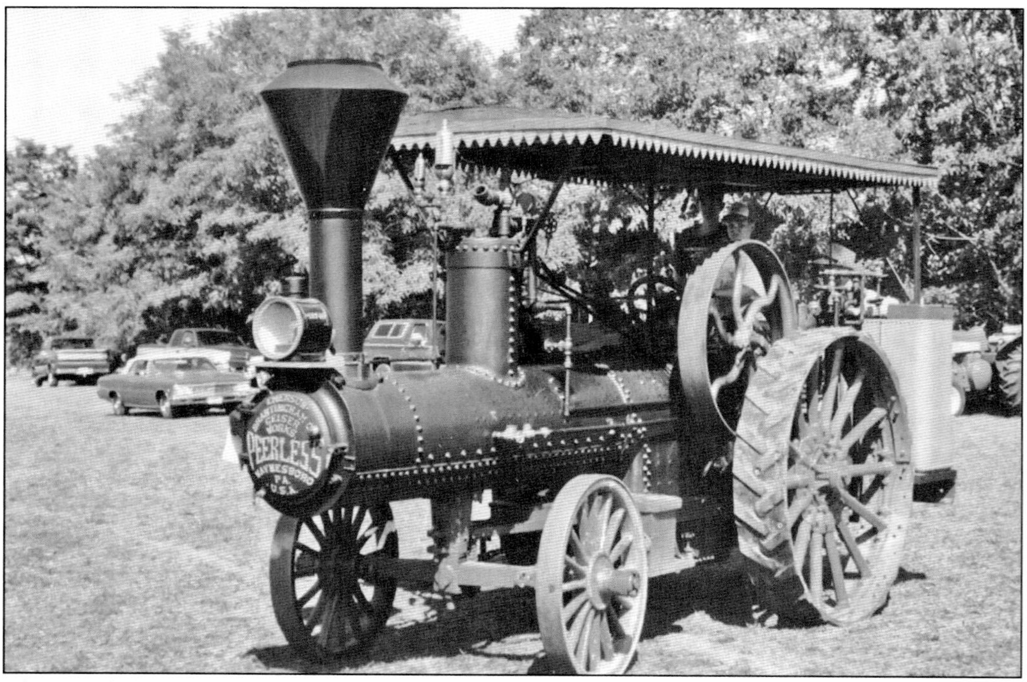

The Smithsburg Steam and Craft Show, held annually, is a huge draw to the area. Pictured here is Peter Geiser's Peerless machine, which he created and manufactured in order to ease the burden on many farmers. (Courtesy of the Smithsburg Historical Society.)

Eight

Community
Have Some Pride

Only one thing in life is certain, and that is change. While each generation brings about a social change, the physical landscape of Smithsburg has not been affected. The Smithsburg Community Volunteer Fire Company has occupied the same piece of land for almost 200 years. Most of the houses along Main Street and Water Street have been standing as long. Traditions such as the Smithsburg Steam and Craft Show and Pride Days occur yearly, as residents and tourists expect. Smithsburg has grown and prospered over the years. The residents of this small town thrive on faith, loyalty, and pride; because of them, Smithsburg has flourished and will continue to do so in the future.

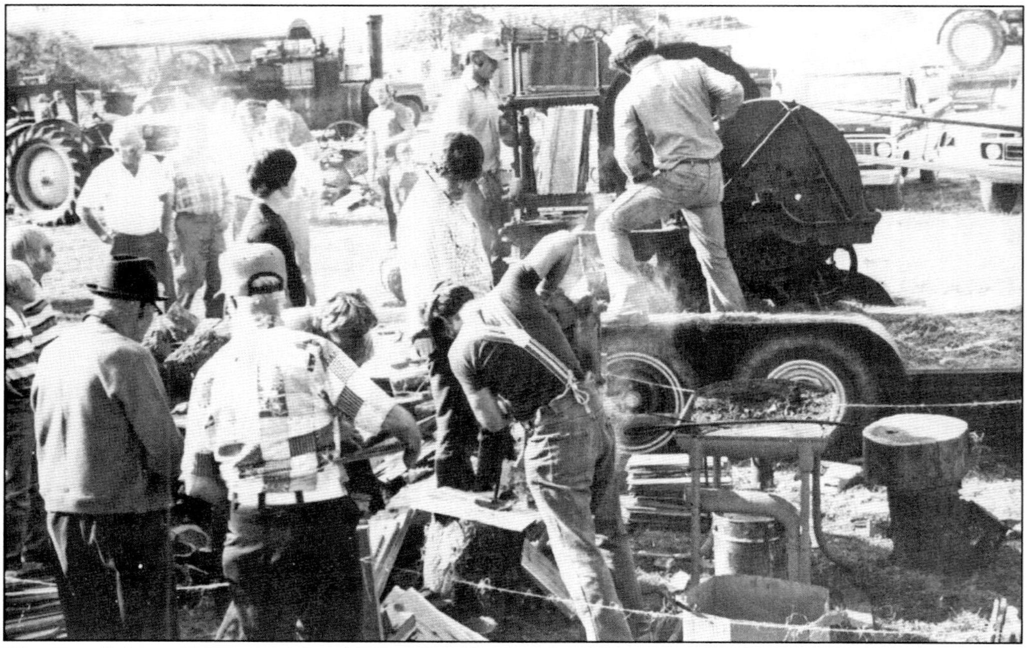

The Smithsburg Steam and Craft Show has been around for many years. Leopard stew (consisting of a mystery meat and other delicacies) and other treats such as funnel cakes, ice cream, and fresh-baked pies and cakes are made and available for purchase. This photograph, taken in the mid- to late 1970s, shows a group of farmers demonstrating their skills to a crowd of onlookers. (Courtesy of *Maryland Cracker Barrel.*)

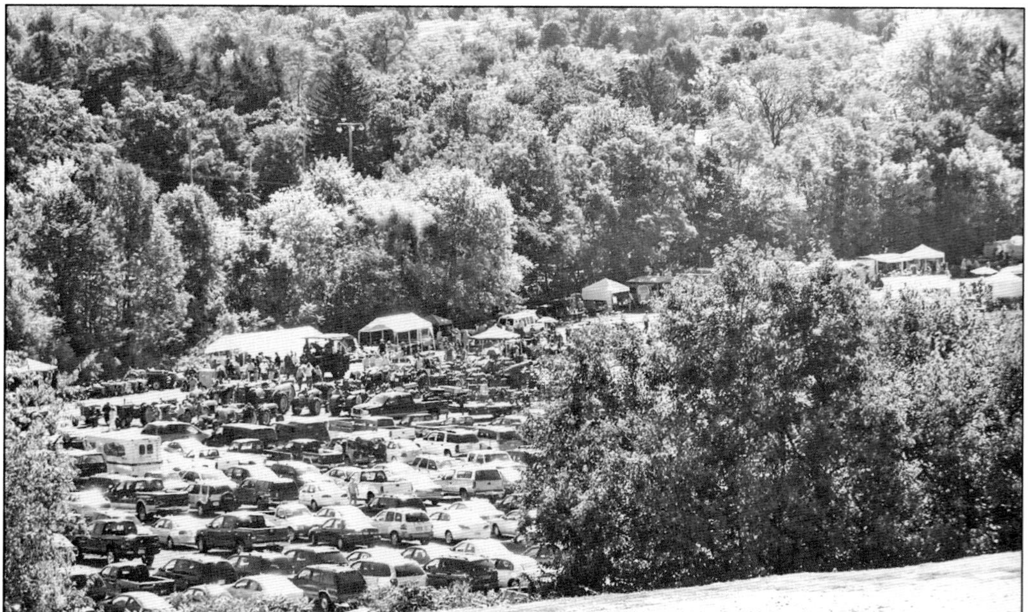

The Steam and Craft Show draws a large number of community members as well as tourists annually. This photograph was taken from the top of Sunset Hill between Smithsburg Middle School and Smithsburg Senior High School by Shay Mace *c.* 2007. (Courtesy of the Smithsburg Historical Society.)

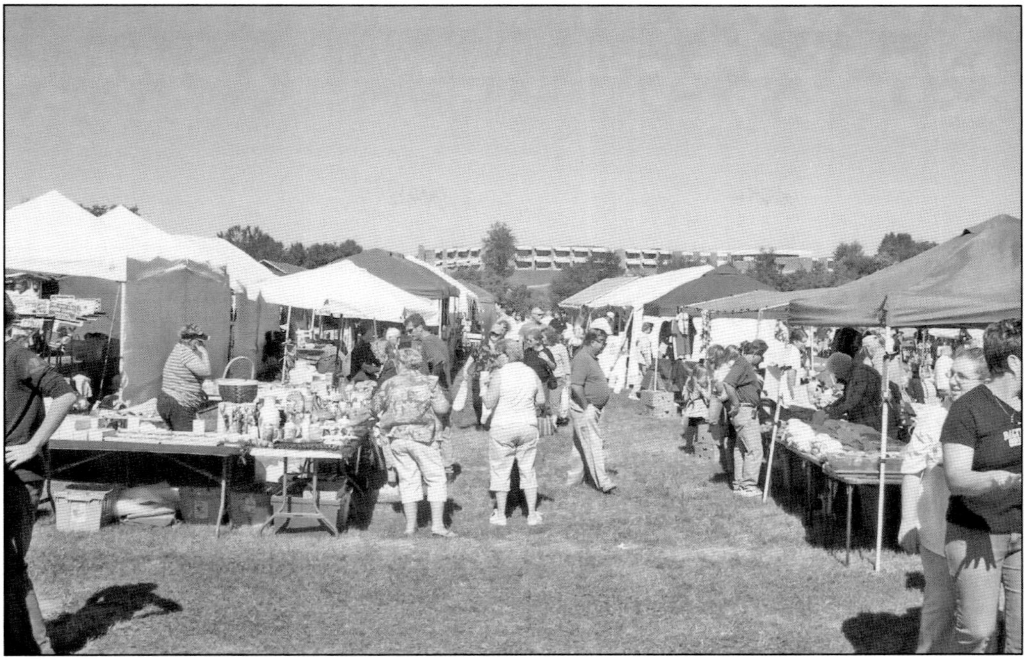

In another view of the annual Steam and Craft Show, Smithsburg Senior High School can be seen in the background on Sunset Hill. The Steam and Craft Show draws a significant crowd of community members and tourists alike. The photograph was taken by Shay Mace *c.* 2007. (Courtesy of the Smithsburg Historical Society.)

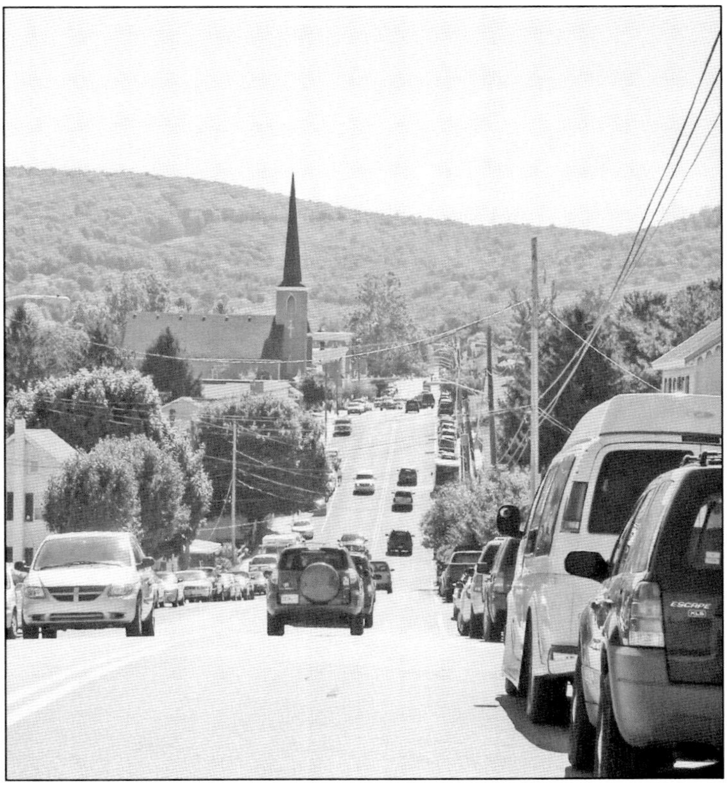

In a recent view of Main Street from the top of Sunset Hill, Trinity Lutheran Church can be seen in the distance. Smithsburg's population has more than doubled its size between 1990 and the time Shay Mace took this photograph in 2007. (Courtesy of the Smithsburg Historical Society.)

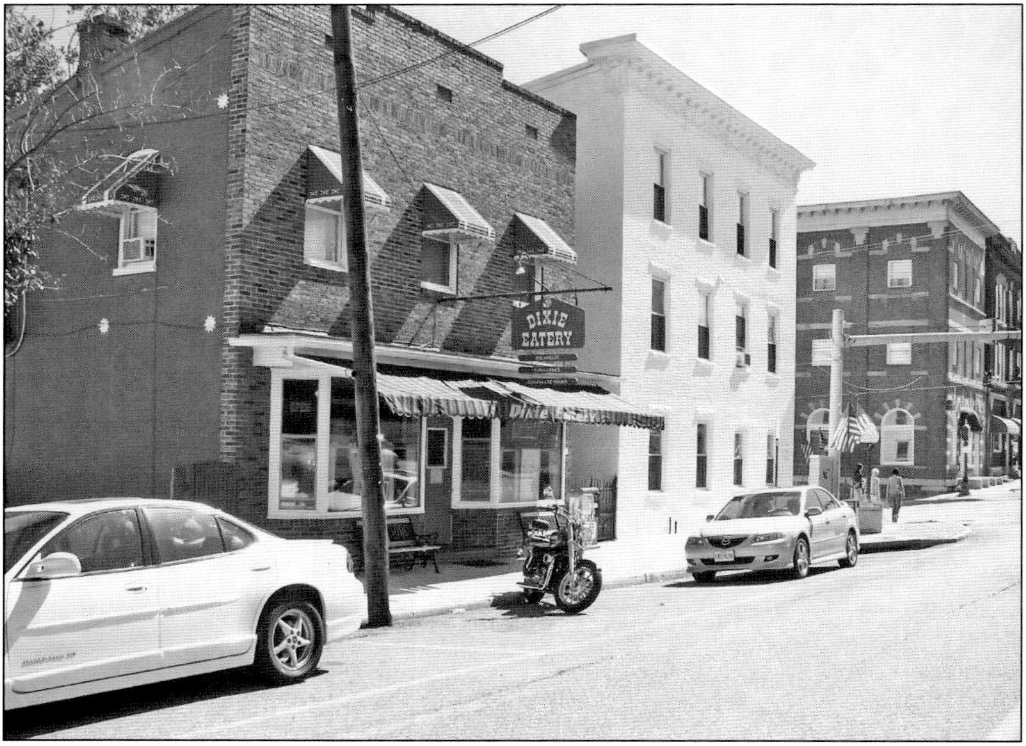

The Dixie Eatery, located at 4 North Main Street, is a Main Street staple of good eats and enjoys a steady supply of customers. The two-story building the Dixie Eatery occupies was bought and renovated to its present form in the 1950s. (Photograph courtesy of Shay Mace.)

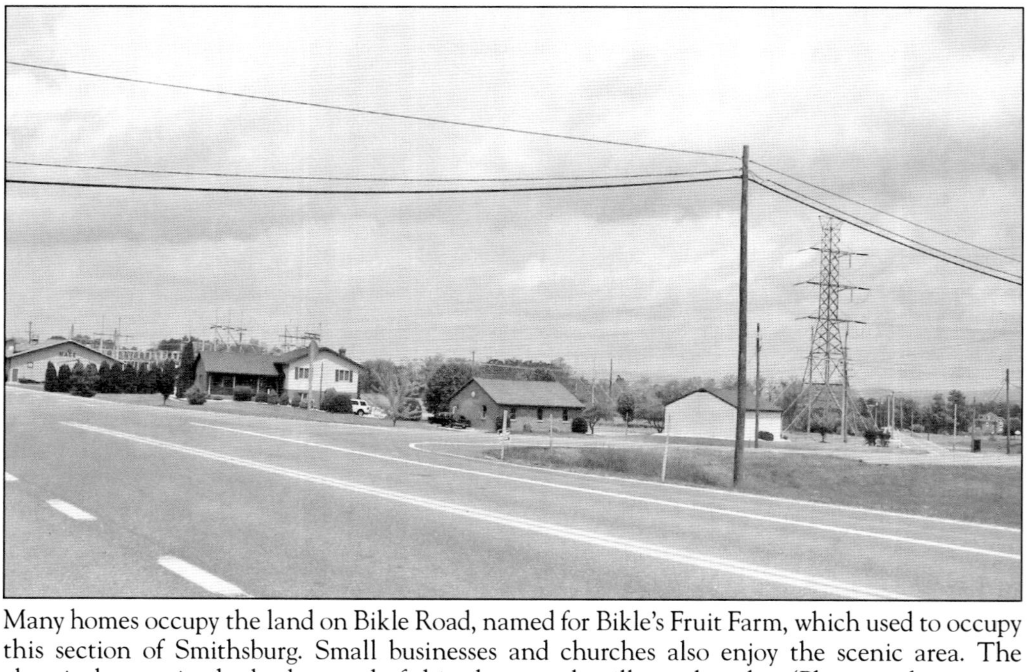

Many homes occupy the land on Bikle Road, named for Bikle's Fruit Farm, which used to occupy this section of Smithsburg. Small businesses and churches also enjoy the scenic area. The electrical tower in the background of this photograph still stands today. (Photograph courtesy of Shay Mace.)

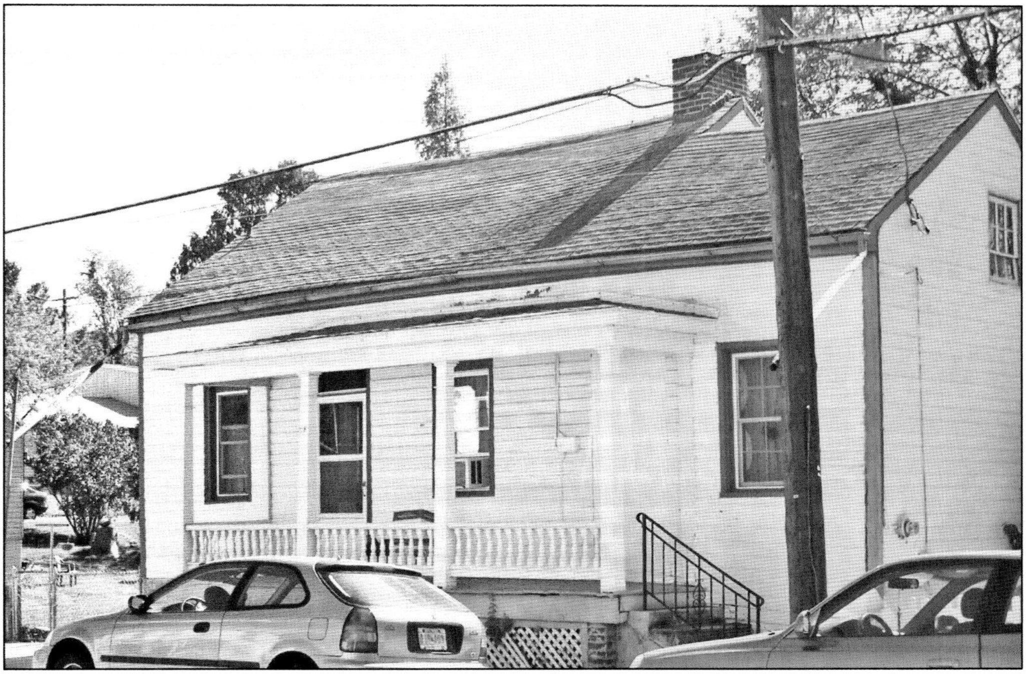

The Kimler Pottery House is seen in 2007. Saturated with history, it is a point of historical interest. It is believed that the house was built by Jacob Frederich Kimler in the 1830s. A pottery shed was built over the stream that runs east of the house. (Courtesy of the Smithsburg Historical Society.)

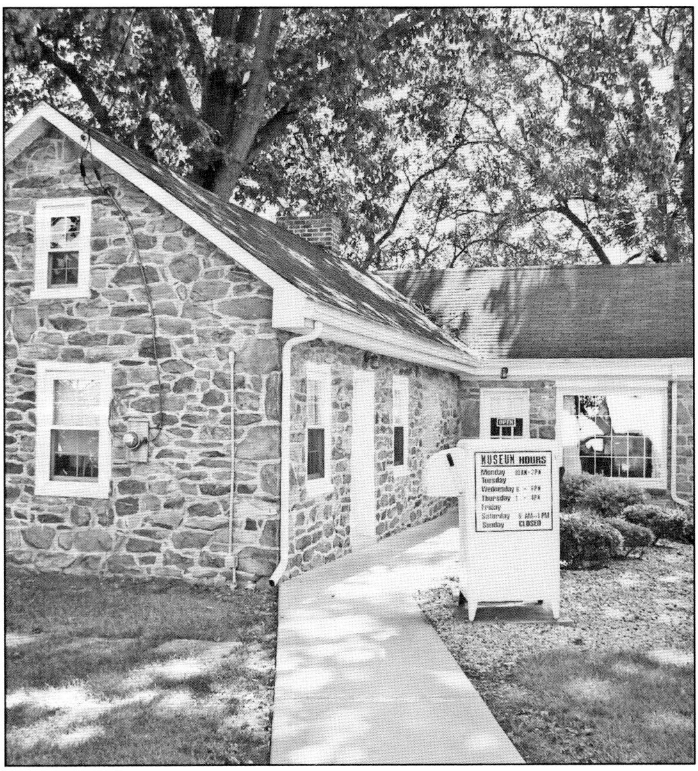

The Smithsburg Historical Society is pictured as it stands today. This stone house was among the first built in Smithsburg. This building has changed hands many times since its construction, some time between 1834 and 1857. At various times, this building has been a jail, a residence, and a library. The Reading Club purchased this building in 1921. In 1945, the building was given debt-free to the town. (Courtesy of the Smithsburg Historical Society.)